ITALO CALVINO AND THE COMPASS OF
LITERATURE

ITALO CALVINO AND THE COMPASS OF LITERATURE

Eugenio Bolongaro

UNIVERSITY OF TORONTO PRESS
Toronto Buffalo London

© University of Toronto Press Incorporated 2003
Toronto Buffalo London
Printed in Canada

ISBN 0-8020-8763-9

∞

Printed on acid-free paper

Toronto Italian Studies

PQ
4809
.A45
Z6527
2003

National Library of Canada Cataloguing in Publication

Bolongaro, Eugenio, 1959–
  Italo Calvino and the compass of literature / Eugenio Bolongaro.

  (Toronto Italian studies)
  Includes bibliographic references and index.
  ISBN 0-8020-8763-9

  1. Calvino, Italo – Criticism and interpretation.   I. Title.   II. Series.

  PQ4809.A45Z57 2003   853'.914   C2003-900839-8

This book has been published with the help of a grant from the Humanities and Social Sciences Federation of Canada, using funds provided by the Social Sciences and Humanities Research Council of Canada.

University of Toronto Press acknowledges the financial assistance to its publishing program of the Canada Council for the Arts and the Ontario Arts Council.

University of Toronto Press acknowledges the financial support for its publishing activities of the Government of Canada through the Book Publishing Industry Development Program (BPIDP).

To Dennis and Domenico

Contents

Acknowledgments

Among all those without whom this book would never have seen the light of day, Professor Darko Suvin has a very special place. It was Darko who first directed my attention to the works of Calvino and guided my research, shaping my understanding of literature in such profound ways that it is impossible for me to say where his teachings end and my own thoughts begin.

Many are the colleagues with whom I spent long hours sharing ideas that have become essential to this book. Among them, I would like to mention in particular Catherine Graham, who never shied away from a good argument, as well as Kees Boterbloem, Joyce Goggin, Susan Mooney, and Andrew Wood.

Over the years, I have also been fortunate to meet a group of friends whose intellectual rigour and commitment to social change has been a constant challenge and inspiration: Andrea Levy, Éric Darier, Steven Jordan, and Qussai Samak and Michael Temelini. The arguments which brought us together have been vehement, enriching, and as important to my work as the friendships that have grown out of them.

Finally, I should briefly speak about the two men to whom this work is dedicated. Domenico Travaglini has been my closest friend for a quarter of a century, though we have spent most of those years on opposite sides of the Atlantic. His intellectual and moral presence has accompanied me through many difficult moments. Dennis McKearney has shared the last seven years of my life and helped me to grow not only in knowledge but also in love.

I would like to acknowledge the financial support that the Social Sciences and Humanities Research Council of Canada provided for the first years of this research.

ITALO CALVINO AND THE COMPASS OF LITERATURE

Introduction

Italo Calvino is unquestionably one of the most widely discussed and admired Italian writers of the second half of the twentieth century. The scholarship on his oeuvre is vast and includes a wide range of book-length studies published on both sides of the Atlantic. In this context, the first question that anyone encountering this volume may ask is, Why another book on Calvino? This is a pertinent question, and answering it allows me not only to explain what differentiates my work from the many other valuable studies, but also to define in a more general way this book's approach to understanding Calvino's achievement.

A perusal of the secondary literature, particularly in English, reveals a marked selectivity both in the works that receive the most attention and in the aspects of these works (themes, concepts, stylistic devices, etc.) that the critics regard as important. The tendency is to focus on the works Calvino wrote after the mid-1960s and emphasize the playful postmodern moments in his fictional narratives. Calvino's oeuvre also includes a considerable body of literary/cultural criticism which has increasingly drawn scholarly attention since the ground-breaking work of Ferretti (1989) and the publication by Mondadori of the two volumes collecting virtually all of the author's essays (*Saggi*, 1995). In this area as well, the postmodern bias leads critics to privilege those theoretical pronouncements that can be closely linked to post-structuralist themes (such as the 'death of the subject' and 'death of the author'). In the end, these lines of enquiry portray Calvino as the most prominent Italian exponent of a kind of global postmodernism, a writer to be studied and understood alongside Borges, Perec, and Pynchon. While undoubtedly some important insights into Calvino's work can be obtained in this way, this orientation seems ultimately limited and potentially pernicious if it becomes the one canonical reading. In order to correct such an imbalance, this book invites the reader to explore anew a different Calvino. My revisitation of Calvino's fictional and critical works discloses his steadfast, lifelong commitment, as an intellectual, to writing as a way of intervening into a particular social and historical situation while taking an ethical and political stance. I will argue that paying close attention to this very modern ethical and political tension allows us to develop a richer understanding of Calvino's achievement, as well as of the legacy he has bequeathed future generations.

This approach to Calvino also leads to a reassessment of which works in his opus are most significant. We have already noted that the majority of studies concentrate on the fictional and critical texts published by Calvino after his move to Paris in 1963, when the playful aspect of his writing becomes dominant. Books such as *Cosmicomics*, *Invisible Cities*, and *If on a Winter's Night a Traveller* and essays such as 'Cybernetics and Ghosts' are major accomplishments, but, from my standpoint, the fantastic trilogy (written in the 1950s and rather neglected by most recent scholarship) and the three major articles of the same period ('The Lion's Marrow,' 'The Sea of Objectivity,' and 'The Challenge of the Labyrinth') represent an equally powerful and, indeed, pivotal moment in Calvino's development. I would go even further and maintain that the significance of the later works can be properly assessed only once the brilliant originality and profound impact of the earlier fictions are fully appreciated. This is the reason why my study refocuses the reader's attention on the five novels published by Calvino in the first two decades after World War II. This corpus, I will argue, constitutes the first complete cycle in Calvino's trajectory as a writer, a cycle that coincides with his formative experiences as an intellectual. Reviving the debate about this body of work is, therefore, a strategic move that leads us to reflect on the foundations of the intellectual project that underlies all of Calvino's undertakings. And by the end of the book I hope to have persuaded the reader that it is precisely this project that endures throughout Calvino's career and yet, paradoxically, forces him constantly to renew his style and choice of genre. The many faces of Calvino all play a role in a single drama.

Calvino and Post-war Italy

Calvino occupies a special place among Italian writers and intellectuals of the second half of the twentieth century. Since his sudden and premature death in 1985, his reputation has continued to grow. In Italy, Calvino is considered probably the most influential figure of his generation: he fathered a school of young and talented writers, whom he himself encouraged and successfully promoted as an editor (see La Porta 1995), while his fictional and critical writings profoundly shaped the very notion of what constitutes valid literary narrative within the Italian cultural milieu. These may seem rather exorbitant claims, but I believe few would object, upon due consideration, that Calvino's legacy as a writer and intellectual was, and continues to be, an unavoidable point of reference for anyone entering the Italian writing scene. The point upon which opinions are bound to differ is whether the long shadow cast by Calvino over Italian letters is a cause for celebration. This question is not directly addressed by this study; and yet I will say that I see no contradiction between, on the one hand, appreciating Calvino's achievements and importance and, on the other hand, recognizing that many other voices have profoundly marked Italian letters in the second half of the twentieth century (figures like Vittorini, Fortini, Pasolini, and Eco immediately come to mind). Indeed, we will encounter some of these other voices as we examine the debates that shaped Calvino, as well as the artistic and intellectual history of the decades that form the subject of this study.

In North America, Calvino's reputation is solidly supported by a body of criticism that is as notable for its quality as for its quantity. This does not make Calvino a household name, but even a cursory and impressionistic survey of the offerings by departments of Italian and modern languages in North American universities confirms that Calvino is widely taught and, in my experience, widely appreciated by graduates and undergraduates alike. And it is precisely the experience of teaching Calvino to a class of North American students that led me to write this book. As I tried to communicate to my students my enthusiasm and passion for Calvino's achievement, I found myself talking more and more about Calvino as an intellectual profoundly preoccupied by his social function. I soon realized that, in order to drive this point home, I had to do much more than simply evoke a historical background that had to be kept in mind when reading Calvino's novels. The problem is that the historical background is not useful if it remains a mere backdrop for diligent students to mention in the introduction of their essays. The so-called background begins to become useful and interesting only when it actively influences one's reading of the fictional work. The text, then, is no longer considered a purely creative act of the imagination, but rather is understood to be a response in an ongoing dialogue: a precisely aimed intervention within a particular social, political, and cultural time and place. This is the thoroughgoing historical approach that I believe Calvino's fictional works demand and that is often neglected by current scholarship.

This book, therefore, attempts to fill a lacuna in Calvinian studies, a lacuna the contours of which came sharply into focus for me after I read Ferretti's excellent *Le capre di Bikini*. Devoting his entire work to a study of Calvino's essays and newspaper articles, Ferretti traces Calvino's *vena oscura* (darker vein) and paints the portrait of a deeply troubled intellectual. I was struck by this picture in part because it was in such stark contrast with the image of the serene and playful storyteller promoted by some critics of Calvino's later postmodern works, and cultivated, as Ferretti well demonstrates, by the author himself. I was also grateful to Ferretti for demonstrating the range of Calvino's non-fictional production, thus drawing attention to a crucial component of Calvino's life work and legacy. Most of all, however, Ferretti crystallized for me the fact that an interpretation of Calvino's non-fictional works was bound ultimately to be unpersuasive if it did not encompass a sustained reading of the fictional works and vice versa. This is not to say that tensions and contradictions may not emerge as the different aspects of Calvino's textual production are taken into consideration, but those tensions and contradictions are alive and operative within each sphere as well as between them. The challenge is precisely to integrate all these different interventions within a discourse that accounts for the overall trajectory of Calvino as an intellectual, and an intellectual who is struggling to work out how to act within an increasingly complex world. Without resorting to the difficult and problematic notion of a dialectic, it is at least possible to speak of a constant and insistent dialogue between different modes of intervention (e.g., novel, short story, essay, newspaper article, etc.), the respective ambit and goal of which evolve over time but which are also all governed by a fundamental impulse: to establish that *presenza morale* (moral presence) which is at the heart of 'The Lion's Marrow,' Calvino's first clear statement of his poetical and intellectual credo.

An intense preoccupation with Calvino's role as an intellectual not only provides a crucial interpretive key to all of his works but also demonstrates how Calvino is in fact deeply rooted in the Italian literary tradition (the first chapter of Jeannet's *Under the Radiant Sun and the*

Crescent Moon is particularly useful in this regard). For my purposes, the most interesting question in this context becomes whether Calvino ultimately emerges as the type of cosmopolitan intellectual criticized by Gramsci or as a new type of intellectual who, having absorbed and digested the Gramscian lesson, is adapting it to a changed world. This is one of the central issues explored in this book, and, naturally, such a project led me to examine the cultural dynamics of post-Fascist Italy and in particular of the decades during which Calvino's formative experiences took place. This was not simply a detour that would enable me to establish a cultural context, but rather a thoroughgoing immersion in a social, economic, and political conjuncture that helped me see the significance of Calvino's work in a new way.

The first decade and a half of the Italian Republic was an exceptionally exciting time. The more one reads about it, the more one comes to feel that this was one of those unique historical and cultural moments when the possibility for real and positive change existed, and when the actions of the political and cultural leadership of the country made a difference to the course of history. It was a time alive with opportunities, and a time whose fascination also lies in the fact that most of these opportunities were squandered and lost. In the first chapter of this book, I have tried to share with the reader this sense of excitement and disappointed opportunity, a sense that is not only my own but also marks profoundly, as I shall argue, the generation of Italian intellectuals to which Calvino belongs. Without pre-empting the discussion in that chapter, it is helpful to point out right away that the legacy of the cultural debates of the 1950s is the difficulty of arriving at a satisfactory rearticulation of the relationship between the political and aesthetic dimensions of literature. This issue functioned as a catalyst for battles over the role of intellectuals and the nature of realism in art. Crucial for the argument in this book is the fact that Calvino participated actively in these battles. His voice grew in maturity and authority until he became recognized as a leading literary figure, a status he was to enjoy for the rest of his life. Many things would change, of course, after the 1950s; indeed, it is my argument that this was a watershed decade during which the seeds of a new world order were sown. However, it is important to remember the struggles that fashioned Calvino as a young writer and intellectual, and recognize that a fundamental aspect of Calvino's originality lies precisely in his complex, mobile, and constantly renewed configuration of the aesthetic and political significance of literature.

Another discovery occasioned by focusing on the post-war years was a readjustment of the traditional segmentations of Calvino's opus. It becomes clear that the central line of enquiry in Calvino's fictional discourse during the 1950s can best be understood by placing the fantastic trilogy (*The Cloven Viscount*, *The Baron in the Trees*, and *The Nonexistent Knight*) at the centre of a quintet that began with the neo-realist attempt *I giovani del Po* (The young people of the Po) and ended with *The Watcher*. This new grouping not only underscores the coherence of, and continuity in, Calvino's artistic development but, more importantly for my purposes, also makes much more clearly visible one key and often neglected dimension of Calvino's work: the ethical and political impulse driving Calvino's use of the fantastic. To do justice to this dimension is the challenge that inspires the remaining chapters of this book and my approach to Calvino in general.

Calvino and Genre

My reading of the works that compose the quintet I have just described is designed to accomplish two basic and interrelated tasks. For my first task I intend to explore the range of options that the literary system of the time made available to Calvino. My second task will be to examine the political significance of the generic choices made by Calvino. This endeavour is based on theoretical presuppositions that need not detain us unduly in this context but should at least be explicitly stated. I am drawing on the work of Claudio Guillén to justify the claim that literature must be understood as a system of genres. At any particular point in its development, this system will exhibit a specific structure based on the power relations between the various genres. This means that there is always a hierarchy of genres, even in postmodernity, where, paradoxically, the dominant genre is the pastiche, which seeks to undermine generic distinctions. Guillén would also maintain that the very definition and effectiveness of genres depends on relations of domination and subordination; for example, an important and irreducible element in the definition of the English novel as a genre is that it is the type of writing which gained ascendancy in the eighteenth century by setting itself against the romance. The importance of this kind of observation is that it allows us to pose the question of genre as a political issue: the dominance of a genre is never politically neutral but represents the ascendancy of a particular world view or ideology. It follows that the generic choices an author makes, deliberately or not, have a political dimension. In the case of Calvino, I will argue that this political dimension is not simply the result of, but also the motivation behind, the formal characteristics of the narrative. In particular, Calvino's shift from the neo-realism of *I giovani* to the fantastic modes of the chivalric trilogy and then back to the neo-realism of *The Watcher* must be seen not simply as vacillations in his poetics but rather as the expression and development of a single and coherent political stance. What changes over this crucial period, then, is not so much Calvino's overall project as a writer and intellectual as the environment in which he is seeking to intervene. It is to remain pertinent and effective within this evolving context that Calvino feels compelled to constantly renew his narrative choices.

It is in the years from *I giovani* to *The Watcher* that Calvino lays the foundations of a style that will sustain all his future endeavours (and it is in the books from this period that Calvino demonstrates a keen sensitivity to the changing historical conjuncture as well as to the shortcomings of his own work). This Calvinian vein, unmistakable in all his works in spite of their considerable range, emerges as much from his remarkable first novel (*The Path to the Nest of Spiders*) and early short stories, which manifest a young and still immature talent, as from the failure of *I giovani*, which, by crystallizing his creative impasse, allows Calvino to understand its causes. This realization is the point of departure for the mature Calvino, who, of course, will keep moving as history moves but within the parameters set at this key juncture in his life.

In the end, the analysis of Calvino's trajectory during the 1950s and early 1960s will show that the impulse driving Calvino's efforts is not, as has sometimes been suggested, a constant attempt to keep up with changing fashions. On the contrary, Calvino is committed to always raising the stakes of the political and aesthetic debates to which he is contributing. His goal is to challenge the dominant assumptions about what constitutes good politics and good literature, as well as the relationship between these two spheres, which for Calvino are indubitably connected but also irreducibly distinct. This is an important lesson, for our times no less than for Calvino's. New information technologies and the globalization of culture in the twenty-first century have put back on the agenda of writers and intellectuals the political dimension of the literary text and, more precisely, the need to rethink the nature and function of literature as a means of intervention in social space. This is where Calvino's lifelong meditations on the role of the writer as intellectual can make an important contribution, a contribution of interest to anyone attempting to understand the cultural dynamic at the turn of the millennium.

These are fascinating issues, in my view, and yet I must warn the reader that this book can only adumbrate them. In this respect, this book is a threshold study. It lays the indispensable groundwork for any assessment of Calvino's later work, which, however, remains beyond my scope. The issue is not simply one of space, though tackling the remainder of Calvino's opus would certainly have required a doubling or, more probably, a tripling of the size of this volume. In fact, ending the discussion in 1963 is strategically important. It makes the point that in 1963 a phase in Calvino's life was complete; there was a real caesura. Calvino's departure for Paris is not a mere coincidence – it signifies, it delivers a message the import of which is explored by my reading of *The Watcher*.

I will conclude this introduction by mentioning that Calvino himself must bear some of the responsibility for the partiality of the scholarship on his works. He treated his own work in the same way any Einaudi editor might have. He was very much involved in the original packaging of his work and in the repackaging that became necessary as new collections or new editions were published. Taking very seriously the task of preparing and influencing the critical and public reception of each new volume, he sought at times to project an image that made perfect sense as a marketing strategy but cannot truly stand up to closer scrutiny. The most obvious example of this, and particularly pertinent to our discussion, is the collection of essays published under the apparently telltale title *Una pietra sopra* (an Italian expression translated in the *Sansoni Dictionary* [Firenze: Sansoni, 1985] as 'let bygones be bygones'). Calvino seemed to say that the concerns which inspired those texts were no longer his, and yet, when a few years later some of the essays in this collection were translated in English and published in North America, the title chosen was *The Uses of Literature* – the connotation could not be more different from the original title and was certainly not lost on Calvino, who was quite prickly and demanding when it came to translations of his work. It is true that the essays excluded from the English edition are precisely the ones Calvino wrote in the 1950s and early 1960s and that are at the centre of the discussion in this book. However, this can best be explained not as a rejection of the fundamental concerns those essays developed but by the fact that in those years Calvino was intervening in peculiarly Italian debates that could not be meaningfully evoked, almost thirty years later and for a North American audience, by a few articles. The fact remains that the translation and republication of essays such as 'Philosophy and Literature,' 'Whom Do We Write For?' and 'Right and Wrong Political Uses of Literature' clearly demonstrate that the title given to the Italian edition must be understood to exhibit more than a pinch of Calvinian irony. This kind of mixed message, by no means unusual in Calvino, points to the fact that over his long years at Einaudi Calvino developed the editorial reflex of promoting the latest product, a reflex that is not insignificant in so far as it points to the material conditions of the intellectual in late capitalism, but which must also be seen for what it is: a negotiation of contradictions that invites a layered and ironic reading. Calvino did always strive to move with the times, but to reduce his constant striving for a constructive engagement with the evolving historical conjuncture to a mere pursuit of intellectual fashions misses the mark. As a whole, the body of work examined in this book represents a towering and fundamental achievement. Rediscovering these works on their own terms extends the horizon traced by Calvino's trajectory and changes in crucial ways the landscape that horizon circumscribes. This wider compass is what Calvino's legacy demands.

CHAPTER ONE

Italy at the Crossroads, 1943–1963

By all accounts the period between 1943 and 1963 was pivotal in the emergence of contemporary Italy.[1] Politically, these two decades are framed by the Resistance to the Nazi occupation of the country and the belated inauguration of the first centre-left government. The former event began in 1943 after the collapse of the Fascist regime and lasted until the end of World War II in 1945. The latter took place in 1962, when the fourth Fanfani cabinet won a confidence vote from parliament thanks to the support of the Partito Socialista Italiano (Italian Socialist Party; PSI), thus establishing the coalition that, in spite of its many transmutations and difficulties, would rule the country until the early 1990s, when Hobsbawm's 'short twentieth century' came to an end. Between these temporal boundaries lie the events that set the parameters for any analysis of Italian society in the second half of the twentieth century: the approval of the republican constitution; the emergence of the Democrazia Cristiana (Christian Democracy, DC) as the dominant political force and the Partito Communista Italiano (Italian Communist Party; PCI) as the only credible opposition; membership in NATO, which settled Italy's alignment with the capitalist bloc; the economic boom, which turned Italy into the seventh largest economy in the West; the launch of the Fiat 600, which did for Italy what the Model T had done for the United States; the advent of television; and so on. In sum, it is during these two decades that 'the Italian case,' as it is sometimes termed, took on a definite shape.

It is well beyond the scope of this book to provide an account of such an intense and indeed electrifying period. However, the arguments I will develop in my reading of Calvino are necessarily intertwined with an interpretation of the historical conjuncture and its unique cultural dynamic. In this chapter, I will make this historical interpretation explicit in the hope that the reader will find it easier to follow the logic of my arguments.

The historical narrative I will present is, of course, extremely selective and will focus resolutely on cultural issues. My reconstruction of the socio-political and, especially, cultural developments in Italy between 1943 and 1963 revolves around four events that were formative for Calvino, as well as for the leading left-wing Italian intellectuals who were his primary interlocutors. The first of these events is the Resistance, while the next three are best identified by the titles of three short-lived but influential publications, namely, *Il Politecnico*, *Officina*, and *Il Menabò*. Also, my analysis will of necessity focus on the two key issues that preoccupied the most influential and original intellectual circles during these two decades: first, the role of intellectuals in a modern society, and, second, realism in art.

The Italian Resistance and the Shaping of the Post-war Italian Intellectual

The Italian Resistance was a complex phenomenon. It arose against the background of a disastrous military and political situation. Mussolini's destitution by the Gran Consiglio del Fascismo (Fascist Grand Council) in July 1943, his arrest, and, only six weeks later, the flight of Victor Emmanuel III and his new Prime Minister, Badoglio, from Rome to the Allied-controlled South, plunged the country into complete chaos. The depth of the crisis of the regime and the virtually complete political vacuum that followed the Duce's deposition are difficult to grasp even in retrospect. The national territory was effectively partitioned between the Kingdom of the South, whose juridical claim to legitimacy would have been meaningless except for the support of the Allies, and the puppet Republic of Salò, whose thinly disguised function was to legitimate the German occupation and attempt to mobilize and exploit the North's industrial base to the benefit of the Nazi war effort. In 1943, Italy was a country fragmented, humiliated, and demoralized in the extreme. Indeed, it could well be argued that if there were a 'year zero,' from which contemporary Italy gradually emerged, it should be 1943 rather than the superficially more obvious 1945, the year that marks the end of World War II in all theatres of operation. How did the Resistance movement emerge from such a catastrophic situation?

The seeds that sprouted in the last two years of the war were sown and resown by the anti-Fascist groups, which, during the dictatorship, operated mostly abroad but also within the country. Among these, two emerged as dominant in the Resistance. The first of these was the PCI, whose members filled the ranks of the Brigate Garibaldine (Garibaldi Brigades), which, as we shall see, Calvino himself eventually joined. The second largest contingent of partisans fought under the banner of Giustizia e Libertà (Justice and Freedom), the movement founded by the brothers Rosselli and organized politically as the Partito d'Azione (Action Party; Pd'A). A significant, though less substantial, contribution to the Resistance was made by Catholic brigades, particularly in the northeast regions of the peninsula.

Clearly, the Resistance was not an ideologically homogeneous movement, though a generic progressive rhetoric was indeed common to all groups. Rather, the sense of an emerging national project and the social cohesion that this project presupposed grew initially out of an urgent and dramatic practical task: fighting a guerrilla war against a powerful, determined, and ruthless modern army. This was the fundamental experience that marked a whole generation.

However, as the fighting continued and spread, acquiring the character of a civil war, the partisan bands' very survival against the Nazi forces depended on their ability to co-ordinate military operations throughout the war zone. Better organization required greater discipline, which in turn led to a greater emphasis on ideological education, as well as military training. In this way, the Resistance acquired an increasingly political dimension. The leadership exercised by the Comitati di Liberazione Nazionale (National Liberation Committees; CLN) presented a positive model of democracy in action – albeit a somewhat deceptive model, as events would later demonstrate.

As a result of these experiences, the Resistance became the foundation for a new democratic consciousness: a new political subject was emerging that would struggle to assert itself in the immediate postwar years. This also explains why the Resistance was primarily a phenomenon of the North. In the South the relatively rapid progress of the Allied forces, as well as the difficult but steady dialogue between the king and his government, on the one hand, and the leaders of the opposition, on the other hand, quickly removed the reasons for armed resistance and for the grassroots politicization that naturally accompanied it. The insurrections that took place here and there as the Allies approached never had time to develop into a new consciousness, with the result that the old Fascist, and indeed pre-Fascist, state apparatuses and mentalities could slowly but surely reassert themselves. In the North, on the contrary, the CLN began in effect to function as a war government, with wide popular support and increasing prestige and legitimacy.

For intellectuals, the key effect of the Resistance was a dramatic simplification: you were either for the Nazi-Fascists or against them, and if you chose to sit on the fence, then you were shirking your basic ethical responsibility. The exemplary figure in this context is Giaime Pintor. The often-cited letter that Pintor wrote to his brother just before leaving for his first partisan mission (a mission in which he was to lose his life) contains what is perhaps the most lucid statement of the position of the intellectual vis-à-vis the Resistance:

> I don't know if I would have decided to commit myself totally to that course [social activism]: individual tastes, indifference and critical thinking were too strong in me to sacrifice it all to a collective faith. Only the war resolved the situation, overwhelming many obstacles, sweeping away many comfortable covers and placing me brutally in touch with a world I could not reconcile myself to ... At some point intellectuals must be able *to transfer their experience onto the terrain of common utility*, each one must be able to take his place in a combat organization ... As for myself, I assure you that the idea of becoming a partisan at this time of year amuses me very little; I have never appreciated as much as today the merits of civilian life and I am aware of being an excellent translator and a good diplomat, but in all likelihood a mediocre partisan. However, this is the only option available and I accept it.[2] (Emphasis added)

There is no enthusiasm here, but a sense of duty and humility in the face of the task ahead. It is especially interesting to note that the duty arises for Pintor not simply from a general humanness that we all share independently of our calling in life, but also specifically from the particular responsibilities of the intellectual. In other words, it is as an intellectual and not simply as a human being, who has momentarily put aside his more particular interests, that Pintor joins the Resistance. Holding the gun and holding the pen are two manifestations in different circumstances of the same effort to grasp and intervene in the historical processes one faces, an effort to participate in the life of the entire national community.

The Resistance was a crucible. The long-lamented division between the intellectual class and the 'people' seemed to disappear in the Resistance movement. It seemed that different social groups could actually talk and understand each other, work together for a common goal, and win together. Following on the heels of the complete and humiliating collapse of the Fascist state, this experience (though hardly idyllic given the violence and brutality it involved) could not but have an extraordinary echo in the consciousness of the country and in particular in the lives of all those who participated in it, Calvino included.

It is also important to note that the experience of the Resistance prepared the ground for the acceptance in the post-war period of a somewhat hurried Gramscian approach to culture and, more specifically, to the role of the intelligentsia. The organic relationship between intellectuals and the working class that Gramsci theorized seemed a real possibility after the experience of partisan warfare, during which democratic political structures had emerged, largely as a result of the cooperation between intellectuals (predominantly party cadres) and a vast popular movement. That the experiences of a war situation could not easily be translated into peacetime would soon become apparent. And yet, as long as the Resistance maintained its appeal, the Gramscian project would provide the peacetime program for recapturing the organic unity that had been achieved in wartime between the progressive forces of the nation.

The difficulties confronting Italy in the post-war period and, in particular, the disintegration of the anti-Fascist front represented by the national unity government of 1945–7 would soon empty the Resistance of political content, turning it into a controversial foundational narrative that no longer expressed a national consensus. Still, for many young intellectuals, the Resistance provided the experiential ground for a social project in which they saw themselves as having a clearly defined and crucial role, a role that seemed to free them from the inertia of a venerable and proud but also stagnant tradition.

Neo-realism is the most immediately striking cultural realization of post-war Italy. Maria Corti (*Il viaggio testuale*, 1978) has persuasively argued that the conventions of neo-realism evolved from the enthusiastic storytelling (both oral and written) that accompanied the experience of the Resistance as it was taking place and that flourished thereafter. After the end of the war, a keen interest in memorial narratives (war journals, eyewitness accounts, etc.) spread to the whole country, propelling the rapid recovery of the publishing industry. Fictional narratives having the Resistance as their theme soon followed, and the critics waited expectantly for the author who would succeed in writing the inevitable great Resistance novel.[3] In cinema, after a long eclipse, Italian neo-realism burst on the international scene with striking images of the devastation brought about by the war and its aftermath.

However, the impact of the Resistance on the cultural discourse of the times goes much beyond the contribution of some obvious war themes for artistic elaboration. Much more fundamental is the fact that the Resistance experience and its first artistic elaborations led to a focus on contemporary history and, more precisely, on contemporary political and social issues. The traditional claims that literature was above history, its forms atemporal in their essence, and that aesthetic value was a transcendent universal were cast aside. Literature had to matter now, had to play a role in the socio-political struggle for a better world. Universal significance remained a goal, but it could be achieved only through a sustained confrontation with the here and now of social and political struggle. This is the approach in which the 'battle for realism' is ultimately rooted.

Serious objections can be raised about the demand that literature become socially and politically relevant. However, my concern is to bring into the foreground the ambiguous role which this approach foisted on the post-war Italian intellectual. The Resistance was held to have proved that commitment was the only way out of the isolation that was the particular predicament of the Italian intelligentsia (Guarnieri 1976, 21–85). But commitment to what? In the context of the black and white dichotomies of the civil war, it was easy enough to gloss over this question. Commitment necessarily meant being on the side of liberty, without which the very notion of commitment (i.e., the underlying ethical imperative) made no sense at all. After the war, however, the notion of liberty revealed all its problematicity (e.g., the 'free' market vs. the planned economy, formal freedom vs. substantive/economic freedom, etc.). It became necessary to provide a much more precise definition of commitment; or, in other words, commitment had to be incorporated in an explicit ideology that would stabilize its meaning.

This is what the PCI tried to do via Gramsci. Commitment, the party confidently stated, meant solidarity with the working class and its revolutionary project. In practice, this meant solidarity or, rather, adherence to the PCI itself, which, following the Leninist rather than

Gramscian model, was deemed to be expression of the self-conscious-ness of the working class. This simple equation resolved the problem of commitment at a political level, thus assuring the PCI hegemony over the left-wing intelligentsia, but it soon became apparent that the party's stamp of approval did not guarantee the quality of intellectual activity. The great Resistance novel never materialized, nor did the great socialist literature anticipated by the party, and Calvino had to remind intellectuals agonizing over this fact that to write convincingly like a communist one first had to learn how to be a communist. It was on that count that writers needed the party, which, on the other hand, should leave writing to writers.

While the Resistance was a crucial experience for the country and the most advanced cohorts of its intelligentsia, it also landed progres-sive intellectuals in a peculiar predicament. On the one hand, they were urged to recognize historical reality and enjoined to keep pace with progress by joining the PCI and adopting its Marxist ideology. On the other, they were criticized for not being able to translate such ideol-ogy into a satisfying imaginative presentation of that reality and pro-gress. They had to have progressive politics, but when progressive politics did not make for convincing literature (or, worse still, made for convincingly 'decadent' literature), then the simple answer was that the fault lay with their insufficient devotion to the cause – their faith in socialism wasn't strong enough.

It is not surprising that a reaction against such a simplification of the issues surrounding intellectual work would soon manifest itself. The Resistance had provided the impetus for a vast movement of social change. However, as the brief neo-realist renaissance faltered, the com-plexity of the Italian socio-political, but also cultural, situation and the shortcomings of the Italian intelligentsia in confronting such complex-ity would begin to show through. It would then become clear that the 'new man' that the Resistance and its literature had allegedly brought into being was still very much in his infancy, and that considerably more effort would be required to move beyond the venerable humanist tradition, which was still the bedrock of Italian culture and the resilient heritage of its intellectuals.

Il Politecnico 1945–1947: Culture vs Politics

The publication of *Il Politecnico* on 29 September 1945 marks the full resumption of Italian cultural life after World War II. This was also the first major editorial endeavour in which Calvino actively participated, establishing his position as one of the 'bright young men' of the post-war generation. *Il Politecnico* was a pivotal experience for our author, as well as for the country as a whole. Accordingly, the journal's trajectory warrants detailed examination.

The tone of Vittorini's famous first editorial for *Il Politecnico*, 'For a New Culture' ('Per una nuova cultura'), left no doubt as to his determination to mark a clear break with the past and inaugurate a new era. Enough, Vittorini was saying, with a culture that could elaborate fundamental principles and preach essential values but was powerless to prevent their utter contradiction and denial in practice. Enough with a culture whose function seemed to be that of consoling humanity from the horrors of history, or, worse still, that of rationalizing barbarism.[4] The task Vittorini set for *Il Politecnico* was the elaboration of a new militant culture that would penetrate and transform every aspect of social life so as to become an effective bulwark against human suffering. Finally, in the last paragraph of his piece, Vittorini made explicit what the whole text in fact implied – the new culture would lay a claim to power and thus abolish once and for all the distinction between the realm of ideas and the realm of political/economic practice: 'Taking care of bread and work is still taking care of "the soul." On the other hand, taking care of nothing but "the soul," while leaving it to "Caesar" to take care of bread and work as it best suits him, this amounts to limiting oneself to a merely intellectual function which allows "Caesar" (Donegani, Pirelli, or Valletta) to have power over men's "souls."'[5]

This editorial caused much debate within the whole intellectual community. Its brash tone was provocative and its 'culturalism' was unashamed: the condemnation of the role played by culture in the past formed the basis for a celebration of the future role of culture. The seed of the polemic between Vittorini and Togliatti, the charismatic leader of the PCI, was sown.

It is clear that the primary purpose of Vittorini's intervention was to provide a rallying cry for post-war intellectuals. It is telling that such a rallying cry was explicitly grounded in the experience of the Resistance: the editorial was accompanied by picture of a dead partisan with a caption stating that 'Those who have fallen for freedom throughout the world dictated to us what we write, ('I caduti per la libertà di tutto il mondo ci hanno dettato quello che scriviamo'). In response to the criticism that the original editorial and photograph had sparked, Vittorini boldly reasserted the vital nature of the connection between the Resistance and his project:

> And you [Vigorelli, a columnist who objected to the photograph and the caption] say that we display, because of this phrase, a rhetorical turn of mind. Has anyone dear to you fallen in the struggle of these last years? I have had three who were extremely dear to me: Giaime Pintor ... Giorgio Labò ... and Eugenio Curiel ... I worked with them and with all of them we often talked of a *new culture* we should search for, of a *Politecnico* we should create. For me, the name of that dead partisan in the photograph is Giaime Pintor, his name is Giorgio Labò, his name is Eugenio Curiel; and everyone who had a friend die in the struggle knows his true name.[6]

The lesson that Vittorini wanted to draw from the Resistance and the war in general is quite interesting, as well as predictably disconcerting to the left-wing circles that were Vittorini's primary audience. The conflict, Vittorini maintained, had demonstrated the glaring inadequacies of traditional culture (and more specifically, one may add, of the old-fashioned humanist Italian culture, whose provincialism Fascism had glorified and aggravated). However, the spectacle of these inadequacies did not provide grounds for questioning a culture's ambition to express universal values. This move would have led to a radical problematization of humanism, and that was precisely the direction in which Italian intellectuals could not yet imagine going. Rather, the inadequacies of traditional culture became the basis for what could easily be characterized as a power grab by intellectuals. The fault lay not in the principles and values that the old culture proposed, but in the powerlessness of the old culture when it came to putting those principles and values into practice. One should note the quasi-Catholic logic: the sanctity of the 'word' remained unquestioned, but the problem lay with its worldly implementation. The solution, therefore, would come not from a re-examination of traditional values in the light of political and economic realities, but in culture staking a power claim, seeking to command historical events, taking over from within political processes – a sort of cultural *ecclesia militans*.

Once the underlying logic of the argument is exposed, questions surface irresistibly: Is Vittorini's argument really as new as his rhetoric protests? Didn't *La Voce* issue a similar call almost four decades earlier when it spoke of the need to organize a party of intellectuals that would govern the country in accordance with the dictates of reason and moral integrity? Wasn't Vittorini simply once more performing the call to arms that was the founding gesture of the modern intellectual from Zola's *J'accuse* to Sartre's post-war fulminations? The answers to these questions must be carefully nuanced.

It would be too simple to dismiss Vittorini's discourse as an old song dressed up in new rhetorical garb. Though the emphasis in recent historiography has been to underplay the discontinuity between pre- and post-1945, I think it is important to remember that the end of World War II remains a fundamental divide. To begin with, then, the world order that provides the backdrop for Vittorini's statement is indeed significantly new, and this world order includes a socio-political situation that in Italy is still remarkably fluid; while *La Voce* clamoured for liberal democratic reforms, *Il Politecnico* supported a socialist revolution. Furthermore, while it is clear that Vittorini is recuperating and refurbishing elements of ideology that had long been part of the Western intellectual tradition, there is a decidedly new element in the way in which he frames the issues: the stark and uncompromising dichotomy between culture and politics. When Salvemini spoke of the party of intellectuals from the pages of *La Voce*, he was essentially claiming that intellectuals would make better political leaders because of their superior intellectual and moral qualities. And yet politics and culture were not opposed and could not be since they belonged to different conceptual categories. It is precisely against this type of distinction that Vittorini spoke.

The question Vittorini asked with such vehemence was disarmingly simple: how is it that when we name the values that, we maintain, define our culture, we get a list of attributes that have very little if anything to do with the actual history of our civilization? His answer was equally simple: because we keep the sphere of culture and the actual organization of our society separate, because we at best allow cultural values to inspire political practice, when in fact we need cultural values to dictate political practice. In this rough but striking way, Vittorini was squarely putting on the table a very important question: what exactly is the function of a culture that proclaims absolute, and absolutely ineffectual, values? This was the truly progressive element of his discourse.

However, the roughness of the dichotomy, though effective as a provocation, also led Vittorini into the trap of theorizing the primacy of culture, a primacy that suggested a hieratic model of society and that many of Vittorini's primary interlocutors therefore found disquieting. Rather than drawing attention to the politics of culture (i.e., the power relations inherent within a given cultural system), Vittorini seemed to be appealing to objective, universal, non-ideological cultural values as providing the principles to which political practice should be subordinated. In this light, the Resistance lost much of its specifically political meaning and became the founding moment of a revolt of culture against unreason.[7] Once the underpinnings of Vittorini's discourse are made explicit, it becomes clear that a confrontation with the PCI leadership was inevitable and could only be postponed by the political exigencies of the moment. In 1945, Vittorini's openness toward the intellectual community in general and the Catholic intelligentsia in particular was perfectly consistent with the PCI's attempt to extend its influence over the largest possible area of society, regardless of the ideological ambiguities that accompanied this project. The dialogue with non-Marxists promoted a widening support for the progressive agenda and thus strengthened the hand of the party that was poised to monopolize it. In Togliatti's view, the intellectuals could play a key role in fostering the party's image as the champion of progress, modernity, and civilization.

That was 1945. By 1947, when the polemics between Togliatti and Vittorini exploded, a series of national and international events (e.g., the beginning of the Cold War, the Marshall Plan, the exclusion of the left from government) had weakened the PCI. This led Togliatti to revise his political and cultural strategy by focusing on two fundamental objectives: first, to ensconce the PCI in the democratic process, thus making its elimination from the political landscape impossible other than by an all-out violent repression, which led to an accentuated political pragmatism (e.g., support for the Lateran Pacts between the Italian state and the papacy); and second, to present a strong and united ideological front to bolster the PCI's claims to legitimacy and project the image of a combat-ready party determined to make the cost of repression very high, which led to a new intransigence on matters of culture (the 'battle for realism') that was clearly inconsistent with the ecumenical approach promoted by *Il Politecnico*.

Both these orientations played a crucial role in ending the honeymoon between the progressive intellectuals and the PCI. The disaffection was mutual. The intellectuals began to denounce partisan oversimplifications of cultural issues, while the PCI's leadership began to demonstrate a growing irritation toward the insubordination of the intellectual community. These differences would explode in the quarrel over *Il Politecnico*.

The opening salvo in the polemics was Alicata's June 1946 article in *Rinascita*. Alicata's complaints included indiscriminate eclecticism and shallow intellectualism: 'Now, for example, it is intellectualistic, in my view, to consider "revolutionary" and "useful" a writer such as Hemingway, whose talents do not go beyond the fragment or the "well-written page"; to consider "revolutionary" and "useful" a novel such as *For Whom the Bell Tolls*, which confirms in every way Hemingway's incapacity to grasp and judge (i.e., ultimately to *narrate*) something that goes beyond his own elementary, immediate, and thus egotistic sensations. It is also intellectualistic to consider "revolutionary" and "useful" an old and superficial journalistic *reportage* about the October Revolution such as Reed's *Ten Days That Shook the World.'*[8] According to Alicata, fully backed by Togliatti, with whom he had discussed the article before publishing it, *Il Politecnico* had lost sight of its original mandate: to bridge the traditional gap between the intellectuals and the progressive forces of the country, thus promoting a vast progressive consensus within the intellectual community. As a result, the cultural renewal that was the cornerstone of Vittorini's original program turned out to be nothing more, in Alicata's opinion, than a superficial and acritical openness to all sorts of cultural products irrespective of their ideological content.

Particularly galling to Alicata and Togliatti was the attempt to claim the revolutionary value of a writer like Hemingway (a translation of *For Whom the Bell Tolls* had been serialized in the first numbers of *Il Politecnico*), whose 'decadent' individualism they considered to be exemplary of the inability of bourgeois thought to grasp a revolutionary experience, such as the Spanish Civil War. Indeed, we should note how carefully chosen were the examples of intellectualism. What do Hemingway and Reed have in common to warrant their choice as the explicit target of Alicata's attack? After all, Hemingway was more of a realist than Joyce or Kafka, and thus presumably more palatable to the left in the years of triumphant neo-realism. Also, Hemingway was less representative than either Kafka or Joyce of the European high modernism that Vittorini wanted Italian culture to confront and that Alicata and Togliatti wanted summarily to condemn. As for Reed, one could hardly think of a figure less deserving of being held up to ridicule by someone trying to rally a vast progressive front. But the puzzlement that these observations provoke dissipates as soon as we realize that Hemingway and Reed are both U.S. intellectuals who had been severely critical of the Soviet Union. Their ideological shortcomings (which were undoubtedly serious from the PCI leadership's point of view) were much magnified by the fact that they could be seen as legitimating the cultural pluralism of a country that since Churchill's 'iron curtain' speech was well on its way to declaring itself as the fundamental ideological antagonist of socialism. If we read a little between the lines, therefore, we can see that Alicata was helping Togliatti set the boundaries of what would be acceptable during the Cold War in the name of cultural experimentation and research.

We should note the subtlety of the manoeuvre. Alicata is appropriating *Il Politecnico*'s project by legitimating its claim to lead the movement for a renewal and modernization of Italian culture and intellectuals. In so doing, Alicata is also redefining *Il Politecnico*'s mandate in Gramscian terms: this modernization must overcome individualism and abstract intellectualism, that is, it must be aimed at establishing 'a "productive" contact between our culture, and the interests and the "concrete" problems facing the great popular masses of Italy' ('un contatto "produttivo" fra la nostra cultura e gli interessi e i problemi "concreti" delle grandi masse popolari italiane') (Alicata 1946, 116). These are hardly the terms of the project defined in Vittorini's original editorial/manifesto. In fact, the heroic humanism – to borrow a term from Hayden White (1978) – that pervades the 1945 article contained all the ideological ambiguities of which Alicata is only now complaining, as he seeks to enforce the PCI's line on culture.

But this is not all. The logical presupposition of the manoeuvre and its most important, though implicit, message is that the PCI through Alicata has the right and authority to evaluate the efforts made by progressive intellectuals to overcome their traditional isolation and political irrelevance. Just as Vittorini's first editorial could be seen as a power grab by intellectuals, so Alicata's article, appearing in the pages of the official review of the PCI and with the backing of its prestigious leader, constituted a counter-seizure by the party leadership of the progressive intelligentsia's intellectual project. Once we take all these elements into account, Alicata's criticism begins to acquire the character of an official admonishment.

It was the more-or-less implicit aspect of Alicata's article that most struck the readers of *Il Politecnico* and irritated Vittorini. As a result, the explicit criticisms moved by Alicata quickly became secondary. Vittorini dismissed them, without further elaboration, as a misunder-standing by Alicata of what *Il Politecnico* was really about, and refocused the discussion on the real stakes of Alicata's intervention: the much larger issue of the relationship between the party and intel-lectuals, or, within the rather unfortunate conceptual framework Vit-torini proposed and Togliatti accepted, between the claims of politics and those of culture.

In his response to Alicata, Vittorini not only set the parameters for the debate but also began to assert explicitly the autonomy of culture that was already implicit in his original editorial. The central argument is an attempt to articulate the difference between culture and political propaganda (from agitprop to its more highbrow expressions). *Il Politecnico*, Vittorini stated, is not an organ of the PCI. Accordingly, the cultural renewal *Il Politecnico* sought to foster could not be judged in terms of the immediate benefits it brought to the PCI's cause. A new culture is not the by-product of political expediency and can only emerge from the cross-fertilization of all the trends in modern thought. This process of cross-fertilization cannot brook ideological precondi-tions, since its purpose is precisely to constantly test all forms of thought (Marxism included) against a multitude of different practices. Vittorini was in effect positing the cultural sphere as the greater inter-active whole of which politics is a part (albeit, a crucial one). Vittorini's reversal of Alicata's perspective could hardly be more striking. We should note, however, that at the end of his response, Vittorini admit-ted with characteristic honesty that his position raised crucial issues he had yet to think through. Unfortunately, this open-mindedness would soon disappear from the debate.

By raising directly the issue of the relationship between the party and intellectuals who either were party members or considered them-selves communist sympathizers, Vittorini raised the stakes of the dis-cussion and virtually ensured a reply from Togliatti. In his letter to Vittorini, Togliatti wished first and foremost to reassert the right of the party to intervene in cultural debates and pass judgment on experi-ments such as the one attempted by *Il Politecnico*. Secondly, Togliatti reiterated Alicata's substantive criticisms, arguing that an authentic and lasting cultural renewal could only be the result of a critical con-frontation with the multiplicity of modern cultural products. But such a critical confrontation in turn presupposed a coherent theoretical approach that would provide the parameters for evaluation and judg-ment. Togliatti expressed the concern that such a theoretical center of gravity had been lost and *Il Politecnico* was drifting toward a shallow interest for the unusual: 'The declared orientation was not consistently followed, instead it was being replaced, little by little, by something else, by a strange tendency toward a kind of encyclopaedic "culture," where the abstract search for the new, the different, the surprising, took the place of coherent choices and investigations pursuing a clear goal, and the news, information (I wanted to say, using an ugly journalistic term, the news "item") overpowered thinking.'[9]

Once again, the impact of the letter lay not so much in the arguments employed (which add little to Alicata's), but in Togliatti's unwillingness to move beyond a rather rigid and undialectical doctrinal response and acknowledge the real issues raised by the debate (one needs criteria to judge, but how does one arrive at those criteria? does the party promulgate them?). Togliatti also seemed determined to ignore the power relations between the two sides involved in the polemic. There is quite a difference between saying that politicians have a right to comment on cultural affairs and saying that the PCI's leader has a right to admonish ex cathedra the editorial board of a journal for ideological waywardness. Between politics and culture (to adopt for a moment the terms of the debate) there is a whole spectrum of possible interventions, carrying different responsibilities – and this Togliatti refused to acknowledge.

Togliatti's letter gave Vittorini the opportunity to further examine his position. The impassioned tone of Vittorini's reply makes it clear that Vittorini considered the issue crucial to his development as an intellectual. Unfortunately, the emotional elan that animates the text is not sustained by a comparable intellectual dynamism. Vittorini struck a deep chord when he reminded Togliatti of the cultural openness inaugurated by the PCI's Fifth Congress and of the enthusiasm that such openness had generated. He was also convincing when he reiterated that a culture reduced to 'beat[ing] the drum of revolution' ('suonare il piffero della rivoluzione') was a humiliated culture that could not help political progress but rather prepared the ground for political catastrophe. And finally, as Forti and Pautasso note, Vittorini provided a key insight when he asserted that 'The line that, in the field of culture, divides progress from reaction, is not exactly the same as the line that divides them in politics' ('La linea che divide, nel campo della cultura, il progresso dalla reazione, non si identifica esattamente con la linea che li divide in politica') (Forti and Pautasso 1975, 134).

However, Vittorini is at his weakest when he tries once more to define the interaction between the cultural and political sphere, while insisting on the autonomy of the former vis-à-vis the latter. One of the fundamental problems with the argument is that Vittorini spends all his energy trying to demonstrate that culture must be autonomous from politics to be vibrant and, in the final analysis, progressive, but very little time demonstrating how that autonomy can in fact function. In the end, and in spite of the lengthy argumentation, he doesn't get much beyond the thesis that cultural research seeks truth and no political agenda has the right to dictate where that truth is to be found (but is there no role for 'truth' in politics? whose truth?).

The last shot in the polemics came not from Vittorini or Togliatti but from Onofri, who, in another letter to the editor of *Il Politecnico*, put his finger on one of the glaring shortcomings of the debate: Vittorini's loose and constantly shifting definitions of culture and politics. Only much later, however, critics such as Ferretti (1968), Fortini (1972, 1974), Forti and Pautasso (1975), and Asor Rosa (1982) will note that Onofri's intervention could have provided the occasion for a useful reconceptualization of the issues. Then the discussion could have moved away from the sterile contraposition of vague and abstract notions of culture and politics toward a dialectical confrontation between, on the one hand, a specific and concrete cultural formation (i.e., the progressive tradition largely inspired by Marxist thought) and, on the other hand, a specific and concrete political agenda (i.e., that of the PCI). It is in this sense that these critics consider the polemic of *Il Politecnico* a lost opportunity and maintain that the failure of Vittorini's experiment had the effect of holding back the renewal of Italian culture as well as the evolution of the PCI's ideology and cultural policy.

While I substantially agree with this proposition, I would like to make it clear that the debate turned out to be a dead end not because Togliatti was wrong and Vittorini was right or vice versa, but rather because neither was addressing the real issue, namely, whether Togliatti's analysis of the conjuncture was right or wrong. After all, Vittorini would have been ready to agree that, as Giaime Pintor had said, there are times when the intellectual must pick up the gun. Might there not also be times when the intellectual would have to wield the pen as a scalpel rather than a sabre?

These observations lead me to another, more fundamental, issue: the presuppositional limitations of the debate. The inability of the participants in the polemics to contextualize their position reveals once more the reflex to seek definitive and universal answers – in short, the traditional humanist prejudice that, as in Vittorini's first editorial, provides the unspoken horizon of the discussion.[10] Both Vittorini and Togliatti were still trying to articulate the absolute or universal value of politics and culture or, to put it in more modern terms, the principles of a science (in the philosophical sense of certain knowledge) of politics and culture without asking themselves whether such a project was viable or even desirable. This is the aspect that, more than any other, dates the polemics surrounding *Il Politecnico*. It shows how the idealist monopoly over Italian culture still prevented progressive intellectuals from absorbing and elaborating the contextualizing sensitivity that was so much a part of twentieth-century philosophical research (e.g., pragmatism, existentialism, critical Marxism) and cultural practices (from high modernism to the avant-garde).

For the intellectuals who had shared Vittorini's dream of a new culture liberated from its traditional constraints, and thus truly and effectively liberating, the end of *Il Politecnico* was a particularly painful setback. Vittorini did not force an open debate about the PCI's cultural politics; Togliatti's *ragion di stato* (reason of state) would prevail. After all, the legislative elections were just around the corner and the left still seemed to have a good chance of success. The intellectuals could perhaps 'beat the drum of revolution' for a little while and put aside their growing uneasiness about Togliatti's ruthless political pragmatism.

And yet, on the central problem that the debate had raised – the relationship between intellectuals and political power – no progress had been made. This was the most negative legacy of the whole episode. On the one hand, Vittorini had been left to argue for an increasingly indefensible autonomy, indeed priority, of culture; on the other hand, Togliatti sounded more and more like the elderly professor putting his students in their place. One is tempted to say that Alicata's article became a self-fulfilling prophecy; by severing one of the key channels of communication between cultural research and political action, it brought about the conditions it had diagnosed. And in so doing it exposed the weaknesses of an intelligentsia that had much work to do to break free of that 'limping humanism' (to cite a felicitous formulation by Fortini) that was its traditional mould.

Officina 1955–1959: The Poetical Potential of Politics

The eight years between the demise of *Il Politecnico* and the birth of *Officina* were crucial to the political, economic, and social development of contemporary Italy. The landslide victory of De Gasperi's DC in the 1948 elections gave the conservatives a clear majority in both houses of parliament, setting the stage for Italy's alignment with the Western Bloc. Benefiting from a largely intact industrial base in the North, Italy's GNP grew by leaps and bounds, creating the economic miracle thanks to which the country would soon rejoin the elite group of Western industrialized nations. But this unprecedented economic growth was hardly painless, since it was accompanied by huge social problems: chaotic urbanization, infrastructural strains, pollution, and so on. Also, the opportunity was lost to take advantage of the favourable economic conjuncture to correct at least the most glaring economic imbalances and rationalize development on a national basis.

Defeated at the polls and facing a frontal attack on its institutions from Scelba, the new ultra-conservative Minister of the Interior, the PCI focused its efforts on consolidating its hegemony over the disoriented left. In this it succeeded. Rent by internal contradictions, the PSI split and was relegated to a subordinate position, clearing the way for the PCI to become the only credible opposition. In the 1953 elections, the DC and its allies failed to win a majority of the votes, making clear that Italian voters would not support a right-wing involution and favoured a cautious reformism. But as soon as the left seemed poised for a renewed offensive, international events plunged it into a new crisis: the Twentieth Congress of the Communist Party of the Soviet Union (CPSU) in 1956 revealed the horrors of Stalinism while the invasion of Hungary dashed the hopes of many communists – like Calvino – in the success of destalinization.

From a more specifically cultural perspective, the period from 1947 to 1955 was in many ways one of very slow movement that began to accelerate precisely in the mid-1950s. *Officina* was both a symptom of, and an element in, the reawakening of cultural debate. After 1948, the intellectuals on the left, seeing no possibility of a dialogue with the ruling government coalition and thus of real political influence, tended to become as dogmatic and insular as the party that claimed to lead them. And yet, since the turn of the new decade, the PCI's cultural politics had not been exclusively obscurantist. For example, in 1951, at the Seventh Congress of the party, Togliatti had asked Salinari to replace Sereni at the head of the Cultural Commission. A member of the old guard who regarded any criticism of the Soviet Union as an intolerable betrayal, Sereni played the role of the watchdog who kept intellectuals in line and ensured their functionality to the PCI's political struggle.

Salinari, on the other hand, was a representative of the younger generation, less compromised with Stalinism, more sophisticated in his style of argumentation, though ultimately just as ideologically uncompromising as his predecessor, particularly in the 'battle for realism.'

What Salinari accomplished was not so much a change in the ideological content of the PCI's cultural politics as a significant and welcome change in tone. Salinari would tirelessly argue in favour of the party line (e.g., on realism), but he would not simply proceed to enunciate a dogma and then chastise the recalcitrant. The most shining example of the new attitude inaugurated by Salinari was the founding, in 1954, of *Il contemporaneo*, which he directed together with Trombadori. This journal played a very important role in reviving the debate about the relevance of Marxist thinking to the study of culture and society, hosting a variety of interventions (many by Calvino), some of which were in fact quite critical of the party's approach to cultural issues. While perhaps overstating the case a little, Albertina Vittoria's assessment of the change in atmosphere can be substantially retained: 'The role of intellectuals took on a different and constructive character. Intellectuals were considered the agents of cultural organizing and the politics of alliances, they became themselves the artisans, as men of culture, of the communist cultural politics: the party, therefore, had to meet them on their own ground and act so as to ensure that the intellectuals themselves became producers of culture and of cultural accomplishment.'[11]

And yet, the message remained mixed. Togliatti could begin a frank and illuminating dialogue with Bobbio about the meaning of freedom in a socialist society while, at the same time, chastise for contravening party discipline those communist critics who had criticized Pratolini's realist novel *Metello*. In the end, the undeniable evolution of the PCI's cultural politics in the mid-1950s did not seem to shake the well-known doctrinal rigidities. Expressing the hesitations and contradictions characteristic of the intellectual atmosphere of the times, *Officina* emerged as an attempt to take a second look at and move beyond the issues that *Il Politecnico* had left unsolved.

Officina inherited from *Il Politecnico* a preoccupation with identifying the distinct contribution of intellectual research to a politically progressive social project. This preoccupation structured the key interventions by Pasolini, Fortini, Leonetti, Romanò, Roversi, and Scalia (the journal's editorial board). Also part of the *Politecnico*'s legacy was the effort to control the solicitations of the intellectual by political agents, an effort that still took the form, in the final analysis, of a claim for autonomy. Between the Olympian detachment from socio-political events that was so much a part of the Italian intellectual tradition, and the 'crude pragmatism' of a certain Marxist tradition that turned the intellectual into a mere instrument of narrow political ends,[12] *Officina* was still struggling to articulate a notion of cultural commitment that harkened back to Vittorini's 'For a New Culture.'

These continuities, however, are outweighed by the discontinuities that mark the evolution between the two experiences. First of all, it is important to note that the abstractness and looseness of Vittorini's term 'culture' was replaced in *Officina* by a focus on literature and, even more specifically, on poetry. Even though the distinction between literary or poetic works and other forms of intellectual work (i.e., work done by intellectuals qua intellectuals) was never explicitly drawn, it is nevertheless clear that the issue was the specific type of engagement appropriate to literature. This narrowing of focus was consistent with the journal's mandate: *Officina* was essentially a literary journal concerned with literary debates. The encyclopedic enthusiasm of *Il Politecnico* and the optimism that prompted it had disappeared.

Another fundamental and striking difference between Vittorini's and Pasolini's journals is that the latter did not claim as its founding gesture a break with the past. On the contrary, Pasolini's famous article on Pascoli, which opened the first number of *Officina*, made it quite clear that one of the tasks of the journal would be to retrieve what was progressive in the literary tradition (with an emphasis, as we have seen, on the Italian poetic tradition). Leonetti's articles on Leopardi and Caducci, Romanò's on Manzoni, Scalia's on Gozzano and *i crepuscolari*, exemplified this historicist reappraisal of contributions that a Vittorinian urgency for change had dismissed too summarily.

A similar operation, in a wider context, was carried out by Romanò in his article 'Observations on Twentieth Century Literature' ('Osservazioni sulla letteratura del Novecento', in *Officina* 11: 417–44), where he proposed the axis Manzoni–De Sanctis–Croce–Gramsci as a point of departure for a reconceptualization of the relationship between culture and reality. Against the historical backdrop of the 1950s, Marchi interprets this 'settling of accounts with the Fathers' ('fare i conti con i Padri') as evidencing 'the "transitional" cultural structure, which can easily be seen as homologous to the reformistic tension characteristic of political life in the Fifties, on the right as well as on the left' ('la struttura culturale di "transizione," che si può facilmente omologare alla tensione riformistica che caratterizzò la vita politica degli anni Cinquanta, sia da destra che da sinistra'; in Migliori 1979, 47). The observation is certainly pertinent, but I would push it in a somewhat different direction by arguing that what emerged in this aspect of *Officina* was a renewed consciousness of limits.

In the wake of the Resistance, Vittorini could believe that a radical cultural renewal was not only possible but within reach. For Pasolini and his friends, who had experienced the defeat of the Left in 1948, the ensuing crystallization of the PCI's cultural positions, and were about to witness the crisis of the Soviet regime in 1956, cultural renewal was necessarily a much more problematic matter.

As Scalia (in Migliori 1979) and Ferretti (1975) noted, *Officina* was engaged in a double confrontation: on the one hand with the hermetic claim for the self-sufficiency of literature, and on the other with the neo-realist claim for the primacy of the 'real,' which it was the function of literature to reflect.[13] Embattled on these two fronts, *Officina* could not simply leap forward (as Vittorini had tried to do), but rather took the position that a new course could only be charted on the basis of a careful reconstruction of new points of reference. The voluntarism of Vittorini's experiment gave way to the keen awareness that a renewed historical consciousness was an intrinsic component of the articulation of the new.

Thus the attempt, in particular by Pasolini, to develop the notion of experimentation and neo-experimentalism as the liberating component of the tradition: experimentation against the flat reporting proposed by neo-realism; experimentation distinct from the ludic indifference of self-referentiality; experimentation for the expanding of poetic experience so that it could include what had traditionally lain outside it. It is in this sense that Fortini's famous sentence must be understood: 'the only true way, then, to desecrate poetry and leave estheticism behind is to make poetry' '(il solo vero modo, dunque, di dissacrare la poesia e di uscire dall'estetismo è quello di far poesia'; in Migliori 1979, 139). However, Pasolini made it quite clear that this operation was always to some degree compromised by objective constraints (e.g., cultural and personal automatisms: Pascoli's obsessions, the division of labour in capitalist society, etc.) that constantly posed the threat of a drift toward the Scylla of the old and the Charybdis of the false new, at the time, (post)hermeticism and (neo)realism. Ultimately, the transitional aspect of the experience of *Officina* seems to me to emerge most distinctly in the sharp sensitivity of its editors and collaborators to the difficulties and limitations of the literary project. One need only think of Pasolini's later renunciation of the word in favour of the image, as well as Fortini's Adornian preoccupations with the endless recuperation of the language of dissent by neo-capitalism, to see the connection between this sensibility and themes that would take centre stage a decade later, in the 1960s.

The examination of the continuities and discontinuities between the experiences of *Il Politecnico* and *Officina* has cleared the ground for an assessment of the degree to which the latter represents a step forward in, rather than simply a recapitulation of, the cultural debate. The answer to this question presupposes a standard of evaluation. For my purposes, this standard is the degree to which the debate in post-war Italy gradually confronted two realities: first, the culture of high modernism, which contained some of the most vital elements of the Western literary tradition; and second, the transformations that unprecedented socio-economic development was bringing about in the country. The application of this standard to *Officina* yields, perhaps inevitably, a mixed verdict.

The major step forward in the efforts of Pasolini and his friends was the dialecticization and historicization of Vittorini's concept of a new culture. *Officina* foregrounded what *Il Politecnico* 'narcotized' (to use Eco's formulation): the new culture could not arise ex nihilo from a generalized and ultimately rather vague rejection of the past, but had to find nourishment and depth from a reinterpretation of the tradition in a new direction. To borrow from the Frankfurt School, the new had to be a *determinate* negation of the old (Habermas 1971). This greater rootedness in history would allow a more systematic, sensitive, and constructive assessment not only of the Italian literary tradition, but also of the European experiences of the preceding decades.

Furthermore, while it has been persuasively argued in the discussions that followed the publication of Ferretti's pivotal work in 1975 that *Officina* inherited some of *Il Politecnico*'s eclecticism, *Officina* did not lack a clearly identifiable theoretical position, namely, historicism (Marchi in Migliori 1979, 48–9). The discussions turned around a relatively clear philosophical centre, and the alleged lack of a more specific focus is an accurate reflection of the fluidity that characterizes this transitional period. In the end, the accusation of superficiality that Togliatti levelled against *Il Politecnico* could not be renewed here.

The second important step forward accomplished by *Officina* is related to the first: a growing awareness, particularly noticeable in

Pasolini, of the problematicity of the role of the intellectual and of literature in the Italian society of the 1950s. Vittorini's captivating naivety and enthusiasm for the possibilities opened by the demise of Fascism was replaced by a critical edge that refused to spare not only the PCI's cultural policy (the attacks on neo-realism such as Scalia's 'Party Literature' ['La letteratura di partito,' *Officina* 2: 51–6]) but also the PCI's political position (e.g., Romanò's 'Observations on Twentieth Century Literature' ['Osservazioni sulla letteratura del Novecento'; *Officina* 11: 417–44]). This more disenchanted attitude toward the PCI laid the foundations for a much more constructive engagement of intellectuals on the side of socialism. In particular, it began to open the eyes of the left-wing intelligentsia to elements of the conjuncture (e.g., the advent of consumer society) that the PCI leadership was slow to register, elements that would eventually become part of the constellation termed neo-capitalism.

The third and final advance in the discourse of *Officina* makes explicit what had remained somewhat implicit in *Il Politecnico*. The battle for a new literature was not a battle for new contents or topics (the polemical target was, once again, neo-realism with its emphasis on the social as the mandatory reality requiring literary elaboration), nor for new formal devices as an end in themselves (the target here being hermeticism and the alleged self-sufficiency of literary expression), but rather for a new style. The teachings of Spitzer and Contini were married to a well-thought-out (re)reading of Lukács.[14] The notion of experimentation that *Officina* sought to develop and practise moved decisively beyond the worn dichotomies of form and content, decadence and realism, subjectivism and objectivity, and toward the reevaluation of the political potential of poetry in terms of the poetical potential of politics (e.g., Pasolini's poem 'Gramsci's Ashes' ['Le ceneri di Gramsci']).[15] It is open to question whether this movement remained for the moment mostly a semantic pirouette, but at least the question began to be posed in more two-directional and complex terms, and in a less abstract and dogmatic way, than the Vittorini/Togliatti debate had done.

Officina's shortcomings, on the other hand, lay first and foremost in what I would term the 'institutional' framework within which the operation was conducted. Vittorini's enthusiasm was certainly naive, yet he at least understood that one of the fundamental aspects of the new culture was its openness not only to a variety of research efforts but also to a new public. *Il Politecnico* attempted to widen cultural discourse and invited the active participation of addressees in a cultural elaboration that had typically treated them as passive recipients. The implied reader of Vittorini's journal was an educated non-specialist who was addressed with a solicitude free of condescension. This attempt to provide an open forum where particular kinds of knowledge could make their contribution to a public elaboration of the common good provides the clearest evidence of the profound connection between Vittorini's program and the cultural and political aspirations that emerged in Italy with renewed urgency in the immediate post-war period.

In *Officina*, however, this tension to expand and democratize intellectual debate was lost. In spite of greater theoretical self-consciousness and rigour, *Officina* remained on one level a very traditional journal for a narrow group of intellectuals discussing their own problems largely among themselves and their peers. The cultural management that becomes central to the role of the intellectual in modern societies, and which Vittorini prefigured in *Il Politecnico*, was replaced by specialist discussions that seemed to manifest a surrender to the capitalist division of labour.[16]

Ultimately, then, *Officina* still demonstrates the degree to which Italian intellectuals found it difficult to overcome the limitations of an ingrained and largely unproblematized humanist perspective. The fixation on the canon, the attempt to define a universally applicable poetic (namely, the poetic of experimentation), and, most important, the slow response to the new challenges facing the intellectual in a mass culture (challenges that become the condition of intellectual production in modern developed societies), all these elements are evidence of the surreptitious persistence of traditional habits of thought. As Migliori argues: 'The limits of *Officina* ... I would like to define them as dialectical. They are symptoms of a dialectic of *disorganicity* that was tried and failed precisely because it contended with ... the cultural-political *synthesis* rather than confronting the root issue of class analysis ... The *error* is the missing class analysis of capitalist society and culture, relying on Marxian instruments which would have made it possible to define the political economy of the intellectual and of *intellectual production* (not only of the intellectual's *function*), as well as of the capitalist mode of production of culture and of the social relations in which culture and literature are produced' (emphasis added).[17]

This kind of criticism needs to be itself historicized (particularly Migliori's rather schematic insistence on class analysis) and, more importantly for my purposes, must be directed at the shortcomings of a whole cultural elite rather than at this journal per se. One only needs to review the discussions of the time, even in a rather uninhibited and leading-edge Marxist publications as *Il contemporaneo*, to realize that the type of 'tools' Migliori talks about were in short supply. The crux of the problem emerges once again: the left-wing intelligentsia were struggling to develop the more sophisticated theoretical apparatus that would allow them to first grasp the socio-economic consequences of the economic miracle, and then to move the political debate resolutely forward on the basis of that new understanding.

Il Menabò 1959–1967: Commitment at Sunset

From a socio-political and economic perspective, the years during which *Il Menabò* was published were characterized by a paradoxical asynchronicity. Governments, following each other in rapid succession as politicians struggled to work out a stable coalition, were increasingly aware of the need for reforms that would bring socio-political institutions more into line with the tumultuous economic growth and the resulting transformations in civil society. And yet this new awareness, which soon turned into a sense of urgency in front of a looming crisis, could not find an outlet. The reformist impetus was repeatedly humiliated by a majority interested first and foremost in maintaining its political hold on the state, a majority whose instincts were necessarily conservative and that was an easy prey of the reactionaries' absolute veto on change. The result was a flurry of initiatives against a background of substantial political stagnation.

After a series of political crises that brought the democratic institutions to the brink of collapse, the DC managed to maintain its grip on government and the state by pulling within its orbit the PSI, a rather reluctant partner. But this was accomplished only at the cost of embracing a cynical new ideology of power at any cost. Endless squabbling among the members of the governing coalition would soon replace any real political debate and stifle any substantive reforms. The gap between political institutions and civil society continued to widen.

As for the PCI, the process of renewal begun in the mid-1950s suffered a severe setback in 1956, the year of Khrushchev's denunciation of Stalin and the Soviet invasion of Hungary. It was not until the 1960s that the whole landscape began to move again (see the major conferences organized by the Istituto Gramsci on *Tendenze del capitalismo italiano* in 1962 and *Tendenze del capitalismo europeo* in 1965). Only then would the PCI finally condemn without equivocation the subordination of culture to immediate political exigencies:

From the beginning of the Fifties, then, the PCI developed a unitary approach to cultural politics. This approach went through a series of often contradictory stages, as well as the cleavage of 1956, but thanks to Togliatti's decisive influence and guidance, eventually led to the thinking of the early Sixties and to the positions elaborated at the [Ninth] and, above all, the [Tenth] Congress [1962 and 1963, respectively]. At this time, it was affirmed unambiguously that if it is up to the party 'to organize around itself the cultural forces that are confronting in a progressive way the problems originating in social life,' it is not up to the party 'to propose solutions to the problems originating in scientific and artistic research' or 'to pass judgment on the scientific or artistic validity of a given solution,' and this was a clear and direct rejection of Zhdanovism.[18]

The fact of the matter is that in the early 1960s, the effects of the second industrial revolution, which had taken place in Italy in the 1950s, could no longer be ignored. Thanks to significant pay increases won by a revitalized union movement, workers' disposable income grew, contributing in a crucial way to creating the necessary conditions for the advent of a consumer society. Television replaced radio as the household window on the world, and with it came not only a whole new world of advertising but also the organization on a truly industrial scale of cultural production. FIAT launched the '600,' the subcompact that would make the motor car massively accessible. While it would be inexact to talk about an affluent society in North American terms, an expanding middle class was gaining access to a standard of living or, perhaps more accurately, consumption levels (from the family car to higher education) previously reserved for a small elite.

In sum, Italian society began to exhibit many of the general characteristics of a modern Western industrial society. Among them, of course, was the venal, superficial, and self-satisfied consumerism of the rising bourgeoisie, which was captured with typical promptness in Fellini's *La dolce vita*. Another was the intellectual restlessness that would be the subject of Calvino's *The Watcher*, as we shall see in the last chapter of this book. This was the new Italy that emerged from the 1950s, the Italy that the experience of *Il Menabò* helps us bring more sharply into focus.

With one foot in the 1950s and the other in the 1960s, *Il Menabò* strad-dled not only two decades but also increasingly divergent ideological positions. By the end of the 1950s, the left-wing intellectuals who emerged from the Resistance and dominated the post-war cultural debates were facing a challenge from the younger generation, which began to question Marxism (Gramscian or otherwise) and show inter-est in the new critical approaches being developed abroad, particularly in France. *Il Menabò* provided a space for the interface of the ethico-political impulses of the 1940s and 1950s (perhaps best represented by the axis Vittorini-Fortini) with the new theoretical apparatuses made available by structuralism, semiology, phenomenology à la Blanchot, and so on. The fallout of this interface was not only a clearer ideologi-cal divide within the new avant-garde itself (Ferretti 1968), but also the first clear symptoms of the radical contestation of neo-capitalist culture that would explode in the late 1960s. As the last major editorial initia-tive by Vittorini, who chose Calvino as his co-editor, *Il Menabò* pro-vides an excellent snapshot of the evolution of cultural debates in Italy at the turn of the decade.

The first *Menabò* appeared the same year that *Officina* ceased publi-cation, and it is hard to avoid the impression that Vittorini, who had remained strangely aloof from the experiments of Pasolini and his friends, was once more picking up the baton of cultural renewal. After the demise of *Il Politecnico*, however, Vittorini had not remained in-active. Even leaving aside his novelistic production, in 1951 he had transferred his editorial interests to the series *I Gettoni*, published by Einaudi. As Roversi noted (*Officina* 4: 158–64), the series, which was termed a *collana-rivista* (a series-cum-literary review), was the expres-sion of a precise editorial project, namely, that of challenging tradi-tional forms of narratives by setting two opposite lines of development against each other: on the one hand, the products of high modernism in the wake of Proust, Joyce, and Kafka, and, on the other hand, the historical novels that, moving away from mere reportage, struggled to provide an imaginative grasp of the conjuncture. Vittorini's involve-ment with *I Gettoni* ended in 1958, and we have Calvino's testimony to the effect that *Il Menabò* was its direct descendant: 'Once the experience of *I Gettoni* could be said to be over, he [Vittorini] felt the need for a publication in which critical discussion had more room, alongside the presentation of new texts. He proposed to Einaudi something in between a literary review and a series of volumes, that is, numbers-volumes appearing at irregular intervals. The publication would contain essays of criticism but would not have the traditional structure of a literary review. Each volume was intended to be large enough to accommodate short novels and collections of poetry. It would not be tightly monographic but rather would be focused on one or two general themes.'[19] Calvino also acknowledges the link to *Officina*: 'In addition to the legacy of *I Gettoni*, *Il Menabò* also inherited some of the concerns of the Bolognese journal *Officina*. From the beginning, Vittorini had close ties with Roversi and Leonetti; and later Leonetti played an important role in defining the approach for the central numbers of *Il Menabò*. Even though they remained on the outside, both Pier Paolo Pasolini and Franco Fortini made crucial contributions.'[20] These observations by Calvino confirm that *Il Menabò* was the last attempt to mediate the differences among a group of intellectuals who had covered a lot of ground together in the 1940s and 1950s, but whose paths had began to diverge.

In the political and socio-economic context of the late 1950s and early 1960s, *Il Menabò* appears to have performed two fundamental operations. First, it finally raised the issue of the industrial organization of cultural production, and the place of the intellectual within it. Second, it sanctioned definitively the PCI's loss of leadership over the most advanced (in the sense of theoretically well-informed and politically astute) intellectuals.

With respect to the first of these operations, *Il Menabò* 4 and 5, which appeared in 1961 and 1962, are the key numbers. And yet the tone of the debate that these numbers sparked and hosted had already been set a year earlier by Calvino's 'The Sea of Objectivity' ('Il mare dell'oggettività') in *Il Menabò* 2. In that article, Calvino posed the problem of the relationship to the 'real' by lamenting the tendency, discerned in the artistic production of the 1950s, to dissolve the tension between the individual, history and nature into a surrender to the magma of things, of objective Being. After noting that such a surrender converged paradoxically with its opposite (i.e., with the dissolution of the objective world in the flux of subjective interiority, which characterized the experimentations, in the previous decades, of writers such as Joyce, Beckett, and even Musil), Calvino attributed the phenomenon to a crisis of revolutionary aspirations and of the ethico-political impulse that was their corollary. He concluded by reiterating the need for a literature determined to confront the complexity of the real with a humility and tough-mindedness that precluded any easy abdication before the merely given.

In the context of Calvino's articulation, the polemics that developed in *Il Menabò* 4 and 5 around the discussion of the relationship between industry and literature becomes clearer. Vittorini's argument in the article 'Industry and Literature' ('Industria e letteratura'), which opened *Il Menabò* 4, was essentially the following: industry is the fundamental objective reality of our times, and yet literature has not yet attempted to penetrate that reality and to develop a cognitive/imaginative grasp of the new conditions of existence that industry has instituted. Mindful of the lessons of *Officina*, Vittorini made it quite clear that literature could not respond to this new challenge simply by making aspects of the industrial world, such as factory life, into a new topic for narrative presentation. Rather, literature could be 'equal to its times' ('all'altezza della situazione') only by transforming its methods and forms, that is, by developing an industrial style: 'The truth of industry lies in the chain of effects that the factory world sets into motion. And the writer, whether or not he deals with factory life, will be at an industrial level only insofar as his gaze and his judgment are permeated by this truth and by the processes (processes of appropriation, processes of further transformation) that such truth encompasses.'[21] It is only by absorbing and metabolizing at all levels of expression the newness of industrial reality that literature could fulfil its function to redeem the industrial world from its alien objectivity and help society as a whole formulate an emancipatory project that was rooted in the understanding of the present.

Vittorini's position was developed with a more rigorous theoretical instrumentation by Scalia's article 'From Nature to Industry' ('Dalla natura all'industria'). Scalia explicitly noted that the use of the term 'objective' to describe industrial reality was a means of facing the fact that it was no longer possible (or, in any event, it was anachronistic) to reject industrial development. Indeed Scalia's position was that industry was the common condition of all developed societies, whether capitalist or socialist. Industry had created a new anthropological condition that needed to be grasped from within so that the processes unleashed by development could be humanly mastered, and the future socially chosen. Literature had a crucial role to play in this reappropriation by humanity of its future. In the end, the two leading theoretical interventions in *Il Menabò* 4 were attempts to articulate the 'how' for the agenda Calvino had set: the redefinition of a human project in the face of the proliferation of industrial objectivities. This project remained closely allied to the Habermassian 'project of modernity':

confronted with the increasingly complex and fragmented world of technical/technological development on an industrial scale, the function of literature was to reappropriate particular forms of knowledge and experience within a public discourse about the 'good life,' within a political project that sought to humanize the machine and democratize decision-making processes. The modern intellectual still has a crucial function to play in the world envisaged by Calvino, Vittorini, and Scalia.

Il Menabò 5 pursued the discussion initiated in the previous number and hosted one of the most radical criticisms of Vittorini's and Scalia's proposals, namely, Fortini's article 'Clever as Doves' ('Astuti come colombe'; *Il Menabò* 5: 29–44). Fortini's attack was based on a Lukácsian perspective that called into question the very presuppositions of Vittorini's and Scalia's discourse. To accept the society produced by industrial development as a given (i.e., as a fact before or beyond ideology), to maintain that the task of the intellectual is that of grasping such a given rather than contesting it, and, finally, to see human liberation as the technical mastering of industry, represented for Fortini a surrender to immediacy, an ideological forgetfulness of the human relations that the objective world of industry dissimulates, and ultimately the very naturalization of industrial reality, which Vittorini and Scalia wanted to overcome:

> The goal is to shed light on the relation between object and user, object and producer. But this should not obscure the human etiology of the objects themselves.[22]

> The goal is not only to privilege immediacy but also, it seems, to conclude that, replaced by the categories of the 'Old' and the 'New,' history does not exist; that there are lacunae in the relations of cause and effect about which nobody must ask – or else one's soul is condemned to death, that is, to *ideology* – what modern industry lives on, who moves it, who produces it, who benefits from it.[23]

In sum, Fortini denounced the reformist presupposition that informed Vittorini's and Scalia's attempt to deal with Calvino's sea of objectivity, and reserved the right to an Adornian negativity: 'Today, every literary expression that portrays enslavement in such a way as to make immediately possible the illusion of freedom, serves an illusory freedom ... Today, I believe it is up to the coherent Marxist and Socialist to mock the noble anguish with which capitalist reformism tries to hide its substantial optimism, the persuasion of having succeeded in assuring progress and democracy to our country.'[24]

In this same number of *Il Menabò*, Calvino and Eco steered a middle course. In 'The Challenge of the Labyrinth' ('La sfida al labirinto'; *Una pietra*, 88), Calvino elaborated the position stated in 'The Sea,' and argued for a literature that would measure itself against the increasing complexity of the industrial world and seek a way out by traversing it rather than by rejecting it wholesale. While Calvino did not support the non-ideological claims of Vittorini and Scalia, he also attacked Fortini's position: 'To those who ask themselves every instant: "But am I not playing capitalism's game?" I prefer those who tackle all the problems of transforming the world with the confidence that what is best serves the best. After all, in this same number the text by Fortini is a document of how a revolutionary tension, if sustained only by a passion for theory and not for practical human action (and for the things that are the instruments and products of that action), turns out to be a choice of nothing.'[25] To Fortini's ascetic denial, Calvino opposes, at the cost of an empiricism clearly of Vittorinian descent, the lucid acceptance of the ambiguous position of the intellectual in industrial society.

Eco, on the other hand, in his long article 'About Giving Form as Engagement with Reality' ('Del modo di formare come impegno sulla realtà'; *Il Menabò* 5: 198–237) develops, as Marchi notes (1973), the theoretical justification for the new avant-garde. Starting from the proposition that language cannot be innocent (i.e., non-alienated, in the parlance of the times) and that 'art knows the world through its formative structures' ('l'arte conosce il mondo attraverso le proprie strutture formative'; *Il Menabò* 5: 222), Eco argues that the writer (Joyce in the specific example) 'alienates himself in the situation [he is confronting] by adopting its modalities. But by making these modalities evident, and becoming himself aware of their form-giving function, he escapes the situation and masters it. He escapes alienation by estranging in the narrative structure the situation in which he has alienated himself.'[26] What kind of writing, then, can be considered avant-garde? 'It is art that, in order to have an impact on the world, descends in it, adopting from the inside the conditions of its [the world's] crisis, and uses to describe this crisis the same alienated language in which this world is expressed. This art brings clarity to the world. *Ostending* it as a discursive formation, this art discloses the alienating nature of this world, enabling us to demystify it. From here the next operation can begin.'[27]

While accepting Calvino's rejection of objectivism (in 'The Sea') and the attempt to evacuate the subject and his ethico-political tension from literature, Eco maintains that such objectivism is in the strictest sense an impossibility. The object is not a metaphysical thing-in-itself radically divorced from the human world, but, rather, 'It is the world of modified nature, of manufactured objects, of relations that we have posited and that we now find again outside ourselves ... Now, this world that we have created contains within itself, not only the risk of reducing us to its own instruments, but also the elements on the basis of which the parameters for a new human dimension can be established.'[28] It is this effort to explore and reassert the human possibilities within reality that demands an open structure for the work of art in our times, and constitutes the only legitimate form of commitment in literature.

The inclusion of Eco's article made absolutely clear that Vittorini was increasingly sensitive to the discourse of the new avant-garde, anticipating the new phase that *Il Menabò* 7 would inaugurate. More than any of the other interventions, 'About Giving Form' drew heavily from the then most recent developments in criticism (Robbe-Grillet) and communication theory (Barthes) that dominated literary studies in France and would soon burst on the international scene. With *Il Menabò* 7 Vittorini could finally steer the internationalist course that had been his vocation from the times of *Il Politecnico*. Though the original title of the publication was retained, the new turn was marked by a new subtitle (*Gulliver*) to signal a difference that Vittorini himself took pains to underline in the opening editorial. With *Il Menabò-Gulliver*, Vittorini was opening the Italian intellectual scene to direct solicitation from abroad and specifically from Germany and France (i.e., Barthes, Blanchot, Enzensberger, etc.). With this gesture, Vittorini could claim that he had fulfilled his chosen mandate: to shake the Italian intelligentsia out of its provincialism and reinsert it into the mainstream of Western European culture. What remains to be established is at what cost such catching up was bought.

I have spent some time outlining the debate that raged on the pages of the two central issues of *Il Menabò* because it seems to me that all the articles in question (though not all to the same degree) provide a spectrum of opinion that represents an indubitable advance over the efforts of *Il Politecnico* and *Officina*. Fortini may well have been right to accuse Vittorini and Scalia of 'Kennedism' and to maintain, some years later, that '*Il Menabò* was the last Italian literary review, according to a notion of literature rightly swept away after '67 ... *Il Menabò* was a successful mistake' '(Il Menabò è stata l'ultima rivista letteraria italiana, secondo una nozione di letteratura giustamente travolta dopo il '67 ... Il Menabò' è uno sbaglio riuscito'; in Marchi 1973, 60n101). The fact of the matter, however, is that the question of the role of intellectuals in modern society had never been discussed in Italy with such lucidity as in the two issues in question.

The Lukácsian and Adornian problematics raised by Fortini himself, the structuralist suggestions of Scalia and Leonetti, the semiological prefigurations in Eco, and, in general, the emphasis on the new function of the intellectual in an industrial society, all witness that the old humanism still championed by Vittorini (though with a neo-positivist twist that was further evidence of Vittorini's constant alertness to fresh stimuli) was no longer a dominant force. The historicism that had been, as we have seen, the trademark of *Officina* was also being seriously questioned by the very people who had propounded it (i.e., Scalia, Leonetti). Still, there was a price to pay for this *aggiornamento*. If we harken back to the atmosphere of the Resistance, which I tried to evoke earlier, and to the enthusiasm of Vittorini's 'For a New Culture,' we realize that what started as a cultural movement with truly revolutionary intent was fizzling out in a theoretical sophistication that justified, at best, reformism and social democracy (except in the case of Fortini, who seemed to prefigure certain aspects of 1968). It is striking how Vittorini, Scalia, and, to some extent, Calvino seem to be providing the ideological legitimation of the new centre-left government and, more specifically, of the PSI's role in it. Long gone are the times for leaps forward, such as the one *Il Politecnico* had attempted. Only Fortini seems determined not to come to any compromise with triumphant neo-capitalism, but then, as Calvino points out, he seems to be unable to propose any real alternative to silence.

Il Menabò marks, then, the last attempt to form a united front of progressive intellectuals vis-à-vis the socio-political conjuncture. This front would no longer involve an explicit political affiliation, as had been the case fifteen years earlier in the immediate post-war period, but rather a consensus at least on the basic nature of the task on which to focus the intellectual energies of the country. For Vittorini and Scalia the focus had to be on the nature and problems of massive industrialization, which they saw as having brought about a distinctly new and inescapable human predicament. Calvino insisted that this predicament be perceived as an ethico-political, rather than merely a technical problem, while Fortini wanted to reject the very parameters of the discussion. And Eco introduced further distancing mediations between literature and the real, shifting attention to the problem of de-alienating language.

It is important to note that in *Il Menabò* a kind of unity was still preserved. From Fortini to Eco, all still saw the role of literature and of the intellectual to be that of contributing to the elaboration of a progressive social project. And yet one already feels that this ethico-political impulse is most authentically felt by Calvino and Fortini, whose interventions, not surprisingly, clashed most directly. On the other hand, Vittorini, Scalia and Eco's interventions seem more interested (and here is where Fortini's criticism hit the proverbial nail on the head) in the technical challenge of mastering the 'brave new world' of industry (for the first two) and of communication theory (Eco). And indeed, after this unsuccessful attempt at establishing a substantive consensus, Vittorini would slide into a neo-positivistic celebration of technical progress, while Eco would find in semiotic theory an ideal vehicle for his theoretical research. As for Fortini and Calvino, they would chart their own independent and, henceforth, largely solitary courses. In the mid-1970s, Fortini would remember this period and regretfully say that each chose to be right on one's own, rather than struggle together.

In the final analysis, then, the experience of *Il Menabò* provided the emerging new avant-garde with the left-wing legitimacy (*copertura a sinistra*) it needed to assert and then consolidate its hegemony over the Italian cultural scene. In 1963, at the much-publicized meeting in Palermo, the new group would attempt to articulate a coherent poetics (see Balestrini 1964) and fail to do so (Asor Rosa 1973, 149–61). Its institutional success, however, was unquestionable and due to the fact that its members understood much better than their predecessors the new managerial function of intellectuals in neo-capitalism. But the function that in the early Vittorini (in spite of all his philosophical naivety) remained strongly tied to an ethico-political tension, now turned, by and large, into corporativist interest. The modern intellectual survived at the margins, while centre stage was taken over by a new figure: the expert. Some of the characteristics of the new dispensation were the retreat into an increasingly and unprecedently esoteric specialistic discourse that abandoned the goal of revitalizing public discourse about the 'good life,' and an institutional activism that sought to colonize the management of cultural production and organize it on an industrial basis, while bracketing issues of ideology. This constellation is beyond the scope of this study, but I mention it because it underlines the significance of the boundary that *Il Menabò* has allowed me to trace. Calvino would play a role in that configuration as well, but he would play it from Paris, where he settled in 1967 after his marriage in 1964 and the birth of his daughter in 1965; interestingly, the historical caesura had a counterpart in Calvino's personal life.

CHAPTER TWO

Italo Calvino: From Neo-realism to the Fantastic

The discussion of the cultural debates that took place in post-war Italy provides us with the intellectual horizon within which Calvino's works need to be situated. It is important to reiterate that Calvino played an active role in all the key moments of the historical narrative that occupied us in the previous chapter. In 1943, Calvino joined the Garibaldi Brigades, which were operating in the mountains near San Remo, the Ligurian city where he grew up. His experience of the Resistance was at first hand and would bear fruit literarily in his widely acclaimed first novel, *The Path to the Nest of Spiders*. In 1945, Calvino became a member of the PCI and one of the core journalists in Vittorini's *Il Politecnico*. In the late 1940s and early 1950s, Calvino struggled to find a mature voice in *I giovani*, which was eventually serialized in *Officina*. And by the end of the 1950s, Calvino emerged as a leading figure in Italian letters with the publication of his fantastic trilogy and a series of essays that seemed to crystallize many of the issues at the centre of the cultural debates of the time. In this perspective, his co-editing of *Il Menabò* with Vittorini amounted almost to a consecration, as the older generation passed the baton to the new one. For Calvino, the trajectory of the Italian intelligentsia during this period is not simply an element in the background; rather, it is inherently related to his own personal trajectory. These, then, are undeniably the formative experiences in Calvino's development as a writer and intellectual.

Calvino and Neo-realism

Before we proceed to an analysis of the first in the series of texts through which, as I have suggested in the introduction, Calvino fashioned the basic elements of his unique style, we need to reflect more deeply on the literary movement whose rise and fall spans the two decades between 1943 and 1963, namely, neo-realism. We have seen how neo-realism was the manifestation in the aesthetic domain of the socio-political aspirations around which the Italian progressive intelligentsia rallied in the immediate post-war period. In its first phase (roughly from 1945 to 1948), neo-realism emerged primarily as an expression of post-war enthusiasm that was shared by large sections of the population and of which the young intellectuals (many of whom had participated in the Resistance movement) became the interpreters. In a famous passage from his 1964 preface to a new edition of *The Path*, Calvino made the point with typical lucidity:

> Italy's literary explosion in those years was less an artistic event than a physiological, existential, collective event. We had experienced the war, and we younger people – who had been barely old enough to join the partisans – did not feel crushed, defeated, 'beat.' On the contrary, we were victors, driven by the propulsive charge of the just-ended battle, the exclusive possessors of its heritage. Ours was not easy optimism, however, or gratuitous euphoria. Quite the opposite. What we felt we possessed was a sense of life as something that can begin again from scratch, a general concern with problems, even a capacity within us to survive torment and abandonment; but we added also an accent of bold good humour. Many things grew out of that atmosphere, including the attitude of my first stories and my first novel. (*The Path*, v)

It is precisely this 'bold good humour' ('spavalda allegria') that breathes life into Pin, the youngster who is the protagonist of *The Path*, and confers on the narrative that surreal, fable-like intensity and levity that constitute its enduring interest, though the novel remains, in my view, an immature work (cf. Re 1990).[1]

Calvino and his contemporaries perceived and responded to a youthful desire to take full advantage of the freedom to speak openly about the dramatic experiences of the war, a desire that was all the more keen because it was a liberation from two decades of Fascist rhetoric and mystification. People wanted to know the truth about the past as well as the present, and they longed for that reality which open and frank communication could disclose.

The Resistance became an inescapable focus of artistic elaboration since its objectively dramatic character not only demanded artistic sublimation but was also ideally suited to function as the founding civic myth for the new Italian Republic. Another aspect of this thirst for the 'truth' and the 'real' manifested itself in curiosity about the way in which people across the country actually lived. An enthusiasm for social change steered this curiosity toward communities that had traditionally been socio-economically marginalized. This spawned a series of novels about the Italian South, whose rural economy and feudal social structures provided an easy opportunity to voice indignation over long-standing injustices, thus legitimating the progressive political project that the vast majority of Italian intellectuals favoured at this time. What is not always acknowledged, however, is that this disclosure of the Italian 'Deep South' also provided a ready-made defamiliarization effect, sometimes reduced to an exoticism whose decadent ancestry did not escape the most attentive critics (see, for example, Alicata's critique of C. Levi's *Cristo si è fermato a Eboli*, in Milanini 1980).

However, as we have seen, by the end of the 1940s the socio-political context had changed dramatically. The polarization of political life leading up to and following the 1948 elections did much to stifle postwar enthusiasm. The anti-Fascist consensus evaporated as the ideological differences between the left and the right gained centre stage, not only nationally but also internationally.

In response to this new conjuncture and its political exigencies, neo-realism ceased to be a movement and became a poetics, that is to say, it was systematized into a fairly precise set of aesthetic principles. The elaboration of a neo-realist poetics, which played a key role in preserving the PCI's cultural leadership over progressive intellectuals during the 1950s, begs two basic and related questions that will ultimately lead us back to Calvino and *I giovani*: first, what conceptual resources were deployed in the elaboration of the neo-realist poetics? And second, why was the poetics of neo-realism so successful in rallying leading intellectuals? I will try to answer each of these questions in turn.

The elements that contributed to the elaboration of a fairly coherent neo-realist poetics had three main sources.[2] First and foremost was the strong humanist tradition that had made historicism its trademark and dominated Italian letters since the Romantic revolution and the teachings of its most eminent interpreter, Francesco De Sanctis. One of the most important aspects of De Sanctis's contribution to the Italian intellectual tradition was to place a renewed emphasis on the notion that literature must be seen as an integral part of, and an intervention into, the social processes that surround it. Consequently, De Sanctis called attention to the importance of the social role of the writer and intellectual. The second source was Benedetto Croce, who played a key role at the turn of the twentieth century in revamping the Italian humanist and historicist legacy. In spite of his insistence on the distinctness of the aesthetic moment and the atemporal universality of poetic value, principles such as the perfect fusion between form and content, the utter individuality of the creative act, and the universality of the poetic word became fully assimilable to the humanist project once situated within Croce's neo-Hegelian historicism. Admittedly, the militant dimension of De Sanctis's teachings was largely lost, or rather transposed, from the realm of national history to the realm of the universal history of Spirit.

The axis along which De Sanctis and Croce were aligned was completed by the third source, Gramsci, whose contribution was seen to be primarily that of providing a concrete and immediately applicable political analysis of the function of literature and the role of intellectuals. By shifting attention away from aesthetics and toward the politics of culture, Gramsci demonstrated the relevance and originality of a Marxist approach, which many post-war Italian intellectuals were eager to adopt. At the same time, his emphasis on culture and education was susceptible of a humanist interpretation that made his brand of Marxism much more familiar and palatable to the Italian intelligentsia. Gramsci's return to De Sanctis's militantism could be seen as providing a needed correction to the aloofness or Olympian stance espoused by Croce during the Fascist regime and now thoroughly discredited, a correction that reiterated the ethical assumptions – particularly in relation to the moral duty of the intellectual – that were among the fundamental elements of continuity in the national tradition. Finally, on a more practical political level, Gramsci's call for a literature that was both national and popular underlined the importance of the cultural battle that socialism had to fight in order to successfully revolutionize bourgeois society, and provided a workable blueprint for a cultural strategy that was sensitive to the realities of modern industrial society.

And yet, the De Sanctis-Croce-Gramsci axis was theoretically too unstable to provide the poetics on the basis of which neo-realism could be systematized and vindicated. Indeed, beyond a set of general though quite basic tenets – about the historical significance of literature, the leadership role intellectuals are called to play in the life of the nation, and the importance of developing a vigorous national tradition – these authors did not have much in common. What made their quite different approaches seem more compatible than they actually were was their common allegiance – by and large, and with significantly different inflections (e.g., Gramsci's interest in popular genres) – to the Italian equivalent of the 'Great Tradition,' that is, a substantial agreement in their literary pronouncements (again, Gramsci's criticism of Manzoni stands out as atypical). In sum, the De Sanctis-Croce-Gramsci line expressed more a literary taste, which these authors had both manifested and shaped, than a well-thought-out poetics. This taste was firmly rooted and indeed stuck in the nineteenth century, and here the parallel between Italy's delayed socio-economic development in relation to Western Europe and the United States, and the provincialism of the Italian cultural scene, becomes unavoidable.

As for the poetics of neo-realism being so successful in rallying leading intellectuals, several reasons may be adduced. Having in general little appreciation for the high modernism of the European avant-garde, the vast majority of Italian intellectuals were culturally conservative at the same time that they were politically progressive (Togliatti's tirades against contemporary art and literature are notorious). This implicit cultural conservatism was a powerful tool in the hands of a master tactician such as the PCI leader. It was precisely by displaying ostentatiously this cultural traditionalism that Togliatti's party sought to obtain the *lettres de noblesse* it needed to reassure intellectuals and win them over, hoping that their support would eventually seduce the reluctant petty bourgeoisie (the social stratum from which these intellectuals predominantly came), whose votes were essential to an electoral victory. After the debacle of 1948 the possibility of such a victory had receded, and yet it remained the fundamental justification of a strategy that had difficulty envisaging other avenues for political struggle in a bourgeois democracy.

The national dynamic was reinforced by the international situation. On the cultural front, the propaganda war between socialism and capitalism took the form of the 'battle for realism' waged by Soviet critics and their sympathizers against Western 'decadence.' The rejection of virtually any type of formal experimentation, the insistence on the Balzacian novel (the quintessential bourgeois genre) as the dominant literary form, the penchant for a neo-Romantic epic of good feelings and healthy, positive heroes, all these elements made it clear that the realism in question was aesthetically conservative. In its most vulgar form it would lead to Zhdanovism, while at a much higher intellectual level Lukács would develop a theory of critical realism that would seriously challenge bourgeois critics (e.g., the French structuralists whose works began to appear in the 1950s), as well as the most brilliant and uncompromising Marxist dissenters (e.g., Benjamin, Brecht and Adorno).

In the end, then, the neo-realist poetics that crystallized in the 1950s was a rather motley composite, blending the national historicist tradition (which, as we have seen, was anything but univocal) with elements taken from Zhdanovism and Lukácsian thought, and made into a fairly solid whole by the conservative taste that was the trademark of the vast majority of Italian intellectuals across the ideological spectrum. It is interesting to note how this poetics displayed many of the weaknesses of a political program that commanded a wide consensus among the members of the Italian intelligentsia. The demands for social justice, peace, and democracy seldom went beyond a rather general progressive agenda that could have easily been supported by any European social democratic party (and, indeed, the PCI often ran the risk of being outflanked on the left by the more lively elements of the PSI). What distinguished the PCI was its staunch support for the Soviet Union on foreign policy matters and its unremittingly Leninist organizational culture. In sum, Togliatti based much of the PCI's strategy on cultural as well as more generally political matters on articulating the progressive moment in the bourgeois agenda. The PCI was trying to become the agent of the bourgeois revolution Italy had never truly had. The problem was that soon enough this agenda was itself overtaken by events. A decade of unprecedented growth catapulted the country into late capitalism, a stage in economic and cultural development that made a bourgeois revolution seem hopelessly anachronistic.

For the purposes of this discussion, the poetics of neo-realism is especially interesting in that it strongly privileged a specific literary genre (i.e., the 'classic' realistic novel) and explicitly articulated the link between such a genre and a theory of the role of the intellectual. The debates surrounding neo-realism explicitly politicized the generic system; never before had the point been so clearly made that the decision to write a novel about the adventures of a partisan brigade rather than about the psychosexual predicaments of a couple of well-off professionals had profound and precise political (rather than simply moral) implications. The simplification lay not so much in the emphasis on the political significance of artistic forms but rather in the assumption that writers could simply choose what form they pleased and instantly translate their conversion to socialism into a new triumphant aesthetic. Gramsci could be used to stigmatize conservative intellectuals as priests of the ivory tower and to woo progressive intellectuals with the promise of an organic relationship with the vital forces of the nation and history (i.e., the proletariat). However, this superficial use of Gramsci sounded increasingly hollow as it became clear that the destruction of the ivory tower and the dialogue with the proletariat would not take place by fiat once and for all, but rather had to be fought for day by day and step by step. The difficulty lay not so much in persuading intellectuals to play a new and progressive political role. The critical task was to fight for a change in the socio-economic conditions that would turn the intellectuals' abstract will for an organic dialogue with the working class into a concrete reality. Until these conditions began to dawn on the horizon, the intellectuals could only live their political commitment as a contradiction,[3] and there was certainly no ground for confidently expecting a socialist literature to suddenly emerge fully formed.

From this perspective it becomes clear that the essential pitfall of the neo-realist poetics was not that it was too Marxist (as non-Marxist commentators have argued), but rather that it wasn't Marxist enough. Taking little note of the actual socio-political situation, it went on to theorize an allegedly socialist literature that, in fact, was nothing more than the literature that suited the immediate political ends and the conservative taste of the party leadership and a rather mixed group of fellow-travellers. In so doing, the most intransigent proponents of (neo)realism demonstrated not only an insufficient understanding of the nature of literature both as a social and as an aesthetic phenomenon, but also a voluntarism that was characteristically idealistic and abstract – and this was the predictable result of reading Gramsci through Croce (Asor Rosa 1972, 245–6; Luperini 1981). In short, neo-realism was essentially the attempt by an intelligentsia that had not yet overcome its humanist and idealistic reflexes, and still lacked the theoretical instruments to do so, to impose from above a poetics that had no concrete social basis. The result was a literature full of good intentions and yet seldom convincingly above the level of competent left-wing didacticism, a literature that might have served some short-term political exigency but that soon caused multiple misunderstandings and recriminations: the critics trashed the books that had been written according to their formulae, authors felt betrayed by the critics and the politicians that had egged them on, and the public soon moved on to the more palatable fare provided by a burgeoning culture industry.[4] Neo-realism had attempted to bypass a critique of the dialectics between ideology and existing social relations, and, in the final analysis, the shortcomings of the neo-realist poetics can be seen to be rooted in the same conceptual framework we saw operating in the polemics between Vittorini and Togliatti about the respective roles of culture and politics. Once again, what emerges is the idealist and humanist bias that made it impossible for Italian intellectuals of the time to confront the material realities facing them with seriousness. Problems, and particularly cultural problems, were articulated in a relentlessly abstract way, as conceptual puzzles rather than historically specific predicaments, so that the solutions envisaged could only be abstract and thus fail the test of practice.

I giovani and the Limits of Neo-realism

We can now appreciate that, by attempting a work such as I giovani, Calvino was positioning himself within a precise and unique political dynamic. I giovani is not just a realist narrative about a young man from the countryside who has come to the city to work in a factory and who is abruptly brought face to face with the realities of modern capitalism. I giovani is also a deliberate attempt to apply a poetics that entailed certain fundamental structural choices/constraints and presupposed a theory of the role of the intellectual. The 'wilful' aspect of Calvino's effort becomes even clearer when we consider that both the constraints and the theory of the intellectual in question ran against Calvino's instinctive inclinations. Why attempt to write a realist novel when all the critics (beginning with Pavese, whose judgment was highly esteemed by Calvino) agreed that the most interesting passages of The Path, Calvino's first novel, were the ones possessing a surreal intensity, a fable-like peremptoriness? Why write about an environment (the factory) and people (newly urbanized workers) about whom he knew very little? (Witness the fact that he had to turn his main character into an intellectual with greater affinities for the middle class than for the proletariat.)

It was Calvino's political commitment that made these choices seem unavoidable. The Cold War mentality prevailing in the 1950s encased neo-realism within an increasingly rigid poetics. The emphasis on the exploration of new domains and ideas that would help to bring forth a new culture for a new man (which had been the program of Vittorini's

Il Politecnico just a few years earlier) gave way to dogmatism. The party had the answers, at least to all essential questions; the time of adventure, so congenial to Calvino, was over – none of *The Path*'s 'bold good humour' is left in *I giovani*. In this context, it is not surprising that Calvino would respond to the call to order issued by the party and demonstrate his commitment to the cause of socialism by attempting to write precisely the type of work that the party critics asked intellectuals like him to write.

I giovani exhibits all the essential attributes demanded by the neo-realist poetics. Submitting to the populist injunction to 'go to the people' (Asor Rosa 1972), Calvino embraced what was considered a 'popular' genre, adopted a middle-to-lowbrow level of language, and supplied the requisite positive hero, whose role was to represent the historical mission of the proletariat, as well as a few violent and spoiled bourgeois adolescents functioning as foils for serious-minded factory workers. These elements may not seem inspiring to begin with, but there is certainly no a priori reason why they should add up to an artistic failure (broken up in this way, any poetics will seem trivial). Rather, the crucial question is what could be done with these elements at a particular historical time by authors who, whether they like it or not, are interrogated by the ideology of the social fraction to which they belong. That is why the difficulties encountered by Calvino in composing *I giovani* can be approached not primarily as the symptoms of personal inadequacies, but rather as a sign of the contradictions and tensions within the ideology of a group: the left-wing intelligentsia of which Calvino was a member. The gap between what ought to have been done and what was in fact accomplished provides a key not only to the limitations of the neo-realist poetics but also, more fundamentally, to the complex interaction and different pace of development between the cultural sphere, in which such poetics was still dominant, and the socio-economic sphere, which had began to pose problems neo-realism failed to deal with. Calvino's great merit in *I giovani* is to operate with a rigour and lucidity that allow these disjunctions to emerge clearly.

What, then, is the substantive thematic concern that Calvino attempts to explore and develop in *I giovani*? What does Calvino add as he fleshes out the general requirements of the neo-realist poetics and shapes his fictional world? The answer is not difficult, even though it has been overlooked by critics blinded by the glaring faults of the novel (its uninspired homage to Pavesian motifs, its equally uninspired neo-realist orthodoxy). Calvino himself provides some important clues when he writes: 'With this novel [*I giovani*], I wanted to express finally in narrative form also those interests and experiences that so far I have only been able to bring to life in a few essay-like pages, namely: the city, industrial civilization, workers; as well as that part of reality and those interests of mine (from which it has always been easier for me to draw narrative symbols), which are nature, adventure, the difficult search for a natural happiness today. *My aim was to give an image of human integration*; instead, the result was an unusually grey book, in which the fullness of life, though much talked about, is barely felt' (emphasis added).[5]

While useful, Calvino's comments need to be elaborated further, and I propose to do so by citing in full a key passage in the novel: the conversation between Nino and the wise old man and trade union activist Bastia. We are now at the end of the novel, and Nino is looking for someone who will understand his predicament and perhaps even provide some advice on how to move beyond it:

'I don't quite understand what you're saying ...' Bastia began, slowly. And Nino was thinking: Of course, he can't understand. Why did I want to talk to him?

'... When it comes to young people like you, I can't follow you very well,' continued Bastia, 'I have a few years on my back, I'm old-fashioned, I had a different life, totally different from yours ...'

Here it is, the usual story ... thought Nino.

And Bastia: 'If I could go back, well, I'd do it all over again ... there was nothing else to do. Sure, the world is a big place ... a man's life is made up of many things ...'

Nino pricked up his ears.

'... We are the kind of people who don't want to give anything up ...'

That's what I wanted to say, thought Nino.

'... but when we find ourselves in the middle of it, what can you do? ... Many things that we like go by the wayside, and one keeps on going nonetheless ... Well ... You're young ... You'll see many things we'll never see ...'

I know, thought Nino, but what I am saying ...

'... Sure it would be better if nothing went by the wayside ... if we did not forget anything ... not even wishes ...'

He understands, he understands everything, the old man! He really understands! Nino was all excited.

'Anyway ... These are the things I thought about when I was in prison, in the early days ... I was just a little older than you ... Five years I spent in there ...'
He wasn't in the habit of digging up his past, Bastia; nor of making long speeches: so he shut up. And it was all over now. But the tone of Bastia's voice told Nino that the old man hadn't disapproved of him, didn't even seem surprised. Everything would go on as before.
They said goodbye. Bastia got back on his bike and pedalled away. Nino had shaken his hand mechanically and stood still on the edge of the sidewalk.[6]

This passage discloses that Nino's predicament is that of human alienation in modern industrial society. As a recently urbanized factory worker, Nino confronts a series of conflicts and contradictions among the various experiences and desires that modern capitalist development produces. First among these is the conflict between Nino's nostalgia for the simple life of the countryside, which he has left behind, and his decision to move to the city and work in a factory, which he justifies in terms of the desire to participate actively in the processes that are reshaping humanity and the world in which he lives. But then this basic opposition gives rise to a multitude of others.

Nino's political involvement, which will eventually result in him occupying a leadership position in the local trade union, comes into conflict with his love affair with Giovanna, the young daughter of a bourgeois family. This doomed relationship is linked to the conflict between work and leisure: Nino takes pride in doing his work efficiently and well, but he also likes to go rowing on the river, even if it means taking the odd afternoon off work by calling in sick. Nino and Giovanna first catch a glimpse of each other on the river and it is there that they begin to meet.

Work plays a role also in another conflict, namely, that between workers and students. Nino pretends to be a student when he first meets Giovanna. When he tells the truth, he becomes the butt of nasty jokes made by Giovanna's student friends. The political meaning of this conflict becomes clear when the neo-Fascist group of which Giovanna's friends are members physically attacks Nino and his co-workers, who are pasting up election posters. And yet Nino's first instinct to identify himself as a student to Giovanna is not simply evidence of class intimidation. It also expresses the authentic respect Nino feels for, and the value he attributes to, knowledge as a means of understanding both one's world and oneself. It is learning as cognition that Nino defends against his friend Nanin's determined anti-intellectualism – 'Fish never ask themselves: "What's the point?" They live like fish, period. They're right. I try to be like them: to live as a man the way they live as fish. It's not as easy as it seems, but it's the only way, believe me'[7] – and the perverse, almost surreal, stupidity of Giovanna's student friends (RR, 3: 1080–2, 1086–8). The search for knowledge, for an understanding capable of integrating all these conflicts and contradictions (and I have mentioned only the most glaring ones), is ultimately what characterizes the subjectivity Nino is attempting to work out. Once we realize that this is the project at stake we can better grasp the difficulties the narrative runs into, as well as their significance for the purposes of this study.

The way in which Calvino sets up the problem of human alienation seems far removed from Marx's analysis of alienated labour in Capital. Nino does not sound like the factory worker brutalized by machine-driven production processes. Rather, he sounds like the humanist intellectual who understands alienation as the inability to provide a conceptual synthesis of what is taking place in the world in which he lives as well as within himself.

It is, then, hardly surprising that the analysis of alienation in I giovani lacks concreteness. We have an extremely sketchy idea of what Nino actually does in the factory, what the conditions on the shop floor are like, and so forth. The novel contains no such descriptions, but instead presents the reader with discussions about what goes on in the factory, or rather about the union's attempt to politicize workers and mobilize their support for its political agenda. The realist (and Lukácsian) precept 'show rather than tell' has no purchase.

Moreover, the foregrounding of reflexive articulation over concrete practice makes it impossible for even the most willing to suspend disbelief in relation to Nino, whose sensibility has nothing to do with the recently urbanized factory worker we are supposed to take him to be, and everything to do with the bourgeois intellectual Calvino was. Beneath the neo-realist veneer, I giovani addresses Calvino's own concerns, which arise within the social fraction to which he belongs. This fraction also constitutes the novel's real audience (and the fact that Calvino allowed the book to appear only in a literary journal is telling). As for the proletariat whose experiences I giovani intended to present, it is wholly outside the horizon of the novel.

The novel's focus on bourgeois experience undermines the neo-

realist project, condemning it to failure. And yet, once this fundamental contradiction is identified, it also becomes clear that the concerns
Calvino explores in *I giovani* are, in themselves, perfectly valid. Understood non-realistically as a parable of the alienation of the modern
intellectual, the novel begins to make sense. Then we can follow the
dynamics of the narrative, which develops in terms of a series of essentially conceptual antitheses: city vs country, workers vs students, river
vs shore, work vs leisure, love vs politics, just to name the most obvious. Nino's problem is not so much that he is torn between these opposites, but rather that he is unable to organize his experience other than
in these binary terms. Nino is a prisoner of his conceptual categories,
which, far from providing a synthesis of the manifold of perception (to
use a Kantian formulation), result in division, alienation, insuperable
conflict, and difference. Nino faces, or rather embodies, an intellectual's problem, and *I giovani* is an attempt to work out an intellectual's
solution.

The attempt was bound to fail because Calvino had locked himself
within a neo-realist form that hypostatized the solution to the problem
rather than truly confronting it. Neo-realism presupposed the possibility of a synthesis that *I giovani* revealed to be not only far from realized
in social reality but actually receding. Nino keeps protesting, in an
interestingly proto-1968 fashion, that he doesn't want to give up either
of the terms of the many binary oppositions he is setting up (he wants
politics and love, the city and the country, to be a worker and a student, etc.), but this abstract will is powerless to find a standpoint outside the binarisms, from which a solution could be imagined. In the
final analysis, the problem is not only that the proletarian transposition
remained too abstract to provide insight into the socio-ecomonic reality of the times, but also that the integral proletarian self, conceived as
the dialectical sublation of the fragmented bourgeois subject, was unimaginable, in realistic terms, by the social fraction Calvino expressed.
Indeed, in the fragmented world of advanced consumer capitalism,
wholeness could perhaps be conceived only as a utopian term by any
subject (be it bourgeois or proletarian). In this context, the project
embodied by *I giovani* manifests an inherently flawed voluntarism,
which once again bears witness to the idealist rather than Marxist
reflexes of even the most sensitive left-wing intellectuals in Italy.

Calvino was struggling with his own ideology, and he paid the price
at every turn. Let us consider, for example, the device of juxtaposing
the third-person narrative with the correspondence (naturally in the

first person) between Nino, the protagonist, and Nanin, the childhood friend who refuses to come to the city and stayed behind in his small native village. At one level, this device provides the ideal space for developing the contrast between the country (the place of memory) and the city (the place of work). And yet we soon realize that the correspondence is primarily a vehicle for the articulation of Nino's self-understanding. In this way, Calvino not only gives himself a further means to emphasize the centrality of self-reflection and the intellectual moment in *I giovani*, but also palliates the lack of a detailed analysis of the character's psychology, which the classic realist novel as a genre requires and which Calvino is reluctant to provide – indeed, the letters that Nino and Nanin exchange are stiff and unemotional. However, the remedy ends up being worse than the illness since the epistolary device further undermines the neo-realist structure of the work.

By introducing a first-person narrative, the exchange of letters destabilizes the objectivity of the narrative. Nanin's remarks flatly contradict Nino's own judgments and perceptions, and while it is true that Nanin's challenge remains purely discursive – he never comes to Turin and we hear from him only in his letters – Nino's authoritativeness is irremediably lost. Lacking psychological depth, plagued by doubts and hesitations, the protagonist of *I giovani* seems to lose consistency as the narrative progresses. He is gradually revealed as a mere function of the narrative, a two-dimensional discursive self whose 'deficit of being' is exemplified rather than remedied by the epistolary exchange. The insurmountable problem is that the classic realistic novel envisaged by neo-realism needs much stronger, 'round' characters to convince us of its objectivity. Calvino, however, is too troubled to believe in such characters, and his use of the epistolary device reveals rather than conceals his inability to imagine them. The end result is a further undermining of the neo-realist form he so wilfully chose.

I giovani began as an attempt to demonstrate that the human alienation that, according to Marxist analysis, is the necessary corollary of modern industrial capitalism can be overcome, or at least significantly mitigated, by siding with the politically active section of the working class in the struggle for social change. The demonstration of this thesis via the evocation of a particular fictional world led Calvino to construct a situation that, somewhat paradoxically, laid bare his ideology but could not be mastered by it. The binary oppositions that propel the narrative and represent the divisive force of capitalism cannot in the final analysis be dialectically overcome. The sense of confusion and impotence continues to grow and the reader soon loses any hope of a synthetic, positive resolution.

Then, abruptly, the novel ends with a car accident that definitively denies the possibility of reconciliation and constructive integration. Thematically, Giovanna's death seals the insuperable divisions between the various spheres of Nino's life and the desires each of these spheres addresses. At a more formal level, Calvino is drawing attention to the arbitrariness of the device that ends the story – within the framework of a realist novel, the death of a main character is the most obtrusive and unimaginative form of closure. This unmasking of the narrative as fiction, in other words, as a literary construct, signals the final collapse of realism and suggests that what concludes the novel, what 'kills' Giovanna, is just a pen stroke, a 'period,' which manifests both Calvino's incapacity to end the story and his desire to stop writing. The sharp distinction between the narrated and the narrating subject is blurred when the latter loses his mastery over the former. Calvino has to face his alter ego and acknowledge his own fissured selfhood, which can no longer be distanced and contained through the representation of the divided self of the fictional 'other.' And this is where the realist strategy oddly backfires, and Nino's failure as a character mirrors directly Calvino's failure as a writer and intellectual: *de te fabula narratur*, as Eco might say. Here also lies the importance and usefulness of the experience.

Calvino's own assessment of *I giovani* is well summarized in a passage from the letter that he wrote to Dario Puccini on 17 March 1954: 'It's all "head," cold, and built with inadequate symbols. It's an essay about problems I care about but expressed in *narrative formulae which don't suit me*, and with which I am uncomfortable. I won't publish it in a book form' (emphasis added).[8] In the end, *I giovani* provides a demonstration of the limits of the neo-realist poetics and of the ideology underpinning it. The attempt to implement the neo-realist program, however, allowed Calvino to become conscious of these limits and in particular of how a bourgeois intellectual could neither produce convincing literature nor contribute to the cause of the working class simply by writing about factories and unions. Still, for the moment, this awareness was predominantly negative in that it manifested itself as a profound dissatisfaction with a given model rather than pointing the way toward a new model. But the seeds were sown, and they would bear fruit in *The Cloven Viscount*, the next work that Calvino would complete and publish. The difficulties encountered by Calvino in *I gio-vani* provide us with the context we need to appreciate fully the novelty and significance of this later work.

The Cloven Viscount and the Resources of the Fantastic

In the 1980 English edition of *Our Ancestors*, Calvino describes the circumstances of the composition of *The Viscount*: 'The fact is that after my first novel, written in 1946, and my first short stories, which told of picaresque adventures in an Italy of wartime and post-war upheaval, I had made efforts to write the realistic-novel-reflecting-the-problems-of-Italian-society, and had not managed to do so. And then, in 1951, when I was twenty-eight and not at all sure that I was going to carry on writing, I began doing what came most naturally to me ... *Instead of making myself write the book I ought to write, the novel that was expected of me, I conjured up the book I myself would have liked to read*' (*Our Ancestors* vii; emphasis added).

The 'realistic-novel-reflecting-the-problems-of-Italian-society' Calvino is talking about is *I giovani*. And in Calvino's comments the atmosphere of the early 1950s, which I have described in the previous section, surfaces once again; a period when the hegemonic pressure of neo-realism was most keenly felt precisely because the inadequacy of its poetics was increasingly apparent (though hindsight may be slanting Calvino's recollections a little).

The most interesting passage in the quotation, however, is the one that I have italicized, and which records a shift in the relation between the writer and his work. This shift is crucial to Calvino's development as a writer and, more importantly for my purposes, provides an invaluable lead for the understanding of the processes that result in the dramatic shift in genre from *I giovani* to *The Viscount* (and to the trilogy as a whole).

In *I giovani* Calvino tried to 'go to the people' and write a book whose interlocutor was a collective subject – the proletariat – to whom Calvino was drawn predominantly because of an explicit political commitment. Calvino chose to write about factory workers in *I giovani* not because he felt any particular socio-cultural affinities with them, but because he felt that it was important to try and look at the world from the eyes of factory workers – the influence of Lukács's 'standpoint' theory (in *History and Class Consciousness*, 1971) is recognizable in this attitude. However, adopting the standpoint of the proletariat (or of any other collective subject for that matter) requires a much greater and more sustained effort than simply constructing a narrative around a proletarian hero. In fact, the idea that one can speak for other social groups simply by making a pure act of will or by a sort of secular conversion could only occur to an intelligentsia that had not yet shed its idealist (Croce) and Catholic automatisms – it is indeed striking how often one finds Italian intellectuals in the immediate post-war period talking about communism as a faith duly equipped with redeeming and epiphanic powers (cf. Gambetti 1976).

In fairness, Calvino and the most attentive intellectuals of his generation hoped to ground their new standpoint not only in artistic practice. For a brief period, the participation in the Resistance movement seemed to provide the concrete grounds for overcoming the traditional and long-standing separation between the intellectuals and the lower classes. After the liberation these intellectuals attempted to keep alive the experience of the Resistance by actively supporting left-wing parties and, in particular, the PCI. In the mid-1940s Calvino became a member of the editorial board of the PCI's daily, *l'Unità*, of which he remained a regular contributor until the mid-1950s.

Reviewing the range of his contributions as a journalist, it becomes clear that Calvino had a rather non-specialist view of his role as a committed intellectual. He published not only fiction, reviews of works by national and international writers, and other cultural reports, but also topical articles on theoretical, social, and political issues.[9] These efforts demonstrate that for Calvino commitment involved a wide range of interventions. His implicit objective was to create and keep open channels of communication between the political leadership, the intellectuals, and that collective subject (i.e., the working class) whose claims needed to be expressed, elaborated, and eventually acted upon in terms of the official party platform. In short, Calvino took a rather encompassing view of the organic function that he was attempting to perform in keeping with the Gramscian injunction.

In the introduction to *Una pietra sopra*, a collection of essays covering the period from 1955 to 1980, Calvino himself noted:

The youthful ambition from that I started was the project of creating a new literature that in turn would contribute to the creation of a new society ...

The character that takes the floor in this book (and that in part rejoins and in part diverges from the self represented in other things I have written and done) comes on the scene in the Fifties trying to provide a personal interpretation of the role that at that time was in the limelight: *the committed intellectual*.[10]

Echoes of Vittorini's 'For a New Culture' are unmistakable and firmly situate Calvino within the progressive section of the Italian post-war intelligentsia. But the problem with the way Calvino and much of his generation went about fulfilling this organic role was, as has been noted (Asor Rosa 1972), that their efforts remained primarily one-directional and thus part of an essentially populist agenda. What was missing (and this constitutes one of the dangerous simplifications of the Gramscian legacy that a rather hurried left-wing intelligentsia was disseminating in the post-war years) was an analysis of the intelligentsia's own position within the capitalist system of production, and of the similarities and differences, that is, the contradictions, between the standpoint of the intelligentsia and that of the working class. (It may be noted, in passing, that this was precisely the problematic that occupied Walter Benjamin and Bertolt Brecht in the 1930s [cf., Benjamin's 1937 essay 'The Author as Producer'].) Paradoxically, then, the intellectual could become organic to the working class only by becoming more keenly aware of the position of the social fraction of which he or she was a member. Only on this basis could a truly two-directional communication be attempted. For the intellectual, joining in the struggle for social change meant first of all taking responsibility and confronting what one was (not so much as an individual but as a social group), so that eventually the intellectual could learn to become 'other' than oneself. Seeking refuge from the self by wearing proletarian garb and adopting working-class postures – thin disguises, as we saw in *I giovani* – was a way to avoid the painful task of questioning one's role, not a way of performing one's function as a progressive intellectual (an uncharitable Sartrian reading would speak of *mauvaise foi*).

After the failure of his populist attempt, Calvino realized that the time had come to turn his attention to the subject with whom the responsibility for that failure rested: the 1950s Italian intellectual, with all her or his weaknesses but also her or his strengths. The challenge then became to let this subject speak in the ways most congenial to him or her and thus most revealing of his or her education, of the *bagaglio culturale* that characterized that intellectual as a type, in other words as the member of a socially significant group. This challenge could not be met by objectifying the type as a mere puppet in the hands of the omnipotent author/narrator. Rather, the narrating voice itself had to become visible, and in a manner that raised the issue of the authorial position. The issue was not simply to portray a 1950s intellectual but to perform his or her stance, a stance that revealed the complexity of the superficially straightforward Gramscian typology, that is, 'traditional' vs 'organic' intellectuals. Only then could the stance be truly played out, confronted, fully grasped. This is the effort that propels the trilogy: 'With these three stories [*The Cloven Viscount, The Baron in the Trees,* and *The Non-existent Knight*] I wanted to find again – and keep in circulation in the real world, keep alive – a tension that is both individual and collective, existential and rational, autobiographical and historical, lyrical and epic; a tension that marked an entire season of world literature, including Italian literature. This seemed the only possible way of remaining true to it.'[11] For us, the challenge is to grasp how the generic resources that Calvino is able to deploy in *The Viscount* contribute critically to the success of the work.

I have argued elsewhere (Bolongaro 1992) that realistic and non-realistic fiction are both informed by two fundamentally different narrative strategies. I have also maintained, relying on the work of Suvin (1979) and Angenot (1979) on science fiction, that one of the best ways of encapsulating the difference between these strategies is to contrast the 'as if' modality of realist fiction with the 'what if' modality of non-realist fiction. This distinction can now help us understand the nature of the generic divide between *The Viscount* and *I giovani*.

We should begin by noticing that the basic thematic concern propelling the narrative remains constant in the two works. In *The Viscount,* Calvino is confronting once again the issue of human alienation in modern industrial capitalism: 'Severed in half, mutilated, incomplete, an enemy against himself, that's contemporary man. Marx called him *alienated*, Freud *repressed*. We have lost an ancient harmony, and aspire to a new completeness. This was the ideological and moral kernel that I consciously intended the story to have. But rather than developing the issue at a philosophical level, I focused on giving the story a skeleton that would function like a well-constructed mechanism, while relying on free lyrical associations for the flesh and blood.'[12] The lucidity of these comments provides a striking contrast to the programmatic generalities that underpinned *I giovani* (the realistic-novel-reflecting-the-problems-of-Italian-society). This time Calvino can name with absolute confidence the thematic core of the story. The self-assurance of the statement indicates not only a clearly formulated authorial intention but also a thematic transparency, which is one of the characteristics of the non-realist strategy Calvino is adopting. In *I giovani*, the theme of the narrative is implicit: I retrieved it by reading between the lines of a discourse that pretends to give access to a real situation, that is, to a set of circumstances that may be interpreted to have a certain meaning, though they are presented as factual and thus to some extent independent of human meaning. The reader's willingness to accept this pretence is one of the key characteristics of the 'as if' modality that marks realistic fiction.

In *The Viscount*, on the contrary, the theme of the story is expressly declared. It appears and draws attention to itself on the very surface of the narrative. The title of the work announces it: *The* Cloven *Viscount*; and so does, most dramatically, the basic 'conceit' around which the work is constructed: the literal splitting in two of the protagonist, which sets up the central confrontation between the evil half and the good half of the unfortunate Viscount. Through this nonchalant and uninhibited literalization of the key metaphor of the divided self the 'as if' modality of realism is replaced by the 'what if' modality of the fantastic.[13] This means that, in evoking a fictional world, the text no longer relies primarily on an analogy with our everyday experience, but catapults us into a world that is explicitly estranged, in other words, governed by 'laws' that to some extent differ from the ones we are used to applying in daily life. The emphasis then shifts from the attempt to represent and critique the categories through which we organize actual experience to the working out of the consequences of the difference that the narrative introduces – herein lies the essence of the 'what if' modality.

Once we grasp the basic nature of the generic shift, we can go on to explore in more detail what specific possibilities the non-realist strategy makes available to Calvino, and then how the text manages to exploit these possibilities. This in turn will give us the elements we need to understand why and how Calvino's development of the theme of alienation finds a much more convincing voice in *The Viscount* than in *I giovani*.

The Viscount is an exceedingly simple story. It begins with the arrival of the Viscount, Medardo of Terralba, at the encampment of the forces led by the Christian emperor against the Turkish infidels. In his first battle, the day following his arrival, the inexperienced Viscount finds himself facing the business end of a cannon with the result that he is left horribly mutilated on the battlefield. The doctors manage to save what is left of the Viscount, namely his left half, while the right half is presumed to have been destroyed. On his return from the war, the halved Viscount demonstrates a singularly nasty disposition, which is soon interpreted to be the result of his mutilation: only the bad half has survived.

Soon enough, however, the good half makes its appearance and the two sides begin a confrontation that comes to a head when they both fall in love with the same girl, Pamela. Finally, facing each other in a duel, the two halves reopen the old wound, thus giving the local doctor a chance to sew the unfortunate Viscount back together. Whole again, Medardo lives happily ever after with the woman both his halves have chosen.

A few geographical and historical references set the narrative against an eighteenth-century background that is more named than shown and whose function is twofold. The blurred historical context reinforces the fairy-tale opening of the narrative: 'There was a war on against the Turks' ('C'era una guerra contro i Turchi'). The nod to the traditional opening line 'C'era una volta ...' ('Once upon a time ...') is clear and immediately establishes a non-realist register. The halving of the Viscount will be perfectly within the logic of the narrative chronotope (borrowing from Bakhtin 1981).

Moreover, the vaguely eighteenth-century intellectual atmosphere provides an ideal setting for sharp allegorical tableaux of the prototypes of modern ideologies. For example, the Huguenot farming community that lives on the harsh slopes of the mountains within the Viscount's domain bears the stigmata of primitive capitalist accumulation under a strict patriarchal rule, though Esau, the youngest son, has already shed the old order and becomes a caricature of the bandit-entrepreneur whose only morality is greed. By contrast, the community of lepers, whose death masks are effete aestheticism and unrestrained sensuality, provides a thinly veiled allegory for the excessive expenditure typical of doomed and sterile elites (a predominantly carnivalesque allegory of the class depicted in much drearier colours by many of Moravia's novels).

While the mixture of fable and allegory suggests levity and the mood suitable to a literary divertissement (a word Calvino himself uses referring to *The Viscount* in his December 1951 letter to Vittorini), the reader is forced to imagine an unexpectedly raw landscape. It is essential to note, however, that this harshness is by no means a realistic residue harking back to certain passages of *The Path*. On the contrary, the images of violence and death with which *The Viscount* opens play a key role in establishing the non-realistic character of the narrative:

> The squire, a dark-skinned soldier with heavy moustaches, never raised his eyes. 'There are so many plague-ridden bodies that the plague got 'em too,' and he pointed his lance at some black bushes, which a closer look revealed as made not of branches, but of feathers and dried claws from birds of prey. (*Our Ancestors*, 3)

> 'Careful Signore,' added the squire, 'They're so foul and pox-ridden [the prostitutes of the imperial army] even the Turks wouldn't want them as booty. They're not only covered with lice, bugs and ticks, but even scorpions and lizards make their nests on them now.' (*Our Ancestors*, 5)

This is not gritty realism, this is grotesque hyperbole, which Emilio Cecchi, in a well-known early review of *The Viscount*, correctly identified: 'a northern, Gothic vein was already obvious in Calvino's first short stories' ('una vena nordica, gotica era palese in Calvino già dai primi racconti') (Cecchi 1954, 311). The analogy with certain scenes in *The Path* holds, then, but far from disclosing a realistic residue, it allows us to see more clearly the fantastic impulse that inspired large sections of the neo-realist Resistance narrative.

This stylization of violence and death distances and 'makes strange' the human spectacle that the narratives evokes. Furthermore, this strangeness cannot be easily mastered by a symbolical interpretation, as the reader's attempt to find a second level significance for what exceeds the register of verisimilitude is often frustrated by laconic understatement and self-conscious literariness.

Let's examine more precisely how Calvino proceeds. The dialogue between the Viscount and his squire, which punctuates the beginning of the narrative, is so matter-of-fact that the reader's inclination, if any, to attribute a deep, hidden meaning to the images evoked finds little purchase. The non-realist elements draw attention to themselves, but the effect is not so much to suggest a secret truth underpinning the text as it is to emphasize the ludic and cerebral quality of the narrative. What confronts us here is an allegorical tableau where the complexity of the human spectacle is compressed in broad strokes of sharp, even stark, colours. The horrors described are neither pathetic nor equivocal, but remain an object of detached observation. The Viscount asks questions and the squire provides the explanations, and the reader is made to observe the observers: 'His eyes kept straying towards the verges of the dark horizon where he knew lay the enemy camp, and he hugged himself with crossed arms in his certainty both of distant and differing realities, and of his own presence amid them. He sensed the bloodshed in that cruel war pouring over the earth in innumerable streams and finally reaching him; and he let it lap him with no outrage or pity' (*Our Ancestors*, 7).

This invitation to read with a detachment that enhances cognitive engagement is further enforced by the self-conscious literariness of the narrative, whose ludic and cerebral character is thus accentuated. How not to notice, even in just these few opening pages of *The Viscount*, the many literary allusions: Cervantes and Stevenson ('The Strange Case of Dr Jekyll and Mr Hyde,' but also *Treasure Island*, as Cecchi notes),[14] as well as Virgil and Dante (the legend of Polydorus in *Aeneid* III: 32–63, and the punishment of the suicides in *Inferno* XIII: 28–51), and, more generally, the prestigious Italian chivalric tradition (Boiardo, Ariosto, Tasso).

This intertextual density provides Calvino's fantastic mode with one of its distinguishing features. Harking back to our original definition of the 'what if' modality, which is the hallmark of non-realist fiction, we can now go further and observe that the deviations from verisimilitude have a different function here than they do in science fiction (cf. Suvin 1979, 1988; Angenot 1979). The 'what if' in *The Viscount* does not produce a narrative driven by the attempt to work out a world in which people could actually live through the Viscount's predicament. Rather, the halving of the Viscount and other deviations from verisimilitude function in Calvino's novel as short cuts that allow the narrative to get more quickly to the thematic concerns propelling it; namely, the modern divided self, the ruthless binarisms of Cartesian nationality, the stark and reductive ideological oppositions of the Cold War. The fictional world evoked by *The Viscount* allows Calvino to make clear at once that he is aiming for a sweeping compression of narrative materials: realism tends to the prosaic, while the fantastic can, at its best, zoom in on the essential. This 'velocity' yields a narrative development that is economical to the point of minimalism, and links the form Calvino is manipulating not only, as it has often been noted, with the classical fable and the eighteenth-century *conte philosophique*, but also, and to my mind more interestingly, with baroque allegory (Benjamin 1977) and, further, with twentieth-century cartoons (of which Calvino was an avid reader in his youth).

In *The Viscount*, the narrative proceeds by short tableaux painted in vivid colours and generally coinciding with chapters: chapter 1, the Viscount goes to war; chapter 2, the Viscount is wounded; chapter 3, the Viscount comes home; chapter 4, the Viscount reveals himself as the bad half; and so on. These tableaux align themselves along a series of binary oppositions: chapter 1, the Viscount and his squire; chapter 2, Christians and Turks; chapter 3, father and son; chapter 4, the Viscount and his subjects; and so on. The opening and closing lines of chapter 3 and of the episode recounting Medardo's courtship of Pamela are exemplary of these techniques, as well as of the overall pattern:

> When my uncle made his return to Terralba I was seven or eight years old, It was late, after dusk, in October, with a cloudy sky. We had been working on the vintage that day and on the grey sea over the vine rows we saw approaching the sails of a ship flying the Imperial flag ...
>
> Next morning when the nurse put her head into the bird-cage, she realized that the Viscount Aiolfo was dead. The birds had all perched on his bed, as if it were a floating tree trunk in the midst of [the] sea. (*Our Ancestors*, 10–14)

> Hitched to the saddle of his high-jumping horse, Medardo of Terralba would be out early, up and down bluffs, leaning over precipices to gaze over a valley with the eye of a bird of prey. So it was he saw Pamela in the middle of a field with her goats ...
>
> Next day they tied up Pamela and locked her with the animals; then they went off to the castle to tell the Viscount that if he wanted their daughter he could send down for her as they on their side were ready to hand her over. (*Our Ancestors*, 35–40)

These passages are typical of a non-realist stylization that relies heavily on familiar topoi in Western literature (waiting for the ship carrying back the hero; the *pastourelle* stalked by the lecherous nobleman), as well as on literary allusions (from Villon's 'La ballade des pendus' to Richardson's *Pamela*). Calvino manages to steer clear of self-satisfied bravura and to infuse this material with an exuberance that manifests the young narrator's irrepressible vitality – here is where the baroque 'allegory of death' (Benjamin 1977) is checked by the cartoons' liveliness. Calvino has found again the 'bold good humour' – albeit now rather more darkly tinted – that animated *The Path*, and of which *I giovani* was so obviously bereft.

The constellation that gradually emerges as we examine the attributes of Calvino's non-realist fiction more closely raises some interesting issues as to the ideological positioning of this type of narrative discourse. The fact that *The Viscount* proceeds by short, almost self-contained episodes or scenes rather than by a steady and well-orchestrated concatenation of narrative units (as the classic realist novel à la Balzac) or by long waves of discursive exfoliation (as the experimental novel of high modernism à la Proust, Joyce, or Svevo) leads in the direction of a poetics of the fragment. This poetics, much touted by the European avant-garde (Benjamin again comes to mind), had a wide following in Italy with the difference that the particular socio-economic and political conjuncture steered the Italian avant-garde movement toward a distinctly right-wing ideology.

The Italian experience clearly exposed the avant-garde's vulnerability to recuperation by Fascism. And while Marinetti's Futurism provided the paradigmatic example, more profound and lasting, as well as subtle, was the influence of hermeticism and of the *prosa d'arte*, which were theorized and practised between the world wars: the former by a whole generation of poets, among whom Montale and Quasimodo, and the latter by the writers close to the literary journal *La Ronda*. These literary currents were the primary targets of neo-realism, which denounced their aristocratic/elitist posture, their rejection of politics in favour of the aesthetic realm, understood as the surest field of universal, atemporal values. Armed with some elements of Gramscian thought, post-war progressive intellectuals identified in the poetics of hermeticism and the *prosa d'arte* the typical ideology of the traditional Italian intelligentsia. And they considered this ideology one of the main obstacles to their progressive political project, which included and, indeed, programmatically depended upon the development of an organic relation between intellectuals and the proletariat. It was therefore as a reaction against this ideology that the neo-realist poetics I have discussed was elaborated (unfortunately, as we have seen, paying more attention to Zhdanov and Lukács than Benjamin and Brecht). In this context, Calvino's open abandonment of the realist register in *The Viscount* was bound to be met with suspicion by committed communist critics (e.g., Salinari 1967). But were these concerns justified? Was *The Viscount* reviving a reactionary aesthetic and the ideology underpinning it?

Even at the time, most critics realized that the renunciation of realism by no means meant a retreat to the Rondist ivory tower. The narrative construction based on well defined episodes did have the effect of fragmenting the narrative, but only in the sense that it imposed on the flux of discourse a precise and self-conscious scansion. What Calvino rejected was not a larger socio-political meaning or significance for the narrative, but the mimesis of reality either by an objectivist or a subjectivist reduction. In *The Viscount*, narrative discourse does not pretend to be either a transparent medium for the mapping of things or coterminous with subjective consciousness (we are not far from the theses defended by Calvino in his famous 1959 essay 'The Sea'). Rather, the opacity of language is acknowledged by generic choices that draw attention to the text as a literary construct. This, however, does not result in an empty, self-sufficient linguistic game. On the contrary, the purpose of the exercise is to establish a critical distance between the narrative and the readers, who are then in an ideal position to take up the cognitive challenge that the narrative provides: to understand the textual mechanism, to experience the pleasure of the mechanism while seeing through it, while grasping the horror the mechanism nevertheless stands for and points to. The analogy with the onlookers of Mastro Pietrochiodo's beautiful scaffold is compelling: 'The rigid corpses and cat's carcasses hung there for three days, and at first no one had the heart to look at them. But soon people noticed what a really imposing sight they were, and our own judgements and opinions began to vary, so that we were even sorry when it was decided to take them down and dismantle the big machine' (*Our Ancestors*, 17).

One of the ways in which Calvino avoids being a Mastro Pietrochiodo is by forcing us to see the machinery for what it is: an object in the world with real effects. Thus the spell of the (textual) machine – another incarnation of what Benjamin (1983) called 'the sex appeal of the inorganic' – is broken:

> But a sorrow always weighed on the saddler's heart. The scaffolds he was constructing were for innocent men. 'How can I manage to get orders for work as delicate, but with a different purpose? What new mechanisms could I enjoy making more?' But finding these questions coming to no conclusions, he tried to thrust them out of his mind and settle down to making his instruments as fine and ingenious as possible.
>
> 'Just forget the purpose for which they're used,' he said to me, 'and look at them as pieces of mechanism. You see how fine they are?'
>
> I looked at that architecture of beams, criss-cross of ropes, links of capstans and pulleys, and tried not to see tortured bodies on them, but the

more I tried the more I found myself thinking of them, and said to Pietro-
chiodo: 'How can I forget?'
'How indeed, my lad,' replied he. 'How d'you think I can, then?' (*Our
Ancestors*, 22)

This is the crucial realization that dictates the generic shift: the need
to expose not simply the machine of capitalism but the machinery of
the fiction that capitalism makes possible. While the strategy of realism
by virtue of its mimetic stylization tends to draw attention away from
the machinery of the narrative, the non-realist strategy brings the artifice of fiction clearly into focus.

There is something paradoxical in these observations: the neo-realist
work that on the surface directly addresses the contemporary situation
seems in the final analysis less imaginatively anchored in the atmosphere of the times than the non-realist story. It is not only that, in *The
Viscount*, the lacerations caused by Cold War political polarization find
an echo that one would be hard pressed to discover in *I giovani*, but
also that the fundamental issues underpinning these lacerations are
much more imaginatively and 'positively' elaborated than in the earlier work: 'We were in the middle of the Cold War, there was a tension
in the air, a hidden rending that did not manifest itself in visible
images but dominated our spirits. And by writing a completely fantastic story, I found myself expressing, without realizing it, not only the
suffering of that particular moment but also the impulse to come out of
it; I did not accept passively the negative situation but rather I was able
to get it moving again, with the swagger, the crudity, the economy of
style, the ruthless optimism that had been part of Resistance literature.'[15]

Only by abandoning the neo-realist poetics can Calvino approach
the ideal of a constructive and active (rather than reactive) criticism of
the historical processes he is witnessing. Still, Calvino's 1960 comments do not provide an answer to another crucial question that the
context raises: why is it precisely this type of narrative that lends itself
to be infused with the qualities Calvino is talking about? Calvino sheds
little light on this issue. And yet all the elements for an answer are
there.

First of all, there is the palpable affinity that Calvino felt for the
material he was handling. Second, the precise geometry of plot development: moving from antithesis to antithesis, we finally come to the
happy ending that sutures the narrative without truly resolving the

conflicts inherent in each polar opposition. Third, the deliberate formal experimentation characterized by the mixing of genres (the fable, the *conte philosophique*, the allegory) and styles (e.g., the Gothic-cum-expressionistic crudity of certain images, elements of the adventure novel as well as of the bucolic pastoral) that have an illustrious history in the Western tradition, with hints of contemporary popular genres (e.g., the cartoon), the whole held together by a predominantly middle-to-lowbrow level of language.

The combination of these elements leaves no doubt as to the fact that, while *I giovani* embodied, at least in theory, an attempt to reach a popular audience, *The Viscount* was explicitly written for a well-educated, intellectual audience.[16] Calvino's statement that he wrote the novel he would have liked to read means not only that he let speak the subject that most strongly interpellated him (i.e., the modern intellectual), but also, and as a corollary, that the text establishes a particularly close relay between writer and reader, the speaker and the spoken to. In other words, the dialogue for which the text provides a site is conducted essentially within a single social group. And yet, far from resulting in narcissistic self-indulgence, the work provides a strikingly insightful image of the social fraction in question: the bourgeous intellectual. The Gramscian project is here reinterpreted: the best way for a bourgeois intellectual to be organic to the proletariat is to grasp his or her own condition. Now nourished by a precise knowledge of the subject, Calvino can move with assurance and insight. While *I giovani* sought to address a theoretical (and largely hypothetical) collectivity, namely, the proletariat in the Marxist-Leninist sense of 'the working class conscious of its historical mission,' *The Viscount* spoke of, and to, a concretely experienced social stratum.

At this point, we can appreciate the full extent to which *The Viscount* is the tale of an intellectual adventure. The problem of alienation, and, more specifically, of the divisions that lacerate the modern self, provides the impetus for an epistemological meditation that is acted out narratively (rather than merely reflected upon) at many levels: by the two halves of the Viscount himself in the tale; by the narrator of the tale who bears witness to the Viscount's vicissitudes and his own; and by the dialogue that the writer sets up with the reader through the telling of the tale. The key passages in this regard are the speeches in which the bad and the good halves of the Viscount discuss their experience of the condition of being divided:

'If only I could halve every whole thing like this,' said my uncle, lying face down on the rocks and stroking the convulsive halves of octopuses, 'so that everyone could escape from their obtuse and ignorant wholeness. I was whole and all things were natural and confused to me, stupid as the air; I thought I was seeing all and it was only the outside rind. If you ever become a half of yourself, and I hope you do for your own sake, my boy, you'll understand things beyond the common intelligence of brains that are whole. You'll have lost half of yourself and of the world, but the remaining half will be a thousand times deeper and more precious. And you also would find yourself wanting everything to be halved like you, as there's beauty and knowledge and justice only in what's been cut to shreds.' (*Our Ancestors*, 34)

Then the good Medardo said, 'Oh, Pamela, that's the good thing about being halved; that one understands the sorrow of every person and thing in the world at its own incompleteness. I was whole and I did not understand, and moved bout deaf and unfeeling amid the pain and sorrow all round us, in places where as a whole person one would least think to find it. It's not only me, Pamela, who am a split being, but you and everyone else too. Now I have a fellowship which I did not understand, did not know before, when whole; a fellowship with all the mutilated and incomplete things in the world. If you come with me, Pamela, you'll learn to suffer with everyone's ills, and tend your own by tending theirs.' (*Our Ancestors*, 51)

In praising their severed condition, both halves of the Viscount insist on the insight they gain as a result of being 'divided against oneself,' an insight inaccessible to those who remain stolidly whole. The biblical echoes with which this argumentation resonates further reinforce the notion that what is as stake is the acquisition of knowledge: the Viscount's predicament is a 'happy fall,' the severance from wholeness is the necessary condition for the birth of a keener self-awareness and the sharpening of one's ability to discern, distinguish, and judge self and world.

And yet this knowledge has a sinister side, which the narrative makes apparent by radicalizing and literalizing the founding metaphor of division/severance/split that underpins the Cartesian and Enlightenment model of knowledge and its relation to the subject. The capacity to know can become the desire to tear apart; the ability to make fine distinctions becomes the fury to make the world conform to the rigid geometry of binary conceptual opposition. In the end, it is life itself that gets in the way, and the murderous fury of the Viscount's evil half is paralleled by the impotent fatalism of his good half. Here is where the issue of the possibility of a higher synthesis inexorably arises. The cognitive gain realized by the two separate halves of the Viscount cannot be translated into an existential gain until the two sides are reunited. Left separate, both the evil and the good Viscount undermine the social fabric of the society they live in: 'Thus the days went by at Terralba, and our sensibilities became numbed, as we felt ourselves lost between an evil and a virtue equally inhuman' (*Our Ancestors*, 64).

At the end of the novel, the Viscount is whole again. And yet is this wholeness a new, higher synthesis? The narrator's final comments leave us very much in doubt:

> He [the Viscount] had a happy life, many children and a just rule. Our lives too changed for the better. Some might expect that with the Viscount entire again a period of marvellous happiness would open; but obviously a whole Viscount is not enough to make all the world whole.
>
> Now Pietrochiodo built gibbets no longer, but mills; and Trelawney neglected his wills-o'-the-wisp for measles and chickenpox. *Amid all this fervour of wholeness I felt myself growing sadder and more deficient.* Sometimes one who considers himself incomplete is merely young.
>
> I had reached the threshold of adolescence and still *hid among the roots of the great trees in the wood to tell myself stories.* A pine needle could represent a knight, or a lady, or a jester; I made them move before my eyes and became rapt in interminable tales about them. Then I would be overcome with shame at these fantasies and ran off. (*Our Ancestors*, 70–1; emphasis added)

The happy ending is ambiguous. Made whole, the Viscount brings a better age to Terralba; but this is a return to normality, not the dawning of a new era. The narrative underscores how this return to normality provides only a veneer of contentment, which on closer inspection appears increasingly flawed. While the narrator may attempt to dismiss his uneasiness in terms of traditional common sense (the proverbial restlessness of youth), his daydreaming in the forest expresses the irrepressible longing for that 'period of marevellous happiness' whose advent the making whole of the Viscount promised but did not deliver.

I would go even further and suggest that at the very end of the novel, as the narrator looks on the ships that are taking the English doctor Trelawney away from Terralba, something more than an unsatisfied longing for wholeness begins to assert itself: 'But already the ships were vanishing over the horizon and I was left behind, in this world of ours full of responsibilities and wills-o'-the-wisp' (*Our Ancestors*, 71). A sense of the complexities of experience is being reestablished here after the fable's stylization. Suddenly, the crystal-clear geometry of the narrative self-destructs under the gaze of a narrator who now knows that multiplicity and complexity are the stuff of life. For a split second the reader wonders whether the whole tale of the cloven Viscount is not precisely one of those fantasies that occupy the narrator as he wanders through the forest.

This somewhat convoluted and last-minute *mise en abîme* destablizes an otherwise fairly closed structure. It opens the horizon of the narrative not simply on a thematic level (where the achievement of wholeness is marked by ambiguity), but also at the structural level in so far as the many planes on which the narrative game has been played are simultaneously exhibited and collapsed. Who is speaking the last phrase? To whom is it spoken? These types of questions force the reader to go beyond the suspension of disbelief and contemplate the fabric of the narrative. Then, what emerges is a schematism that could be termed *the figure of reason*. The binary oppositions that are thematically at the centre of the story are now revealed as providing also the fundamental principle of composition.

The non-realist stylization of experience pursued in *The Viscount* allows Calvino to move freely from one term of opposition to the next without regard for the mediation of verisimilitude, a mediation that was inescapable within the confines of the neo-realist form of *I giovani*. Calvino can then deploy without fetters the cleverness and intellectual brilliance that is his but also so much a part of the heritage of the traditional Italian intelligentsia. In other words, Calvino is here in his element, and he is operating at the level at which he has been educated to operate. His discourse is more abstract than the neo-realist poetics recommends, and yet the loss of experiential density is amply compensated by a sharper cognitive focus. Calvino no longer has to pretend to speak for some other collective subject; he can speak openly for the subject that is shaping him, and thus recognize that the contradictions that the narrative experiment brings to the surface are first and foremost his own.

The critique of alienation takes on a much less abstract character when we realize that Calvino is primarily concerned with the embattled Italian intelligentsia. Medardo, the Viscount, is less a petty political leader than an intellectual, as the speeches expounding the condition of being split in half amply demonstrate. To be more precise, Medardo is a figuration of the petty-bourgeois intellectual whose typical foibles he exhibits: a perverse wilfulness (the bad half) and a bleeding-heart Christian meekness (the good half). Moreover, the exalted title of Viscount, in addition to its role within the conventions of the genre, may be read as a manifestation of the megalomania that often underpins the political ambitions of petty-bourgeois intellectuals and that is directly proportional to their political ineffectiveness.

What is important here is not the sketchy portrayal of the given social group, but the precise delineation of what was fundamental in the historical conjuncture: the still vivid lacerations brought about by the war of liberation; the attempts to stitch together a deeply divided country not in the name of the social project that the Resistance put on the agenda but, after 1948, in the name of a vague national myth that emptied the Resistance of political meaning and denied its promise; finally, an intelligentsia that, faced with Cold War polarization, tended on both sides to accept a humiliating bloc discipline that glossed over the complexity of the situation. In this context, the authentic synthesis that neo-realism demanded and in fact presupposed could not be accomplished: this is the crucial message of *I giovani* and the point of departure of *The Viscount*. What could be performed without mystification was the appearance of synthesis. But then, to avoid being swallowed up by despair and defeatism, this appearance had to be assumed, and infused with the raw exuberance that the negative can possess. This is what *The Viscount* proposes not only, and not even primarily, at the level of the tale itself – what Ricoeur (1981) would call the level of 'sense' – where the geometric play of oppositions bears witness to a rather cerebral energy, but mostly at the level of the referential significance of the tale – Ricoeur's level of 'reference' – where the complex interplay between narrator, writer, and reader suddenly bursts open the narrative and tears apart the basic optimism that was the bedrock on which the neo-realist edifice was built.

The Viscount liquidates neo-realism by demonstrating what neo-realism could not grasp: the complex, contradictory, and irreducibly open-ended dynamism of a country that was well on its way to becoming one of the most industrialized nations in the world, while its cultural, social, and political institutions remained in many respects indifferent to the spirit of modernity. The synthesis that neo-realism sought to accomplish was consistent with and a development of the project of modernity (Habermas 1983). To that extent neo-realism played a progressive, modernizing role. However, the progressive moment gradually dissipated as neo-realism became the poetics of the complacent belief in the ineluctable progress of history and imminent demise of capitalism (an optimism driven underground but not truly shaken by the 1948 electoral defeat of the Popular Front). The project of modernity issues from the crisis of modernity, from the realization that a valid social synthesis can never be taken for granted but rather must constantly be reinvented from within. Neo-realism dogmatically hypostatized a synthesis that, on the contrary, was precisely what needed to be invented.

The non-realist genre allows Calvino to keep alive the progressive moment of the neo-realist poetics (the value of wholeness and human integration), while rejecting the complacency that undermined it, a complacency that was increasingly out of step with the historical situation. When the Resistance seemed still capable of providing a viable blueprint for true democracy, it might have seemed reasonable, though in retrospect naive, to believe that socialism, justice, freedom from alienation, and so on, were just around the corner, and that literature should begin to celebrate the new man and the new culture arisen from the ashes of Fascism. Five years later, it was obvious that the balance of power had changed; progressive forces were everywhere in retreat; everyday experience was that of a reactionary restoration to which the name of Scelba, then the Christian Democrat Minister of the Interior, is notoriously associated. How could one write about the glorious future of socialism when striking workers were being massacred in the streets? The positive hero had no credible role to play in the trench-warfare atmosphere of the Cold War. And, finally, the exigencies of East-West polarization left little room for the emergence of the truly organic and thus inherently critical intellectual Gramsci had theorized. After the heroic years of the Resistance, when a productive dialogue between the intellectuals and the progressive forces of the nation seemed a real possibility and a realizable project, what remained was only the awareness of one's inherently compromised position and the realization of one's political marginality.

The Manichean oversimplification of social life that characterized this period exerted an overwhelming pressure on anyone attempting a realistic stylization of experience. In an age of ideological dogmatism, when everything that did not fit within one's framework was ipso facto deemed to belong to the enemy, the kind of pragmatic 'thick description' that is the lifeblood of realism was virtually impossible. Calvino's way out was to explore the cognitive potential of a form that made of simplification a strength rather than a weakness. Through the sharp contour of a *conte philosophique* without precise philosophy, an allegory without a definitive grid to guide interpretation, a chivalric romance where the possibility of synthetic knowledge is at stake, Calvino succeeded in effectively responding to the particular demands of the conjuncture. In the estranged world of *The Viscount*, the predicament of personal and social alienation acquires not only an exemplary quality but also the power of the negative. What finally emerges in *The Viscount* is the figure of the modern Italian intellectual, increasingly aware of the asymmetry between the past and the present, between a social role defined by an oppressive cultural tradition and a social role dictated by progressive parties, but also capable of the lucidity necessary to overcome this predicament. By fostering this movement toward a full and authentic awareness of the post-war Italian intellectual's situation, *The Viscount* fulfils a key cognitive function. Therein lies its importance and its enduring appeal.

CHAPTER THREE

The Baron in the Trees: The Utopian Moment in Calvino's Fantastic Trilogy

The Baron in the Trees is the second work of the fantastic trilogy that occupied Calvino during the 1950s. Approaching this novel after our discussions of *I giovani* and *The Viscount* allows us to see the evolution of Calvino's concerns and appreciate elements of continuity and discontinuity that might otherwise have eluded us. In fact, it is striking how the final configuration reached by the narrative in *The Viscount* provides the point of departure for *The Baron*.

As we have seen, at the end of the first novel of the trilogy, the lucidity and energy of the narrator's discourse suddenly give way to a sense of loss and impotence: 'I felt myself growing sadder and more deficient' (*Our Ancestors*, 71). The happy ending is marred by an atmosphere of nostalgia for the fantastic past, when the two halves of the Viscount enforced a clear-cut binary logic that made the world seem a simpler and more dynamic place. The final note is one of resignation to the uncertain realities of existence, whose claims re-emerge at the suturing of the protagonist, and of the narrative. Once remedied in the character of the Viscount, the division reveals its true nature: it is a split within the narrator himself, an inability to overcome the binary oppositions that his lucidity deploys. In the concluding paragraphs of *The Viscount*, this constantly renewed and inconclusive geometry is predicated, significantly enough, on the binarism between the world of the city and the world of the woods. Upon closer examination, it becomes clear that this closing figure contains many of the essential narrative terms that *The Baron* will seek to develop.

It is important to note that in *The Viscount* the usually punctual narrator misses the final appointment with the denouement of Dr Trelawney's departure for a new world beyond the sea: 'I was deep in the *wood* telling myself stories and had seen nothing' (*Our Ancestors*, 71; emphasis added). The paradoxical aspect of this 'missing the boat' is that the woods in which the narrator is hiding and the world beyond the horizon toward which Trelawney is sailing evoke similar associations: they both represent the hankering for adventure, the longing for a world that is fresh and new, for a consciousness that feels clearly its difference from nature but experiences this difference as an ever-renewed active synthesis rather than as a reflective moment of division against itself – in sum, a life-world not yet stamped by self-doubt and alienation. But while the same longing is at stake, it is already clear that the response that Trelawney and the narrator give to this common impulse is quite different, as their diverging paths signal: 'But already the ships were vanishing over the horizon and I was left behind, in this world of ours full of responsibilities and wills-o'-the-wisp' (*Our Ancestors*, 71).

Trelawney has once again chosen to escape. He stands for a subjectivity that considers its social function (in this case, the practice of medicine) a burden, a hindrance to its own imaginative fulfilment. Thus he flees from the all-too-ordinary pains of all-too-common people. The narrator would have followed him but for the woods, which claimed him first and hold him back, forcing him to confront the ordinary world to which he seems in effect to resign himself. Still, the stage is set for a different answer: the way of the forest need not lead back to the city and to resignation. It may also lead to the struggle to recover a problematic equilibrium between the demands of imagination/desire and the realities of ordinary life. This seems a more promising strategy than flight into fantasy, when the goal is to discover the conditions of possibility for the authentic overcoming of alienation. The fanciful stories that the narrator of *The Viscount* tells himself in the woods could turn into explorations of the possible, into a utopian moment grounding social practice and having little in common with the engaging but fleeting dreams of Dr Trelawney. The possibilities of the utopian moment: this is the thematic crux at the heart of *The Baron*.

We do not have to go far to find evidence that the character of Cosimo di Rondò and his adventures are the narrative expression of a utopian longing. Only a typical Calvinian bashfulness veils an otherwise explicit statement: 'In his fantasies, he managed to avoid specifying where it would happen; on earth, or up in the element where he lived now: *a place without a place*, he would imagine; a world reached by going up, not down. Yes, that was it. Perhaps there was a tree so high that by climbing it, he would touch another world, the moon' (*Our Ancestors*, 194; emphasis added).

The narrative underscores the importance of the passage by eventually granting Cosimo his wish, though not quite in the way he imagined. At the end of the novel, the dying baron is able to keep his promise never to touch the ground: 'The dying Cosimo, at the second when the anchor rope passed near him, gave one of those leaps he used so often to do in his youth, gripped the rope, with his feet on the anchor and his body in a hunch, and so we saw him fly away, taken by the wind, scarce braking the course of the balloon, and vanish out to sea ...' (*Our Ancestors*, 283).

To recognize the utopian longing that propels *The Baron*, however, is only a first step along the path that I intend to explore by asking three basic questions. First, what type of utopia is Cosimo pursuing? Second, what are the generic resources that Calvino is able to mobilize in order to examine this particular type of utopia? And third, what are the links and interfaces between these resources and the socio-cultural moment from which they emerge and which they address?

Cosimo's Utopia

As we attempt to identify the specific kind of utopian impulse Cosimo embodies, we should note that the entire narrative originates from one founding gesture: a refusal. Meticulously presented and elaborated throughout the first chapter of *The Baron*, Cosimo's refusal to eat a dish of snails invites close scrutiny.

What exactly is Cosimo rebelling against? The most obvious answer is that Cosimo is rejecting his father's authority. One might even be tempted to pursue this line of argumentation further and say that, in rejecting the traditionally sanctioned paternal authority, Cosimo is rejecting the traditional order and perhaps even authority per se. It is easy to see how these initial observations set the stage for a discussion not only of the nature of the utopia Cosimo is pursuing but also of the role the intellectual plays in that pursuit. But before we rush down such a tempting path, we need to look more closely at the narrative situation, which is in fact significantly more complex than this preliminary interpretation would suggest.

There is merit in the view that Calvino is playing with the topos of the adolescent rejection of parental authority. While Cosimo seems a bit young for the role of rebel according to North American standards (Cosimo is twelve – one year short of being a teenager), the narrative makes clear that he is no longer considered a child: 'A few months before, Cosimo having reached the age of twelve and I of eight, we had been admitted to the parental board; I had benefited by my brother's promotion and been moved up prematurely, so that I should not be left to eat alone. "Benefited" is perhaps scarcely the word; for really it meant the end of our carefree life, Cosimo's and mine, and we regretted the meals in our little room, alone with the Abbé Fauchelafleur' (*Our Ancestors*, 77). The narrator's reflections on the age-related promotion to the parents' table explicitly points to a conflict based on different evaluations of the same fact: what in the parents' language – more correctly, the father's language – seems a promotion becomes in the boys' language the end of an arrangement that is perceived as preferable precisely because it sheltered them from a family dynamic that appears to be characterized by resentment ('the intimate grudges' and 'family resentments' [*Our Ancestors*, 78]).

In this context it seems prudent to briefly invoke a straightforward Lacanian reading, which might at first seem compelling. The father is laying down the law, but this law seems to have little to do with the family romance (a somewhat cold and sour picture in *The Baron*) or with the pre-symbolic (neither the boys' mother, la Generalessa, nor the boys' tutor, Fauchelafleur, are likely candidates for the maternal *kora*). Finally, the only 'non/Nom' is pronounced not by the father, but by the son who resolutely refuses the dish of snails. If the utopian impulse Cosimo embodies has something in common with Lacan's Imaginary, Calvino is not cultivating the analogy, which would have to be established, if at all, by a very different and much more elaborate route.

On the other hand, it would be an oversimplification to understand the conflict between the parents' and the boys' views of the situation as a further manifestation of a standard generational conflict. The narrative relies on this familiar thematic construct only as a starting point for a much richer configuration, which begins to emerge as we ask: Whose point of view does the generational interpretation ultimately espouse? Is the reader who stops at this interpretation ultimately on the father's side *or* on Cosimo's? And how does the narrator situate himself in relation to this alternative?

Seeing Cosimo's challenge of paternal authority as a typical expression of adolescent rebelliousness describes quite accurately the ideology that Cosimo's father manifests. It is from the father's point of view that Cosimo's behaviour is an immature wilfulness expressing the childish desire to avoid the responsibilities of a more mature age. Such a challenge must be met with severity to teach the child respect for the authority that he will in due course himself wield. The father must impose his authority in order to preserve the sanctity of authority per se. And yet the bond the father invokes to legitimate his authority is also a keenly personal one. The stakes are high and involve the whole social order, not simply a quarrel between individuals; but at the same time, the nature of the relationship between the two individuals is very much in the foreground: the social and the familial are intimately connected in the father's ideology.

There are a number of interesting observations to be made about the narrative presentation of the father's point of view. First, we should note that Baron Arminio's logic is distinctly feudal. In his eyes, Cosimo is calling into question his personal/familial allegiance, which is one and the same thing as his social allegiance to the established order. The public and private spheres have not yet fissured as they will later do in bourgeois consciousness. At one level, this can be seen to be consonant with the pre-bourgeois setting of the novel. However, this reading fails to come to terms with the fact that the father sounds to Italian ears less like a dinosaur from a past age than a well-known type in the traditional repertory: the authoritarian paterfamilias. This means that the figure of paternal authority reaches the reader laden with the blessings not only of literary tradition but also of common sense, of the familiar cultural constructs of which the archives of such tradition (e.g., a repertory of human types) are the repository.

In the end, then, what underpins the father's standpoint and grounds his authority is a whole *Weltanschauung* that goes well beyond the fictional world Calvino evokes and appeals to the reader by bringing into play a familiar and ideologically overdetermined narrative syntax. The interpretation of events this syntax ultimately legitimates is the father's, and, more surprisingly, the mediator of this attempt to lull the reader into accepting a traditional reading is none other than Biagio, the narrator himself.

In the conflict between father and sons, the narrator, being one of the sons in question, seems to side with the latter against the former. And yet it is precisely by framing the conflict in this traditional way that the narrator blunts the radical edge of Cosimo's challenge. If at the root of the conflict there is indeed only a nostalgia for the unruly food fights that the permissive Fauchelafleur did not stop, then the father's conduct may be excessively brutal, but his understanding of the situation is at bottom correct. By emphasizing the brutality of the father, the narrator shifts attention away from the fact that in the end he shares the father's logic and only disagrees with the latter's conduct in the particular case: the law is not questioned, it is just the particular application that is found faulty. It is through this shift of perspective that the narrator's analysis not only legitimates itself but also ultimately vindicates the father's position.

And yet there is an irreducible 'otherness' in Cosimo that troubles and seduces the narrator into a telling admission: 'Then I was eight, everything seemed a game, the struggle between us boys and grown-ups was the usual one all children play, and I did not realize that my brother's stubbornness hid something much deeper' (*Our Ancestors*, 78). But whatever constitutes this 'something much deeper' remains beyond the ability of the narrator to say directly, and before we examine the ambiguities and tensions within the narrator's position, we need to push our analysis of the father's discourse a little further.

I have said that the father's discourse – the discourse that reduces Cosimo's rebellion to childish wilfulness – reaches the reader with a narrator-mediated metafictional authority that draws upon the great reservoir of cultural constructs that is common sense. This characterization gives away the line of argument I want to pursue. The analysis of common sense played a key role in Gramsci's theory of hegemony (1975), and it is by relying on some Gramscian suggestions that we can flesh out further the significance of Cosimo's refusal.

The father's discourse presupposes an order and a law that go beyond the circumstances of the case. As we have seen, it is the distinction between a particular application and the underlying principle that allows the narrator to support the father's discourse while on the surface disagreeing with it. By taking his brother's side the narrator paradoxically takes the conflict back within the established order. And the mechanism to accomplish this reassimilation of a potential difference is to inscribe the events within a well-established system of beliefs. Within that system Cosimo's rebellion has a simple and straightforward meaning, being nothing more than the manifestation of a natural intergenerational dynamics; all is well with the world. In short, the narrator speaks the discourse of hegemony: the accepted wisdom that legitimates established power relations by naturalizing them. The reader who enjoys the text as a reiteration of familiar types falls victim to the seductions of hegemony, of which the narrator is the largely unsuspecting exponent.

And yet, as we have seen, the narrator himself adumbrates that there is more to Cosimo's rebellion than common sense can acknowledge or grasp. Once we realize that our first interpretive reflex is precisely the one that hegemony dictates, we begin to see that beneath an at times gothically humorous surface the whole first chapter of *The Baron* is an elaborate and roundabout attempt on the part of the narrating voice to avoid a single interpretation, to leave open the significance of the event described. It is as if the narrator's discourse keeps alternating between two registers. On the one hand, there is a timid reflective register that often focuses on the limitations of his father's world view: 'Our father the Baron was a bore, it's true, though not a bad man: a bore because his life was dominated by conflicting ideas, as often happens in periods of transition. The movement of the times makes some people feel a need to move themselves, but in the opposite direction, away from the road; so, with things stirring all round him, our father had set his heart on regaining the lapsed title of Duke of Ombrosa, and thought of nothing but genealogies and successions and family rivalries and alliances with grandees near and far' (*Our Ancestors*, 78). When operating on this register, the narrator's awareness of the anachronism of paternal concerns does not lead him to question the unstated principles on which those concerns are based. In fact, as we have seen, the discourse that distances the father's eccentricities plays an important role in allowing those principles to remain out of sight and unchallenged. The narrating voice expresses here an attitude toward history that is passive and contemplative, and thus essentially conservative. Biagio will do his filial duty and eat the dish of snails not so much, as he claims, because he has no courage, that is, because he is less strong-willed than his brother, but rather because he has no vision to sustain his refusal. Ultimately, this discursive register is designed to demonstrate how a lack of imaginative vision constitutes a serious cognitive limit, a limit that the narrative as a whole will constantly attempt to overcome.

On the other hand, by far the greater part of the narrator's discourse, even in this opening chapter, focuses on relating Cosimo's vicissitudes rather than enquiring explicitly into their wider meaning or significance. This is what I would term the storytelling register.[1] And here is where the narrative flux grows strong and confident. The narrator finds a sure footing and his discourse acquires the breath and pace it needs to carry the reader through the longest story Calvino ever wrote. The reader can feel the author's closeness to the material as the boundaries between the various masks that the speaking subject wears become blurred. In Calvino's own words: 'In *The Baron in the Trees*, my problem was to correct my impulse to identify too strongly with the protagonist, and here I put to work the well-known Serenus Zeitblom device; from the very beginning I sent ahead as "I" a character which was antithetical to Cosimo: a down-to-earth brother full of good sense.'[2]

At times the voices of the narrator, the protagonist, and the author vibrate with a shared pathos that endows the narrative with an emotional quality that is unique in Calvino's oeuvre. In no other work of his is the reader's empathy so manifestly solicited. One of the early passages describing Cosimo's first steps in his arboreal world provides an excellent example of the contained lyricism with which the author seeks to make the reader share the marvel of looking at the world from a distinctly new perspective: 'But the whole garden was scented, and although Cosimo could not yet see it clearly, because of all the thick trees, he was already exploring it by smell, and trying to discern the source of the various aromas which he already knew from their being wafted over into our garden by the wind: and these seemed an integral part of the mystery of the place. Then he looked at the branches and saw new leaves, some big and shining as if running water were constantly flowing over them, some tiny and feathered, and tree trunks either all smooth or all scaly' (*Our Ancestors*, 89). Attention-getting lyrical passages such as this awaken the reader to the fact that the narrator's desire to share, recover, and grasp his brother's experience breaks through the timid bounds of his analytical discourse, and impels him to attempt quite a different route for understanding: the 'feeling with,' the sympathetic re-evocation that storytelling makes possible. Storytelling then becomes the means through which the narrator's discourse struggles to surpass the cognitive limits of common sense – the cognitive limits imposed by hegemony. It is here that the seductions of Cosimo's utopia bubble to the surface. In order to understand Cosimo's rebellion from a point of view other than that of hegemony, it is to this storytelling discourse that we must turn, and then read against the grain to hear what the narrative voice speaks somewhat in spite of itself, in spite of the authority it does not know how to challenge directly.

The narrator punctuates his account of Cosimo's fateful refusal of the dish of snails with a series of lively digressions evoking episodes from the childhood the brothers shared. The image of Cosimo that emerges from these stories is that of an imaginative young boy full of life and adventure. The most interesting aspect of his character is duly flagged by the narrator as he recalls the occasion on which Cosimo was punished for toppling the statue of one of his ancestors: 'And Cosimo, who felt innocent because the fault had not been his but the Abbé's, came out furiously with the phrase: "A fig for all your ancestors,

Father [*signor padre*]!" a pre-announcement of his mission as a rebel [*vocazione di ribelle*]' (*Our Ancestors*, 82).

Speaking of a 'mission as a rebel' constitutes another endorsement of the father's analysis, if not of his methods. And yet Biagio's discourse begins to give us the elements to develop a different point of view. What the narrator does not and cannot see is that far from being an abstract rejection of authority in general, Cosimo's invective denies the legitimacy of a specific form of authority, namely, one based on ancestry and lineage. Cosimo is not contesting his father's right to impose discipline. After all, he still addresses his parent as *signor padre* with a point of irony that does not exclude respect. Rather, Cosimo's sentence contains in embryo an argument against a feudal understanding of authority and in favour of a new model of legitimation. What Cosimo is trying to say to his father is that they live in a world in which ancestry and lineage are rapidly ceasing to be unquestioned and unquestionable sources of value and legitimacy for the exercise of power. And nothing is more symptomatic of the legitimation crisis besetting the old patriarchal values than the father's own obsession with titles and family alliances. In the episode in question, this obsession blinds the father to the merits of the case and leads him to wield authority in a typically unreasonable and brutal manner. And for Cosimo, it is precisely this arbitrariness and brutality, this inability to weigh causes and effects and act according to reason, that saps the father's authority, making it as hollow and brittle as the stucco statues of the family patriarchs that Cosimo has accidentally knocked over.

Cosimo's retort, 'A fig for all your ancestors,' not only makes clear that those hollow icons can no longer command his allegiance, but also that the very question of allegiance is beside the point in the situation at hand. Cosimo seems to say to his father that these statues are cheap false idols, and that he makes himself ridiculous by venerating them; that but for the clumsy intervention of the Abbé Cosimo would not have knocked the statues over; and that by punishing Cosimo without cause the father undermines his credibility and invites rebellion. In short, Cosimo is not prepared to accept an authority structure based on status alone. On the contrary, he suggests that in order to be legitimate, the exercise of power must be grounded in reasoned conclusions based on stated principles and on investigation of the perceivable facts. Cosimo is in fact attempting to provoke the authority figure into giving reasons, and thus becoming explicitly accountable, for his exercise of power.

How does authority respond to this challenge? While the narrator does not relate any reply to Cosimo's barb, the father's voice finds an echo (perhaps I should say comes through as an 'interference') in the narrator's description of his brother's statement as a 'ferocious invective,' a characterization that redeploys the father's procedure of personalizing the offence while eluding the ethical debate.

When the matter of the dish of snails brings the tension between father and son to a head, the father has to respond. Cosimo is now explicitly refusing to obey an injunction that he considers petty, arbitrary, and unreasonable. The father's insistence on imposing his authority on the ground that he is the father, and for that fact alone entitled to be obeyed, runs against a determined and immovable denial for which Cosimo takes full responsibility: 'Cosimo said: "I told you I don't want any, and I don't!" and pushed away his plateful of snails. Never had we seen such disobedience' (Our Ancestors, 77). At first the father does not seem to offer a verbal response, though once again we can hear his voice in the narrator's comment. This silence underscores the fact that the father will not tolerate any questioning of his authority and thus refuses any discussion whatsoever on the matter. The boys will receive corporal punishment without any further explanation – as a crime of lese-majesty demands according to this logic. But when such punishment fails to yield the desired result and the situation escalates further, the father finally speaks: 'Leave this table' (Our Ancestors, 77). This speech is in and of itself an admission of defeat. And the moment Cosimo succeeds in forcing Baron Arminio into discourse the latter has lost, because the father's claim to authority rested on enchantment, on the a priori principles of the aristocratic world view, which demand the unquestioning acceptance of established power relations. By entering into discourse, the father himself becomes subject to its inescapably dialogic nature consisting of contradiction, argument and counter-argument, explanation and retort – the moral order becomes subject to rhetorical deployments, to nonpersonal standards of validity.

Indeed, the father's words fail to articulate an argument. The father cannot explain, cannot even understand what explaining would involve. He still tries to give orders and issue threats. But the spell is broken: the world has not come to an end even though the sacred parental authority has been refused. Cosimo becomes a thorn in the side of the old order, a public sign of contradiction.

These observations allow us to begin to appreciate that 'something much deeper' which Cosimo's rebellion contains. But in order to go further we must remember our earlier discussion of the ambiguous role played by the narrator in guiding the reader's interpretation of the story. We discovered that the narrating voice played a key role in shifting attention away from the questioning of the foundations upon which the father's authority rested. We noted that it was precisely by criticizing the father's conduct that the narrator reasserted the law that the father had perhaps erroneously applied but that remained itself unscathed by events. In this way, the brother attempted to grasp Cosimo's refusal by resituating it within the established cognitive framework. And in the end I argued that the narrator was thus blunting the radical edge of his brother's negation and restoring hegemony under the cloak of common sense. We can now see clearly how Cosimo's rebellion against his father is in the final analysis a rebellion against hegemony, and more specifically, a rebellion against the very mechanism that allows hegemony to exercise its power.

Hegemony that has to speak its name, that has to justify itself and argue for its legitimacy, has already lost its absolute power and fundamental character. It has ceased to be what 'goes without saying,' the limit of the sayable and the thinkable. It has descended to the status of an ideology, which can be attacked, contradicted, found wanting. If it must argue its case, hegemony can no longer operate behind the scenes as the unstated and thus unquestionable set of presuppositions that defines the discursive field. The conclusions it dictates may still sound commonsensical, but they are no longer beyond scrutiny. All of this is what Cosimo has achieved by refusing his dish of snails. This is the real scandal that the narrator can dimly sense but is unable to articulate.

We are now in the position to formulate another crucial question. We have seen that Cosimo's refusal is a determinate negation both of a particular type of authority and of the mechanism of hegemony, but is Cosimo also suggesting an alternative? Does his refusal have a more positive content, albeit in an embryonic form?

I believe this question must be answered in the affirmative. First, what moves Cosimo to rebel against his father's authority is a sense of injustice. In the case of the shattered effigy of the ancestor, the narrator specifies that Cosimo '*felt innocent* because the fault had not been his but the Abbé's' (*Our Ancestors*, 82; emphasis added). And when it comes to the dish of snails the narrator notes that 'Cosimo considered his father's behaviour an *unjust* attack on him' (*Our Ancestors*, 86; emphasis added). That 'superhuman tenacity which my brother showed throughout his life' (*Our Ancestors*, 85), as the narrator puts it, is then based on a moral stance: authority is legitimate and the exercise of power warranted when they are predicated upon just principles and a sound analysis of the circumstances of the case.

So far, however, we are within what Taylor (1989) would call a procedural definition of justice. But Cosimo goes further. The justice of the principles that legitimate the exercise of authority must be open to discussion and cannot be simply taken for granted. While this demand remains within the procedural, it begins to hint at a positive notion of the *good*: the touchstone of value cannot be tradition, but rather an argumentation that persuades most of all by encompassing a fuller picture of the situation being judged. In other words, the narrator and the reader find Cosimo's sense of wrong justified because he is shown to have a much more complete understanding of events than the father, who, obsessed with improbable political intrigues, can only see the world through increasingly narrow filters. What begins to emerge here is Cosimo's pragmatism, which, far from engendering laxity and ethical confusion, leads to an unwavering attention to events and an inflexible intellectual discipline of which the determination never to touch the ground is the perfect objective correlative.

And this is not all. In fact, if we pursue this line of thinking and analyse more closely the story the narrator relates, we can see that a substantive notion of justice is beginning to emerge in Cosimo's conduct. Let's pay careful attention to what the brother is able to tells us: 'It was as a protest against this macabre fantasy of our sister's that my brother and I were incited to show our *sympathy* [*solidarietà*] *with the poor tortured creatures*,[3] and our disgust, too, for the flavour of cooked snails – a revolt against everything and everybody; and it was from this, not surprisingly, that stemmed Cosimo's gesture and all that followed after' (*Our Ancestors*, 83; emphasis added). Once again, we have to filter the narrator's description and be particularly wary of the tendency to reduce Cosimo's behaviour to a generalized, undifferentiated rebelliousness. The phrase I have italicized slips through the narrator's own filters and provides us with an opportunity to develop our analysis further.

What flags the statement is its unusual character. Using Eco's categories, one would say that our encyclopedic entry for invertebrates in general and snails in particular does not contain an indication that their contribution to the human diet is likely to occasion an outpouring of human compassion, even less of solidarity. In a narrative that relies heavily on well-established topoi, Cosimo's unexpected sympathy for snails is designed to attract attention, particularly when it is paradoxically coupled with the culturally sanctioned repulsion for snails – viscous, mucus-producing lumps of organic matter – which plays an important part in their culinary allure.

At first, one may want to explain Cosimo's rather odd object choice as a pathetic counterpoint to the Gothic viciousness of his sister Battista. And yet, once again, we must be careful not to close the matter too quickly. A counterpoint to Battista, yes, but not simply a face-off on the axis of Gothic sensibility. The confrontation with Battista takes place on quite a different plane as we discover by harking back to another rather puzzling statement by the narrator.

Immediately after the description of the incident that led to Cosimo's outburst of 'A fig for all your ancestors,' the narrator begins a new paragraph with these words: 'Our sister felt the same at heart. She too, though the isolation in which she lived had been forced on her by our Father after the affair of the Marchesino della Mella, had always been a rebellious and lonely soul' (*Our Ancestors*, 82). Up to this point Battista had been presented to the reader as someone with whom the brothers had nothing in common. Now, suddenly, the narrator recognizes that in her way she is just as much a rebel as Cosimo. And yet the antipathy between the two clearly suggests that their rebellions are very different. And, indeed, their behaviour is in many respects antithetical. Stinging statements mark Cosimo's rebellion, while Battista's is silent. Cosimo chooses to break with paternal authority in the most explicit way, not only verbally but going to the extent of establishing a physical barrier between himself and his father. Battista accepts confinement within the home and eventually marries well, much to everybody's surprise.

Battista's grim rancour manifests itself first and foremost in her extravagantly grisly cuisine. The essence of her rebellion is an emphatic and theatrical transgression against taste: 'In fact, most of these peculiar dishes of hers were thought out just *for effect*, rather than for any pleasure in making us eat disgusting food with her. These dishes of Battista's were works of the *most delicate animal or vegetable jewellery*; cauliflower heads with hare's ears set on a collar of fur; or a pig's head from whose mouth stuck a scarlet lobster' (*Our Ancestors*, 83; emphasis added). While Cosimo's revolt is based on a sense of injustice and constitutes a moral challenge to the father's authority, Battista's is grounded in sensibility and takes essentially the form of an aesthetic challenge. Cosimo denounces 'common sense'; Battista assails 'good taste.' He is the moralist, she is the aesthete. And here we are reminded of a figure we have encountered in *The Viscount*: Mastro Pietrochiodo, who built beautifully intricate gallows and tried to forget the use to which they were put by concentrating on the aesthetic quality of his cruel inventions. Battista also takes pride in her cruel artistry, but her sensibility takes her much further than Mastro Pietrochiodo. Far from attempting to block out the cruelty that her art involves, she revels in it and makes it an integral part of her artistic performance: in her baroque composition, the lobster is tearing out the piglet's tongue.

The interpretive thrust of these observations is further strengthened by the aura of sensual excess that surrounds Battista's circumstances. Not only does the incident to which her confinement is due involve an allegation of attempted rape, but the narrator also makes no mystery of his serious doubts about the official family version and suggests that the victim of the attack might in fact have been the alleged rapist. In addition, the fact that, in order to save her own as well as the family's reputation, Battista has to wear a nun's attire, though her religious vocation is at best dubious, immediately evokes the dissolute nun of Monza in Manzoni's *I promessi sposi*. In the end, it becomes clear that while Cosimo demands justice based on reason, Battista demands the right to sensual satisfaction.

Once we understand the nature of Battista's transgressions, Cosimo's antipathy for her and the products of her artistry becomes considerably more meaningful. We can now see that, for Cosimo, the dish of snails is not only a pretext to provoke the father into discussing the moral basis of his authority but it is also a direct challenge to Battista. Cosimo tried to free the snails and thus save them from Battista's murderous hands. The plan failed, Battista discovered the intrigue, and Cosimo and his brother were duly punished. Now readmitted to the family table, they are presented with a full-course meal ... of snails: snail soup, a main dish of snails. The narrator succeeds in making the reader feel the glee with which Battista had prepared the courses.

If Cosimo ate the snails his defeat would be complete: he would become an accomplice to the carnage in the most physical and sensuous way. With every contraction of his mandible, he would submit to the logic of the performance Battista has engineered. She would watch and feel his repulsion, feed on it. Battista expresses the sadistic impulse of the aristocratic libertine, and nothing could be more antagonistic to Cosimo's ethical discipline.

By refusing the dish of snails, Cosimo puts an end once and for all to the sophisticated games Battista is trying to drag him into. In the end, then, the stakes are higher than the father or even the narrator realize. Where the father would, or could, see only an act of insubordination, where the narrator could see only an obscure obstinacy of the will, there is actually a demand for justice (for a reasoned exercise of power pursuant to just principles), and a sober ethics based on solidarity with living creatures. This is the ground that, from the very beginning of *The Baron*, Cosimo begins to stake out for himself, and where his utopian vision begins to take root.

A Finer Fantastic

The first chapter of *The Baron* is a particularly rich text. With disarming stylistic simplicity, it introduces the reader to the fundamental thematic tensions that propel the narrative. Having analysed this chapter in quite some detail, though by no means exhaustively, I should take Cosimo's own implicit advice, that is, find a vantage point at some distance from the textual world below and pause a moment to consider the wider significance of the story we are being told. In the context of this study, our vantage point is easy to find: genre and the role of the intellectual.

I began my discussion of the *The Baron* noting that there is a clear thematic nexus between the second work in Calvino's heraldic trilogy and the first. And it is interesting to note at this point that in an early version of the manuscript a statue of the Viscount Medardo of Terralba was included in the gallery of ancestors whose effigies stood perilously at the end of the balustrade that Cosimo liked to use as a slide. We can now focus on the equally evident stylistic similarities. For example, the story is told through the eyes of a young boy,[4] which translates linguistically into the use of a very informal level of language marked by a loose paratactic structure and punctuated by colloquial expressions: 'Having our father and mother always there in front of us, using knives and forks for the chicken, keeping our backs straight and our elbows down, what a strain it all was! – not to mention the presence of that sister of ours [*quell'antipatica di nostra sorella*], Battista' (*Our Ancestors*, 78).

On the other hand, from the very beginning *The Baron* presents the reader with a significantly different modulation of the genre with which Calvino is experimenting. Setting the opening sentences of the two works side by side clearly makes the point:

There was a war on against the Turks. My uncle, the Viscount Medardo of Terralba, was riding towards the Christian camp across the plain of Bohemia, followed by a squire called Kurt. (*Our Ancestors*, 3)

It was on 15 June 1767 that Cosimo Piovasco di Rondò, my brother, sat among us for the last time. And it might have been today, I remember it so clearly. We were in the dining room of our house at Ombrosa, the windows framing the thick branches of the great holm oak in the park. It was midday. (*Our Ancestors*, 77)

While the opening of *The Viscount* immediately signals to the reader the non-realistic character of the ensuing narrative (as we noted in the previous chapter), the opening of *The Baron* leaves the reader somewhat more in doubt about the generic register of the narrative discourse. The reference to a specific date typically invites realistic expectations. On the other hand, the pathos of the passage and its ostended (again to use one of Eco's formulations) melodramatic tone evoke a Gothic atmosphere that opens up the possibility of a non-realist development. As we read on, this not unpleasant sense of finding oneself at the edge of different generic registers never quite leaves the reader and ultimately becomes one of the fundamental characteristics of the work as a whole. In fact, in a 1957 interview, Calvino himself noted: 'I believe that in my work one can find not only two souls and poetics but many. *The Cloven Viscount* and *The Baron in the Trees* are two fantastic stories, but of different shades of fantasy. And in each of the two books (especially in *The Baron*), shifts in the gradation of fantasy can be found between chapters (and that's a serious defect).'[5] While we may well disagree with Calvino's evaluation of the generic complexity of *The Baron* ('a serious defect'),[6] which may also be ironical, his diagnosis points us in the direction my analysis is taking.

The stylistic continuity in difference and the thematic nexus between *The Viscount* and *The Baron* set the stage for an extremely fruitful and revealing generic comparison, which I should begin by noting that the structural principle or device that organizes the narrative is once again the literalization of a central metaphor. In *The Viscount*, the divided self of the increasingly alienated post-war Italian intellectual was represented by the predicament of the protagonist, cloven in half by a cannonball and compelled to confront life from that odd vantage point until the narrative forcibly sewed his two halves back together. In *The Baron*, Cosimo's ascent into the trees literalizes the utopian impulse to which his whole life will bear witness. However, while at the level of narrative syntax we recognize the identity of the procedure, the real interest of the comparison lies in the differences that emerge as we examine the meaning and significance of the device.

We have seen that the representation of the Viscount's predicament allowed Calvino to grapple with issues that preoccupied the progressive Italian intelligentsia in the post-war period. The problematic of the role of the intellectual within a society in the throes of an unprecedented capitalist development took centre stage in *The Viscount* through the mediation of a genre that allowed the author to avoid pat ideological answers. That genre was a highly personal fantastic form that combined elements from allegory, romance, fairy tale, the adventure story, and even comic strips. The bold and uninhibited way in which Calvino proceeded to manipulate these generic resources had a great deal to do with the vivacity and interest of the final product, while the brevity of the narrative made it easy for Calvino to master stylistically the disparate elements. However, as some of the early critics noted and as Calvino himself understood, this form had serious limitations.[7] It permitted, as I maintained, a radical compression and simplification of narrative material, which in turn allowed an incisive and brilliant presentation of the basic terms of the problem. And yet, as the inevitable happy ending confirmed, it could not go far when it came to imagining a way out of the cloven condition *The Viscount* had boldly foregrounded. At the close of the story, the Viscount is whole again and the narrative implodes, as if to demonstrate that the generic seams can no longer contain it. One of the key problems facing Calvino in *The Baron* is precisely that of developing a form robust enough to accommodate a more sustained imaginative elaboration of the issues *The Viscount* put on the table.

The narrative core of *The Baron*, and of which the whole book is in a sense the exfoliation, is Cosimo's decision to retreat into the trees. For us the question now is: what is fundamentally different about this basic narrative fulcrum from the halving of the Viscount which was at the heart of the earlier work. The first difference is that the departure from verisimilitude is less striking in the former case than in the latter. It would be tempting to argue that while in *The Viscount* the reader is catapulted into a fairy-tale-like logic, in *The Baron* the suspension of disbelief required of the reader is much less taxing: Cosimo's adventures are at the edge of verisimilitude but not over it. This line of argument is not completely without merit; it points in a direction worth

pursuing as long as we correct the danger of considering verisimilitude, or the lack of it, as ontological rather than discursive categories.
In other words, the important point is not that, everything else being
equal (and this is a huge assumption), our historically situated sense of
what is empirically possible is less disturbed by a story about a young
boy who climbs into the trees and decides never to walk on the ground
again than one about an aristocrat who spends part of his life cloven in
half by a cannonball. Rather, the point is that, within the world evoked
by *The Baron*, Cosimo's ascent into the leafy world of treetops plays a
much more complex role than the protagonist's predicament in *The
Viscount*.

In *The Viscount*, the image of being literally divided against oneself
functioned as the precise objective correlative of the simple binary
logic that propelled the narrative. By the end of *The Viscount*, we have
exhausted the resources of that logic. The problematic of alienation
evolves; it is no longer symbolized through the literalization of a split
within the subject, rather, it is socialized and presented as a multiplicity of distances that the subject has to negotiate. The subject is no
longer divided against himself, rather, multiple divisions are seen as
constitutive of the process through which the subject comes to being
and seeks to define himself. And here is the place where I can bring to
bear the results of the detailed analysis of the first chapter of *The Baron*.

Unlike the accident that caused the Viscount's mutilation, Cosimo's
retreat into the trees marks a separation that is deliberately chosen, and
the whole narrative revolves around the attempt by the narrator to
understand Cosimo's motivation. In relation to *The Viscount*, it would
then seem that the narrative axis would have to shift dramatically from
allegory to psychology, which would in turn explain the more realistic
feel of the later novel. But this is not the case. The discussion about
motivation, rather than leading to psychologism and to the fathoming
of the depths of interiority, is externalized and projected into a public
space where Cosimo's utopia and the ethical project it manifests is
endowed with a socio-political significance that becomes the object of a
shared cognition.

The break with the father is dictated not by an Oedipal dynamic or
other personal trauma, but by a demand for reasons, for an argument
that would necessarily have to address an issue of wide socio-political
significance: the legitimation of the established order of which a certain type of father/son relationship is one of the central pillars. Indeed,
as the two later encounters between Cosimo and the old Baron make

abundantly clear, Cosimo does not rebel against the figure of the Father but against this particular father and his particular logic:

'You are making yourself a figure of fun!' began the father, bitterly. 'Really worthy of a gentleman!' (He called him by the formal *voi*, as he did for the most serious reprimands, but the use of the word now had a sense of distance, of detachment.)

'A gentleman, my lord father, is such whether he is on earth or on the tree-tops,' replied Cosimo, and at once added: 'If he behaves with decency.'

'An excellent maxim,' admitted the Baron gravely. 'And yet only a short time ago you were stealing plums from one of our tenants.' (*Our Ancestors*, 131)

'Good day, my lord father.'
    'Good day, son.'
    'Are you in good health?'
    'Considering my years and sorrows.'
    'I am pleased to see you so well' ...
    'Do you realize that you could lead [*comandare*] noble vassals with the title of Duke?'
    'I realize that when I have more ideas than others, I give those others my ideas, if they want to accept them; and that to me is leading' ...
    'Do your remember you are the Baron of Rondò?'
    'Yes, lord father, I remember my name.'
    'Do you wish to be worthy of the name and title you bear?'
    'I will try to be as worthy as I can of the name of man, and also of its every attribute.'
    'Take this sword, my sword' ...
    'Thank you, lord father ... I promise I will make good use of it.'
    'Farewell, my son.' (*Our Ancestors*, 178–9)

These laconic exchanges indicate Calvino's mastery of style: we are witnessing a measured and precise game of chess played by unyielding adversaries, a subtle verbal duel that yet succeeds in being humorous (e.g., the inescapable emotional blackmail: 'Considering my years and *sorrows*'; emphasis added) and even touching.

These dialogues also make clear that, for Cosimo, the break with the father entails cutting himself off from the network of social relations that the established order has configured. As we soon find out, this rejection has a high price. Cosimo finds himself in the position of having to reinvent his social being, and his vicissitudes are ultimately the record of his attempts to carve out a new social role for himself. The determination to persevere on this arduous path and the belief that only in so doing can he live up to his ethical aspiration are the lifeblood of the utopian longing that is Cosimo's trademark.

How does Cosimo go about defining a new relationship with the world, a new world view? As we have seen, the first impulse is a negation and a distancing. The existing regime of common sense is denied legitimacy, and this rejection is externalized through the literalization of the metaphor of distance (cf. Cases, 1970). Cosimo sets himself apart from his father, his family, his community, but, and this is a critical observation, he does not sever all ties with them.

Just as the break with the father is never complete, as the passages I have quoted clearly demonstrate, Cosimo remains in close touch with his family and, in particular, his community. Normal relations are disrupted, but the social bond with individuals and groups is maintained throughout Cosimo's life: 'In fact, Cosimo, despite that escape of his which had upset us all so much, lived almost as closely with us as he had before. He was a solitary who did not avoid people. In a way, indeed, he seemed to like them more than anything else' (*Our Ancestors*, 136). As the narrator notes, the seductions of a radically 'other' nature are rebuffed: 'Certainly the continual contact with the barks of trees, his eyes trained to the movement of a leaf, a hair, a scale ... all those forms of life so far removed from the human ... those borders of the wild into which he was so deeply urged, might have moulded his mind, made him lose every semblance of man. Instead of which, however many new qualities he acquired from his community with plants and his struggle with animals, his place – it always seemed to me – was clearly with us' (*Our Ancestors*, 149).

Though determined to preserve his position at the margins of civilized life, Cosimo remains a member of the human commonwealth. Indeed, one of his exploits will be to reawaken, with the help of fleas, the lethargic French troops that the forest threatened to swallow: '"Instead of which my intervention [Cosimo is speaking] was providential; the itching of the fleas quickly kindled in the hussars a human and civilized need to scratch themselves, search themselves, delouse themselves; they flung away their mossy clothes, their packs and knapsacks covered with mushrooms and cobwebs, washed, shaved, combed, in fact reacquired a perception of their individual humanity and regained the sense of civilization, of enfranchisement from the ugly side of nature [*la natura bruta*]"' (*Our Ancestors*, 271).

From this perspective we can begin to see more clearly the significance of deploying a genre that, while retaining a fantastic edge, is less taxing on the reader's sense of verisimilitude. The ability to take up suggestions that the narrative material offers to the author's lively imagination is preserved by the fantastic quality of the story. Episodes such as Cosimo's bloody encounter with the wild cat, his excursion to Olivabassa where the momentarily 'deterritorialized' Spanish nobles also live on trees, or the already cited intervention to bring back to life the Republican troops, exemplify the freedom of movement that the non-realist form affords.

However, in the context of *The Baron*, it is just as important that this freedom be guided and nourished by the social constraints that, in the given socio-historical context in question, are embodied at the formal level by the conventions of verisimilitude. Cosimo's struggle to reinvent his social being between the temptations of brute nature and the injunctions of the existing order is paralleled in the author's struggle to reinvent a genre in the interstices between fantastic stylization and social realism. For this reason, much of the narrative is devoted to exploring in quite verisimilar terms what it would take to organize one's life in the trees. Cosimo is a kind of Robinson Crusoe: 'Those first days of Cosimo's on the trees were without aim or purpose, and were dominated entirely by the desire to know and possess his new kingdom. He would have liked to explore it to its extreme limits, to study all the possibilities it offered him, to discover it plant by plant and branch by branch' (*Our Ancestors*, 117). And he has to resolve such basic problems as adequate shelter, food supply, and even conveniences – all dealt with in chapter 10.

These passages are not simply the occasion for some typically Calvinian light humour, but also, and more importantly, a way to instal and experiment with a new and cognitively significant standpoint. Cosimo's ascent into the trees is not only allegoric and symbolic, it is also a thought experiment that permits the defamiliarization of common sense and the hegemonic power common sense conceals. It is by trying to deal with the actual problems his new condition poses, that Cosimo develops a vantage point from which to develop a different world view: 'While down below our world lay flattened, and our bodies looked quite disproportionate and *we certainly understood nothing* of what he knew up there – he who spent his nights listening to the sap germinating from cells, the circles marking the years inside the trunks, the mould enlarging its patches quivering under the north wind, the birds asleep in their nests quivering then resettling their heads in the softest down of their wing' (*Our Ancestors*, 142; emphasis added).

The lyricism of this and other narrative catalogues describing Cosimo's kingdom expresses the narrator's attempt to *feel with* his brother as a means to overcome the limitations of his own 'terrestrial' standpoint, limitations that are explicitly characterized as being cognitive in nature. We re-encounter here the same strategy we noted in the opening chapter, where the narrator's empathetic accounts of the childhood episodes (i.e., his vigorous storytelling) overcome the ideological limitations that are responsible for the commonsensical predictability of the explicitly reflective passages.

What, then, are the concrete effects of this alternative vantage point from which Cosimo views the world? At first it seems that rebellion has not brought clear advantages, cognitive or otherwise. When pressed by his father in chapter 8, Cosimo cuts off the conversation with one of his lapidary pronouncements: 'But I can spray water further from the trees' ('Ma io dagli alberi piscio più lontano!'; *Our Ancestors*, 131–2). The statement owes much of its incisiveness to the fact that it is a brilliant non sequitur. Not only does it not in any way answer the father's argument – 'Rebellion cannot be measured by yards' (*Our Ancestors*, 131) – but it also constitutes a sharp break in genre. The conduct accompanying the impertinent outburst underscores this point: 'he [Cosimo] suddenly got bored with all this solemnity, [stuck out his tongue] and shouted' (*Our Ancestors*, 131).[8]

And yet, the apparently nonsensical statement does in fact carry an important message. However, this 'sense' only emerges once the statement is contextualized. The encounter between father and son takes place after Cosimo has challenged the local urchins to a stone-throwing game. As we have seen, in the opening salvo the father expresses his objections to the company Cosimo is keeping ('You're making yourself a figure of fun!') and reminds the son of his status ('Really worthy of a gentleman!'). In this context, the response with which Cosimo puts an end to the conversation constitutes an unequivocal reiteration of his rejection of the social role his father demands of him. Cosimo is speaking as one of the urchins he was playing with would speak, and his words sound almost like a battle cry: 'As though they had heard the phrase, a shout went up from the urchins round Porta Capperi. The Baron of Rondò's horse shied' (*Our Ancestors*, 132).

Cosimo demonstrates his ability to speak a language other than that of his class and to rally support from its social antagonist. And this is a clear indication that his standpoint has yielded a new knowledge, a cognitive and, indeed, political gain. It is worthwhile to note that while at the level of conscious reflection the narrator is unable to grasp the wider significance of Cosimo's sentence 'a phrase without much meaning, but which cut the discussion off short' (*Our Ancestors*, 132), the story he nonetheless tells allows us to go beyond that first level of meaning and appreciate Cosimo's new power of insight. Once again, storytelling allows the narrator's discourse to overflow the analytical-cum-ideological cage within which it operates reflexively.

As the narrative progresses, the paradoxical nature of the distance Cosimo has established between himself and the land where his fellow human beings live comes increasingly into the foreground. Marginality has a price; the realistically explored complications of a life in the trees make that abundantly clear. Marginality also has advantages; freed of his social obligations, Cosimo lives for a while the wondrous freedom of the explorer of a new world, in which every moment is still adventure and excitement.

The real paradox, however, is that marginality emerges as the efficient cause of Cosimo's growing role in the history of his community. No longer encumbered by the constraints of his status as the first-born son of a pretentious baron, Cosimo is free to let his lively intelligence seize on the stimuli that surround him. He consorts with local urchins and begins to see the privileges of his class through their eyes. He sees the peasants working and learns of their needs. He fraternizes with the coal merchants from Bergamo living in utter poverty in the woods. In short, from the trees and, in fact, thanks to his being in the trees, Cosimo has access to a much wider range of experiences than would otherwise have been the case.

These experiences are not exclusively of a practical nature. On the contrary, Cosimo also meets an unlikely intellectual mentor: the brigand Gian dei Brughi, whose insatiable appetite for literature eventually teaches Cosimo what familial discipline had vainly tried to inculcate: 'From the period in the brigand's company Cosimo had acquired a passion for reading and study which remained with him for the rest of his life' (*Our Ancestors*, 169). Only after this encounter does Cosimo's relationship with the Abbé Fauchelafleur become cognitively stimulating, though the order of 'seniority' is now reversed: 'Thus the relationship of pupil and teacher between the two was reversed. It was

Cosimo who became the teacher and Fauchelafleur the pupil' (*Our Ancestors*, 170). From this moment on, Cosimo's intellectual life becomes as intense and essential to his character as his participation in the life of the community. There is no conflict or antagonism between these two types of activities, the meshing of which constitutes his life's fabric. The manuscript *Project for the Constitution of an Ideal State in the Trees* is exemplary of this rich, complex life, which in the final analysis is the content of Cosimo's utopia: 'At that time he began to write a *Project for the Constitution of an Ideal State in the Trees*, in which he described the imaginary Republic of Arborea, inhabited by just men. He began it as a treatise on laws and governments, but as he wrote his impulse to invent complicated stories supervened and out poured a hodge-potch [*sic*] of adventures, duels and erotic tales, the latter inserted in a chapter on matrimonial rights. The epilogue of the book should have been this: the Author, having founded the perfect State in the tree-tops and convinced the whole of humanity to establish itself there and live there happily, came down to live on an earth which was now deserted' (*Our Ancestors*, 212).

The final twist to this utopia is a further indication that even utopia must contemplate its own dialectical overcoming: history does not stop and the social role of the intellectual is never complete. This complex blend of experiences overwhelms and breaks down the rigid binarisms that led to the impasse of which *The Viscount* was an eloquent record. And for a moment, the synthesis that the previous work could not sustain seems within reach. But there is one further challenge Cosimo has to meet, the challenge of an intelligence and sensibility to match his own but moved by a different logic: Viola.

The love affair between Cosimo and Viola – fairy-tale conventions have suggested it since the two characters first met in the distant chapter 2 – finally gets off the ground in chapter 21, at the beginning of the third and last part of *The Baron*. Once again it seems useful to let Calvino's own words serve as a point of departure for the discussion: 'The protagonist, the Baron Cosimo di Rondò, broke out of the burlesque frame, and was turning out to be a moral portrait with precise cultural connotations; the research carried out by historian friends of mine about the Enlightenment in Italy and Italian Jacobins became a precious stimulus for the imagination. Even the female character (Viola) joined in the play of ethical and cultural perspectives: *in contrast with Enlightenment exactitude,* [she represented] *the baroque and later Romantic impulse towards the absolute* [il tutto], *which always runs the risk of becoming a destructive impulse, a race toward nothingness.'[9]*

Viola is in a way also a rebel, but the force that drives her rebellion is imperious desire and passionate abandon. Telling Cosimo what she has done in the years that she has been away from Ombrosa, she explains: '"From now on I'm staying here, where I was a child. I'll stay here as long as I feel like it, of course, then I'll go off; I'm a widow and can do what I like, finally. I've always done what I liked, to tell the truth; even Tolemaico I married because it suited me to marry him; it's not true that they forced me to, they were determined to make a martyr of me, and so I chose the most decrepit suitor I could find. 'Then I'll be a widow sooner,' I said, and so I am, now"' (*Our Ancestors*, 226).

Viola and Cosimo do share a certain peremptoriness of judgment, a stubborn determination to pursue their goals, and also a restlessness that manifests itself in the desire for adventure. However, these qualities of the will are sustained in Cosimo by a sober and stringent ethical discipline based on two fundamental principles: first, justice and truth are contextual, and thus the result of a reasoned understanding of the specific circumstances of each case – this is the principle that emerged from our analysis of Cosimo's original rebellion against his father's authority; second, human beings are part of nature, and it is in reasoned interaction with the natural environment that they fulfil their aspirations and desires – and this is the aspect that the love affair with Viola makes clear: 'With you I make love. Like picking, or pruning' (*Our Ancestors*, 231). Cosimo is a pragmatist and an empiricist whose reason is affectively nourished by a controlled lyrical empathy with natural phenomena.

Viola, on the other hand, strives for totality and therefore for transcendence. She will not accept her love being placed on the same level as picking fruit and pruning. She demands absolute devotion, which is not, and cannot be, of this world. Her demands are, a priori, beyond the possibility of satisfaction. She is trapped in a logic that commands her to constantly test Cosimo, in order to exact the total abnegation of self in a love whose final horizon is death.

Cosimo resists – 'But he never threatened to kill himself, indeed he never threatened anything, emotional blackmail was not in him' (*Our Ancestors*, 232) – but he is troubled: 'The more he tried ... to reacquire command of passions and pleasures in a wise economy of mind, the more he felt the void left by her or the fever for her return. In fact his love was just what Viola wanted it to be' (*Our Ancestors*, 236).

Ultimately, however, Cosimo will not repudiate the principles that have informed his conduct since he declined the dish of snails and left the surface of the earth:

And she: 'Don't you think that love should be an absolute dedication, a renunciation of self?' ...
'There can be no love if one does not remain oneself with all one's strength' ...
'Be yourself by yourself, then.' (*Our Ancestors*, 245–6)

As a result of the dramatic end of his love affair with Viola, Cosimo momentarily loses his reason – another nod to the chivalric tradition from Ariosto to Tasso – and with it his humanity: 'If before he went about dressed in furs from head to foot, now he began to adorn his head with feathers ... and apart from those on his head he scattered feathers all over his clothes' (*Our Ancestors*, 248). The equilibrium between reason and nature on which Cosimo's philosophy of life is based is breaking down. The synthesis that seemed within reach is now receding, and the reader gets the impression that something has snapped for good. Suddenly, Cosimo's parable becomes a descending one, in the narrator's words: 'Yes, it was a sad decline' (*Our Ancestors*, 250).

Still, Cosimo eventually recovers his reason. An invasion of wolves during a particularly rigid winter will allow him to demonstrate his inventiveness as he helps the community one more time. He will also take up his studies again and his utopian impulse will once more come to the fore:

What he had in mind was an idea of a universal society. And every time he busied himself collecting people, either for a definite purpose such as guarding against fire or defending from wolves, or in confraternities of trades such as the Perfect Wheelwrights' or the Illuminated Skin Chandlers', since he always got them to meet in the woods, at night, round a tree from which he would preach, there was always an air of conspiracy, of sect, of heresy, and in that atmosphere his speeches also passed easily from particular to general, and from the simple rules of some manual trade moved far too easily to a plan for installing a world republic of men, equal, free and just. (*Our Ancestors*, 258–9)

But these efforts are now clearly depicted as powerless to change the world of the narrative. Cosimo's utopia has lost its purchase. This involution has a counterpart at the generic level. The effort to weave together the various generic strands that the narrative has exploited relaxes, as each of the final episodes pursues its own generic suggestions and the narrator increasingly lets Cosimo speak for himself. In chapter 25, it is the Gothic element that prevails in the confrontation with the Jesuit Don Suplicio. In chapter 26, the French Revolution's repercussions in Italy are narrated in a tone of chatty realism. In chapter 27, the tone turns to heroic fable as Cosimo tells the story of how he helped the French Revolutionary Army beat the Austrian forces. Then the chapters become shorter, their raison d'être being primarily to suture the narrative by tying it in with history and literary tradition. Cosimo meets Napoleon, the emperor who betrayed the Enlightenment dream of justice, freedom, and equality, and yet whose defeat will usher in a truly reactionary restoration. But before we let ourselves be deceived by the accumulation of historical references, the fantastic character is restored by Cosimo's meeting with the melancholy Prince Andréj from Tolstoy's *War and Peace*, with whom, in fact, he has a much more meaningful conversation than with the French Emperor:

'You see ... War ... For years now I've dealing as best I can with a thing that in itself is appalling; war ... and all this for ideals which I shall never, perhaps, be able to explain fully to myself ...'

'I too,' replied Cosimo, 'have lived many years for ideals which I would never be able to explain to myself; but I do something entirely good; I live on trees.' (*Our Ancestors*, 280)

In the end, Cosimo's pugnacious wit and once inexhaustible verve as a storyteller are silenced: 'Now he could scarcely speak' (*Our Ancestors*, 281). What remains is a sense of discipline and commitment anchored in an experience whose value is personally felt but can no longer be explicitly analysed, then communicated and shared. What remains is the determination to bear witness to the last to a utopian longing to which others will have to give a specific meaning. The narrator, who at the very end of the novel comes closest to one brief insight, expresses it as follows: 'Now that he is no longer here I seem to have to worry about so many things, philosophy, politics, history; I follow the news, read books, but they fuzz me, what he meant to say is not there, for he understood something else, something that was all embracing, and he could not say it in words but only by living as he did. Only by being so frankly himself as he was till his death could he give something to all men' (*Our Ancestors*, 281).

And yet, the hurry to submerge all that Cosimo stood for in an undifferentiated totality that cannot be put into words exhibits once again the cognitive threshold the narrator is incapable of crossing. There is more to Cosimo's legacy than a mere longing for a better world. What emerges from the stories that make up his life is a precise ethical trajectory, or perhaps I should say a parable, whose meaning is necessarily a matter of interpretation but has less to do with absolute and all-encompassing principles than with the possibilities of a particular socio-historical configuration. By depriving it of its specificity and retreating into nostalgia, the narrating voice demonstrates once again the seductiveness of the standpoint of common sense and hegemony, to which Biagio surrenders with naive, oblivious candour: 'Such thoughts I confide to this notebook, nor would I know how to express them otherwise; I have always been a balanced man, without great impetus or yearnings, a father, a noble by birth, enlightened in ideas, observant of the laws' (*Our Ancestors*, 280).

The prosaic tone and plodding rhythm of the passage provide in themselves an excellent picture of the grey though excruciatingly well-meaning discourse that the narrator speaks and is spoken by. But before we dismiss Biagio too quickly, we should remember that within the economy of the narrative, this rather dull prop is essential not only at the syntactic level as the conduit through which the story is told, but also at the pragmatic level. It is the narrator who takes care of the family's affairs and provides Cosimo with the minimal but essential resources the latter needs to lead his life in the trees: 'I was just twenty-one and could make whatever use I liked of the family patrimony, as my brother needed very little ... My brother had asked to sign a Power of Attorney in my favour over all our possessions, on condition I gave him a monthly allowance, paid his taxes, and kept his affairs in order' (*Our Ancestors*, 213).

At critical moments in Cosimo's life, the brother helps out: playing the go-between between Cosimo and his parents, filling the occasional order for supplies, providing a warm meal to the aging sibling. And finally, the nameless narrator remains the most diligent witness of Cosimo's vicissitudes. It is through him that Cosimo's stories reach us, carrying a meaning that goes well beyond the cognitive horizon of the narrating voice. In spite of all his limitations, then, Biagio represents a value that will have to be accounted for as we move beyond the fictional world evoked by *The Baron* and seek to examine the way in which this fictional world meaningfully engages the socio-historical conjuncture.

Engaging the Socio-cultural Moment

In the note to a 1995 Italian edition of *The Baron*, Mario Barenghi informs us that '*The Baron in the Trees* ... appears in 1957, No. 79 in the series *Coralli* published by Einaudi ... The period of composition is indicated at the bottom of the last page of the volume: December 10, 1956–February 26, 1957. Rather quickly written, therefore, almost a happy, sparkling interlude ... which interrupts the difficult preparation of "A Plunge in Real Estate."'[10] Calvino himself, in his postface to the 1960 edition of the trilogy *Our Ancestors*, remarks: 'Here as well [in *The Baron* and *The Viscount*] the composition date sheds light on the mood. It's a period during which the role we can have in historical development is being rethought, while new hopes and new disillusionments alternate. In spite of all, the times are getting better; the problem is finding the right way to connect individual conscience to the course of history.'[11]

From the standpoint of the Italian and European intelligentsia of which Calvino was a member, two crucial events mark 1956: the Twentieth Congress of the CPSU, during which Khrushchev denounced the abuses of Stalinism, and eight months later the USSR's invasion of Hungary, which put an end to the liberalization process Khrushchev's report had encouraged. These events plunged the PCI into its most serious crisis since the end of World War II. Images of Soviet tanks crushing the resistance in Budapest had a devastating impact on all those for whom the Italian Resistance remained a founding event and the socialist revolution a program for human liberation. The hopes and expectations raised by destalinization were swept aside by what seemed the rankest kind of realpolitik. The PCI's attempt to give credit to the Soviet thesis that in Hungary the liberalization process had been hijacked by reactionary forces failed to convince even the CGIL (the powerful communist trade union), which publicly broke party line and expressed solidarity with the Budapest insurgents. Calvino was deeply scarred by the experience, which he remembered in 1980:

> But when Khrushchev denounced Stalin before the Central Committee and then before the Party Congress, we thought: now peace will blossom, now the fruit of socialism will come, that oppression, that secret anguish that we [Italian Communists] felt, will disappear ...
> Old Stalinists were being replaced by Communists who had been in jail

and had been excluded from all party functions. We saw in all of this the confirmation of our hopes, a real renewal, a turn of historical importance ...

That was for me a decisive evening ... His voice [Gianni Rocca's, editor in chief of *l'Unità*] was interrupted by sobs. He told us: tanks are entering Budapest, there is fighting in the streets. I looked at Amendola [at the time the second in command within the PCI]. All three of us were in shock. Then Amendola murmured: 'Togliatti [then the PCI's leader] says that there are moments in history in which one must take sides ...'

I did not want to quit the party when it was facing a particularly difficult moment, but my mind was made up. I left without much noise in the summer of 1957.[12]

Calvino's case is exemplary. The honeymoon between the Italian progressive intelligentsia and the PCI, which began to turn sour with the experience of *Il Politecnico*, continued to deteriorate as a result of the political polarization and ideological intransigence of the Cold War years, and was briefly revived by the Khrushchev report, was now definitively over.

And yet, the more specifically Italian political scene was not bleak. The defeat of the fraud law (legge truffa) in the 1953 elections had once again raised the issue of a centre-left alliance, that is, the inclusion of the PSI in the governing coalition.[13] It was becoming increasingly clear that only such an alliance could yield a stable government in terms of a parliamentary majority and its social base – the type of government that could undertake the modernization of state institutions necessary to bring Italy in line with the other members of the elite group of highly industrialized Western democracies. In short, we are at the tail end of the Scelba years, and even the dramatic advance of the neo-fascist and monarchist far right in the 1953 elections could be seen as purging the DC of its most reactionary elements. Under the leadership of Fanfani and Moro, the architects of the DC's prudent left course, the Christian Democrats did begin to adopt a more modern and progressive agenda. Also, strengthened by dazzling economic growth and high employment levels, the trade union movement re-emerged as a major social force. The political landscape would have seemed mixed but far from hopeless from the point of view of an intellectual of Calvino's leanings.

As for the Italian literary scene, the second half of the 1950s is marked by three major events: the publication of Pratolini's *Metello* and Pasolini's *Ragazzi di vita*, both in 1955, as well as the brief but intense experience of *Officina*, the literary journal founded, as we have seen, in 1955 by a group of young intellectuals led by Pasolini. Pratolini's work sparked a bitter diatribe within the progressive intelligentsia. While the polemic evolved more about the artistic value of this particular novel than about a general aesthetics, the consensus was that in order to remain viable neo-realism had to move beyond Zhdanovian social realism toward the theoretically much more sophisticated and defensible Lukácsian critical realism. The debate brought to the fore the impasse Italian post-war literature had reached and the crisis over the kind of Marxist criticism the PCI was sponsoring (Asor Rosa 1972, 253; Romano, 1977, 54–7). By focusing on the issue of good vs bad realism, the polemic surrounding *Metello* effectively shifted attention away from a much more fundamental issue, namely, the need to come seriously to terms with, and move beyond, the opposition between realism and decadent bourgeois avant-gardism. This increasingly barren opposition not only prevented a fruitful confrontation with the more mature works of the European avant-garde, from Proust to Kafka and Joyce, but also created the ideal conditions for a sudden and supremely undialectical reversal. The boomerang effect would not be long in coming – the triumph of the neo-avant-garde was just around the corner.

Pasolini's *Ragazzi di vita*, on the other hand, reopened the 'language question' ('questione della lingua') that has preoccupied the Italian intelligentsia for centuries. Pasolini's uninhibited use of dialect – the language of the subaltern social strata – to replace the literary Italian of the educated classes and their intellectuals had an unmistakable political import. Pasolini was taking the Gramscian condemnation of the traditional intellectual a step further. The notion that the educated language of literature was in itself one of the key institutions at the command of hegemony would lead Pasolini to argue that no radically oppositional discourse could speak standard Italian and only dialect could give a voice to a revolutionary subject. This line of argument was bound to disconcert orthodox Marxists, particularly those sharing Togliatti's predilection for the great bourgeois literature of the nineteenth century, and therefore the canons of good taste and decorum that informed it. Pasolini's practice seemed a provocation not only because in its condemnation of tradition it came perilously close to avant-gardism, but also because it proceeded to portray the Roman lumpenproletariat in all its 'decadence' (i.e., violence, corruption, homosexuality, etc.) – hardly an exemplar of the subaltern as the revolutionary-subject-conscious-of-its-world-historical-function. The PCI critics' suspicion of Pasolini would take years to dissipate.

Finally, the founding of *Officina* revived the debate about the function of intellectuals within a progressive and modern political project. The journal played an important role not only in putting back on the cultural agenda issues that progressive intellectuals desperately needed to confront (especially in the wake of destalinization and of the Soviet invasion of Hungary), but also in continuing the movement for the de-provincialization of Italian intellectual life, which arguably constituted the most positive element in the *Politecnico*'s legacy.

Calvino's response to this historical, socio-political, and cultural context was marked first of all by a growing concern about his function as a committed intellectual. After the success of *The Viscount* in 1952 and four years later of his *Italian Folktales*, Calvino, just over thirty, was emerging as one of the leading figures of the young writers orbiting around Vittorini and the Einaudi publishing house. His activities as a journalist and essayist continued, acquiring a new depth and breadth. In 1955 he published in *Paragone* 'The Lion's Marrow,' the first of a trilogy of essays, including 'The Sea of Objectivity' (1960) and 'The Challenge of the Labyrinth' (1962), that constitute the most sustained effort by the young Calvino to define his poetics in encompassing theoretical terms. The significance of these interventions is perhaps best appreciated if we remember that Calvino would not feel the need to repeat the exercise until 1984, when just before his death he would compose the six texts for the Norton Lectures he had been invited to deliver at Harvard University.[14]

In 'The Lion,' Calvino grapples with the issues that would fuel the polemics surrounding *Metello* and *Ragazzi di vita*. With respect to the 'language question,' his position ran clearly counter to the one expressed by Pasolini, with whom Calvino would continue to disagree when they both took a leading role in the 1964–5 debate.[15] As to the neo-realist movement, Calvino, who had gone through the negative experience of *I giovani*, was clearly moving beyond the antithesis of realism vs formalism, and attempted to shift the emphasis onto the cognitive function of literature, a literature of intelligence and nourished by an ethico-political tension. For Calvino literature mattered when it empowered action through understanding:

We too are among those who believe *in literature as an active presence in history*, in literature as education, one that is irreplaceable in degree and quality. [The men and women who believe this, it is of them that we are thinking] ... Literature must speak to these men, must, as it learns from them, teach them, be of use to them, and can be of use only in one thing: in helping them to be always more intelligent, sensitive, morally strong. *The things that literature can explore and teach are few but irreplaceable*: how to regard others and oneself, how to establish connections between personal and general events, how to attribute value to things big and small, how to judge limitations and faults – one's own and others' – how to find proportion in life, and the place of love in it, with its force and rhythm, and the place of death, how to think or not to think about it ... The rest one should learn elsewhere, from science, from history, in the same way we all must continue to learn it.[16] (Emphasis added)

Calvino's stance is transparent: to preserve the lesson taught by the Resistance ('literature as an active presence in history'), and turn the ethical tension and political commitment that are its legacy into the force propelling the literary imagination. For Calvino the stakes of literature are high ('the things that literature can explore and teach are few but irreplaceable') and have much more to do with the disclosing of new cognitive horizons than in adhering to a narrowly defined fetishized poetics.[17] In short, leveraging the success of *The Viscount*, Calvino is setting parameters that leave him more room to manoeuvre.

And finally, in 'The Lion,' Calvino's attempt to develop a poetics that avoided, on the one hand, a decadent curiosity for the crude and irrational and, on the other, reductive sociologism, came very close to the spirit that would inspire *Officina*, whose first issue was also dated 1955. Calvino would in fact contribute to Pasolini's journal his *I giovani* together with the key explicatory note we already cited. The fact that *Officina* agreed to publish this rather problematic work clearly demonstrates that Calvino's interests and aesthetic experiments intersected with the preoccupations of the editorial board. In sum, Calvino came of age in the 1950s, and, as a leading figure of the left-wing Italian intelligentsia, he felt the pull of Vittorini's trajectory, which was steering him away from the PCI and toward structuralism and semiotics.[18]

In 1956–7, when *The Baron* was being written, the conditions that would lead to the developments we have examined in our discussion of *Il Menabò* were in the making, and it is important to recognize that 'The Lion' already contained some of the key terms that Calvino's later essays would develop. Particularly relevant to our discussion is the fact that Calvino's first major theoretical intervention recentred the debate about (neo)realism in terms of a *discussion of the subjectivity that a narrative proposes*. This was a brilliant move that allowed Calvino to engage one of the basic credos of the neo-realist poetics, namely, the necessity of entrusting the narrative to round, positive characters. Calvino argued that such positive heroes were by all accounts imaginary, at best an expression of a human ideal (and a rather simplistic version of Lukács's 'world historical individual' – see his *The Historical Novel*) and at worst thoroughly unbelievable, anacronistic figures. In turn, by putting the issue of subjectivity on the table, Calvino was able to show that we can retain the values or the ethico-political impulse that underpins neo-realism without adhering to its aesthetic choices. And, refocusing the discussion on the 'I' underlying the narrative, Calvino elegantly sidestepped the barricades that were being built on each side of the divide between realism and formalism:

> Because, among the opportunities literature has to intervene in history, this is the one that most belongs to it, perhaps the only one that is not an illusion: to understand for that type of man the multiform, contradictory labour of history is preparing the battlefield, and dictate his sensibility, his moral reflex ...
>
> Clearly, this type of man, whom a work or an entire literary epoch presupposes and implies, or better proposes and invents, may well not be one of those round characters that are the prerogative of the novel or the theatre. This type of man lives also and perhaps above all in that *moral presence*, in that protagonist, by no means harder to identify, whom even lyrical poetry or moral prose possesses, that true protagonist who even in many a novelist, to begin with Manzoni and the best Verga, is not identified with any of the characters.[19] (Emphasis added)

From this point of departure, Calvino develops a daring defence not only of hermeticism but also of Joyce and Kafka, that is, the leading European authors around whom the battle for realism raged. Even more interesting, from our vantage point, is the fact that Calvino attributes much of the weakness of contemporary Italian literature (the novel in particular) to a crisis in the role of the intellectual. Long in maturing, this crisis leads the Italian intelligentsia to a paradoxical self-loathing combined with megalomania. On the one hand, 'it would seem that in Italy being a intellectual is considered a misfortune' ('si direbbe che in Italia il fatto d'essere un intellettuale sia sentito come un guaio'; *Una pietra*, 7), while on the other '[T]he writer, almost as if he were jealous of the political leader ... tries to repeat the things the political leader does ... and deludes himself into thinking that he is giving lessons ... This illusion to which writers and, above all, critics are subject has its roots in the old social-democratic way of thinking, which identifies preaching with practice, and education with revolution.'[20]

The accusation is this: the evacuation of the author's subjectivity in the realistic narrative can become a means of maintaining the intellectual in an ivory tower. It is relatively easy for writers to assign to rounded protagonists the heroic role of subjects capable of shaping historical processes, while themselves hiding behind the alleged objectivity of the story, which allows authors to refuse to take responsibility for what they have done to the text and to the world by shaping the narrative in a particular way. From this standpoint, writers can preach in safety, but their claim to reach reality remains empty, first and foremost because they do not confront the issue of what writing *does* to the world.[21]

For Calvino the solution to the impasse that Italian literature seemed to have reached in the mid-1950s lay in a reassessment of the creative role of intelligent self-consciousness, and of the ethico-political commitments it brings into play:

> To come back to a calmer understanding of the role of ideas and reason in creative works will mean the end of a situation where the writer's 'I' is perceived to be a kind of malediction, a kind of punishment. And this will happen perhaps only when the intellectual accepts himself as such, feels integrated into society, one of its functioning parts, and no longer has to escape himself or society, to disguise or punish himself ...
>
> [O]ur strength will not lie in the thirst for transcendence, nor a drama of interiority, given the magnitude of the external drama confronting us; our strength can only lie in the experience of this dramatic reality, and in that *extremely cold judgment*, in that *calm will of defending our nature* of which Pintor gave us such a clear example.[22]

I have quoted at some length from 'The Lion' because I believe that this essay, in addition to its intrinsic merits, provides a key mediating link between the socio-historical context and the narrative text. Armed with this keener understanding of the historical conjuncture and of Calvino's response to it, we can now return to *The Baron* and consider how the narrative fits into this complex configuration. It is striking how one key problematic keeps re-emerging in Calvino's interventions, namely, the role of the intellectual in its many incarnations: as political activist, as critic, as writer. It is in fact around this basic concern that a dialogue among different discourses and experiences is established and develops. We have seen the beginnings of this dialogue in *I giovani* and then in *The Viscount*, where the process seemed in the end to reach a momentary impasse: the focus on the divided nature of the modern self leads to an abstract longing for wholeness that can only be satisfied by a final deus ex machina.

As a prelude to taking a leap forward and breaking the impasse, *The Baron* takes a step backward from *The Viscount* in returning to the Gramscian concerns of *I giovani*. Cosimo is once again the committed intellectual attempting to establish an organic relationship with the subaltern classes. However, Calvino demonstrates that he has learned from the failure of the neo-realist attempt, as well as from the success of *The Viscount*. Intellectuals are no longer disguised in the clothes of the class whose concerns and moral claims they seek to interpret and make their own. Rather, intellectuals recognize their social situatedness, namely, that their education and training, their *bagaglio culturale*, has matured and developed in the womb of the dominant class. Also, they squarely face the fact that their traditional function is to perpetuate the dominant culture and the logic of hegemony. This we have seen in *The Viscount*, where class is one of the binarisms around that the narrative revolves and that ultimately knows of no resolution other than an *ideal* one – the Viscount made whole again will be a *just* ruler.

In *The Baron*, the impasse of separation is overcome by a moral choice: class situatedness is not destiny but rather constitutive of the field where moral action can occur. Cosimo's rejection of his father's authority can now be understood in its full import: by rejecting the logic of hegemony and the authoritarian role it assigns him, Cosimo is resolutely distancing himself from his class and placing himself in the position of having to look for other allegiances.

Let us note that Cosimo's rejection of his class is dialectical. He does not seek to deny his origins and obliterate, as it were, everything associated with them. Implicitly aware that the education and outlook inherited from his class position cannot be overcome by a pure act of will, Cosimo is also determined not to indiscriminately jettison the good with the bad: he puts his ideology to the test of experience, to thresh out what can be of use; he does not simply throw it out in favour of an act of faith in another ideology. As the arguments with his father have demonstrated, the negation is not of an abstract totality but of concrete and determinate values, attitudes, and behaviours. Cosimo's choice is to remain at the periphery of his family and class, as well as of the subaltern class that he observes, learns from, and occasionally leads, but always refusing a fusion with either class, a fusion which would be as hypocritical as a submission to the irrational demands of his father. Cosimo's balancing act in the trees corresponds to a balancing act of socio-political positioning.

This balancing act is a continuing activity rather than a simple choice, and the narrative provides Calvino with the opportunity to explore how it can be sustained. What are the costs as well as the advantages of the type of subjectivity that this project entails? We can now see that many of the characters Cosimo encounters embody proposals of subjectivity that Cosimo has to confront as he attempts to articulate his own proposal and define what I referred to earlier as his new social being.

Given that Calvino's overriding concern is a mimesis of the Gramscian problematization of the role of the intellectual, what the reader faces is a gallery of possible intellectual positions. This is a living gallery that Cosimo can set against the stucco gallery of ancestors his father had to offer. The first of these figures is his sister Battista, whose effete aestheticism Cosimo disdainfully rejects, as he refuses the dish of snails. And the narrative ultimately vindicates Cosimo's dismissal of Battista's proposal: her marriage to the son of the Count of Estomac demonstrates that hegemony can easily recuperate her rebellion, unlike Cosimo's, by providing a socially acceptable outlet for desire – an interesting comment on the aesthetic of excess and transgression to which Calvino was never attracted.

On the other hand, Gian dei Brughi, the outlaw who develops a devouring love of reading, caricatures the intellectual: he has such a passion for the fictional worlds words can create that he ultimately forsakes the human community to retreat into the shadows of his imagination. Yet he makes a great teacher and communicates to Cosimo not only his passion but also, paradoxically, a social conscience: 'Now on the other hand he found coming over him a need to do something useful for his neighbour. And this too, if one analyses it, was something he had learnt from his friendship with the brigand; the pleasure of making himself useful, or doing some service indispensable to another' (*Our Ancestors*, 172).

It is the experience of friendship that teaches Cosimo the value and pleasure of solidarity. Gian dei Brughi does not preach it, nor does his life exemplify it. Rather, the common interest in books creates a bond that allows Cosimo to experience directly the joy of pursuing a common project. It is the joy of productive human interaction that creates the environment in which the seed of solidarity can sprout – not sermons, not even exemplary conduct, but pleasure. The fact that Gian dei Brughi is of humble origin is also rich in suggestion. In addition to the somewhat obvious jab at the dominant classes and their presumed monopoly on culture and education, the most significant suggestion for our purpose is that fictional discourse can seduce and communicate value across class boundaries. In other words, storytelling can accommodate a cognitive 'thickness' that can overcome ideological prejudice and enable the reader to surmount their ideological blind spots. One can always read against the grain (as I have done in relation to the discourse of *The Baron*'s narrator). And therein perhaps lies the greatest potential and danger of fictional discourse, the truly serious transgression for which Gian dei Brughi, outlaw and autodidact, has to pay with his life.

That intellectual pursuits are a dangerous business is also made clear by the fate of the Abbé Fauchelafleur, whose arrest is the result of Cosimo's adventurous readings:

> Among his breviaries they found the works of Bayle, still uncut, but this was enough for them to put him between them and take him away ...
>
> ... The Abbé spent the rest of his days between prison and monastery in continual acts of abjuration, until he died, after an entire life dedicated to the faith, without ever knowing what he believed in, but trying to believe firmly until the last. (*Our Ancestors*, 171)

The price of intellectual adventurousness may have to be paid not only by oneself but also by one's pupils. The stakes involved in the dissemination of knowledge are higher than one might naively think.

It is also interesting to note that in the midst of a social discourse in which the role of the committed intellectual is at the centre of heated debate, *The Baron* contains a clear and unmistakable warning against the romantic and idealist dream of the intellectual leading the people to the barricades and taking a leadership role in a revolutionary situation:

Cosimo, too, felt a new strength and content [*contentezza*]: he had discovered his ability to bring people together and to put himself at their head; an aptitude which, luckily for himself, he was never called on to abuse, and which he used only a very few times in his life, always when there were important results to be carried out. (*Our Ancestors*, 176)

'I realize that when I have more ideas than others, I give those other my ideas, if they want to accept them; and that to me is leading.' (*Our Ancestors*, 178)

Finally, the protracted confrontation with Viola is all about the rejection of a proposal of subjectivity for which Cosimo feels such a strong attraction that he almost succumbs to it. In this episode as well, social position plays a key role. Viola's seductiveness has a great deal to do with the fact the she shares with Cosimo a class upbringing that has deeply shaped both characters' sensibilities and desires. They speak a common language, they are bound by profound affinities, and their intimacy yields a knowledge that is also self-recognition: 'They knew each other. He knew her and so himself, for in truth he had never known himself. And she knew him and so herself, for although she had always known herself she had never yet been able to recognize it as now' (*Our Ancestors*, 228). And while it can be argued that Calvino's control of the narrative weakens as he indulges the whimsical and frivolous colours of this feminine portrait, Viola's contribution to the gallery of intellectuals remains clear. Her longing for the absolute, her restlessness, her mysticism are all elements derived from the baroque sensibility of an essentially decadent intelligentsia whose rebellion is vitalistic and irrational, and thus doomed either to self-destruct in its excessive (libidinal) expenditures or be recuperated (accepting the neurotic position). Viola teeters at the edge of self-destruction but ultimately surrenders to nostalgia: 'The Revolution broke out, then the war; first the Marchesa took an interest in the new course of events (she was in the entourage of Lafayette), then emigrated to Belgium and from there to England. In the London mists, during the long years of wars against Napoleon, she would dream of the trees of Ombrosa. Then she remarried, an English peer connected with the East India Company, and settled at Calcutta. From her terrace she would look out over the forests, the trees even stranger than those of the gardens of her childhood; every moment seemed to see Cosimo moving apart the leaves. But it would be the shadow of a monkey, or a jaguar' (*Our*

Ancestors, 246). Unable to establish solidarities beyond the class confines that they allegedly reject, decadent intellectuals like Viola cannot sustain their critique of the established order and escape to an exquisite nostalgia that is quite harmless.

In contrast to Viola, we can see clearly that Cosimo's rebellion is informed by an always productive moral tension. One of the strengths of Calvino's characterization is that his hero's introverted personality is blended with a constant desire to engage the material world. Even love is, for Cosimo, a matter of things done, more than of things felt in the inner sanctum of one's soul; thus the conflict with Viola, whose extroverted personality is a child of the Catholic examination of conscience (see Foucault, 1980–6) and centres on the study of the slightest stirring of 'inner' desire and inclination, her own as well as others'.

Cosimo's imagination, on the contrary, is oriented to practice and concrete results. The attention to results emerges even in the grander expressions of Cosimo's intellectual inquisitiveness, expressions that are not abstract philosophical treatises but rather attempts to describe what a utopian social order might actually look like. Even at his most theoretical, Cosimo is the very antithesis of the contemplative traditional intellectual whose conservatism Gramsci identified as one of the main contributors to the cultural and socio-political backwardness of the Italian bourgeoisie.

Cosimo, then, manages to learn from his encounters with all the proposals of subjectivity proffered by a gallery of intellectual positions that is much richer and seductive than in any of Calvino's previous works. From this angle, *The Baron* can be seen as having a narrative structure that inverts the traditional picaresque model. Rather than taking to the road and moving from encounter to encounter, Cosimo takes to the trees and encounters come to him, as it were.

Evoking the picaresque model also allows us to distance *The Baron* from the Bildungsroman with which one might be tempted to associate it. While there is evolution and growth in *The Baron*, and Cosimo is by no means a static character, Calvino is primarily interested in using Cosimo as a device to develop and test the limits of a utopian argument, rather than in pursuing the mimesis of an individual and his moral development. Cosimo exists as a moral tension or a basic stance that manifests itself at the beginning and waxes and wanes during the course of the narrative but never changes qualitatively. In this, Cosimo resembles much more Tom Jones than he does Madame Bovary.

Yet Cosimo fails, and at the end of our discussion of *The Baron* we must confront two final questions. First, what are the possible meanings we can construct by situating Cosimo's failure within its socio-historical context? Second, does failure at the thematic level correspond to failure at the generic level; in other words, is Cosimo's failure in part a result of Calvino being unable to meet the generic challenge he has himself orchestrated?

If we understand *The Baron* as a parable about the situation of the post-war progressive intellectual, and in particular about the possibility for that intellectual to develop a productive organic relationship with the most conscious elements of the working class, then Cosimo's final failure would seem to suggest that Calvino had lost hope in the progressive project spawned by the Resistance. By 1956, Calvino had matured enough, precisely as the type of intellectual he is writing about, to have a much more complex understanding of what it would take to walk this path successfully. In *The Baron*, the reader senses that Calvino is giving it his best shot, is really trying to work out imaginatively the organic synthesis that is central to the Gramscian project. His closeness to the material, of which we spoke earlier, means also that Calvino was marshalling all his resources – the landscape he loved, the historical background for which he felt the greatest affinity, and so forth – to unravel the artistic as well as the cognitive knot with which he had been struggling since *I giovani*. For a while, until Viola re-enters the scene and renews her relationship with Cosimo on an adult basis, it almost seems that the synthesis is possible. Up to that point the paradox of solidarity and distance that the ascent into the trees signified seems to provide a viable solution. The intellectual could contribute to the progress of his community without forgetting himself – in fact, exactly by not forgetting himself, and constantly fighting against the irrational privileges of his class – while exploiting to the maximum the opportunities for understanding that his class position nevertheless affords. Cosimo seems to be the image of that 'intellectual [who] will accept himself as such, will feel integrated into society, one of its functioning parts, and will no longer have to escape himself or society, to disguise or punish himself' (see note 22) whom Calvino prefigured in 'The Lion.'

The essay, however, was written in February 1955, almost two years before Calvino began writing *The Baron*.[23] The period the two texts delimits is marked by the events of 1956, which plunged the left-wing intelligentsia into a serious crisis. As we have seen, Calvino lived this crisis close to the front lines. Can we detect traces of this experience in the narrative and, in particular, in the collapse of the dream Cosimo seems so close to realizing?

On the surface of the narrative there is in fact remarkably little to suggest that the 1956 crisis had a major impact on the formulation of the issues and concerns the book addresses. Specifically, even when we come to the collapse of the synthesis Cosimo seems on the verge of accomplishing – the place where the after-effects of the crisis could be expected to be most clearly felt – there seems to be no relation between Cosimo's ultimate failure and the historical conjuncture. In fact, at first blush it would seem that while the utopia Cosimo embodies resists the temptation of decadent interiority that Viola represents, the effort to overcome such temptation irremediably saps utopia of its energy. Cosimo temporarily loses his reason, and when he finds it again through social action – the episode in which he devises a scheme to protect the land from the wolves – the active power of his resistance seems mostly spent.

Is Calvino suddenly reverting to the most superficial cliché of 'romantic' literature, in which disappointed love empties the protagonist's life of meaning? A keen awareness of generic considerations allows us to immediately foreclose this avenue of interpretation. The point of reference for the presentation of Cosimo's love pains remains non-romantic. In keeping with the chivalric tradition dear to Calvino and that the protagonist's brief madness clearly evokes, the narrative does not linger on Cosimo's inner feelings but rather on his conduct, on the exteriorization of the topos of lost love, which becomes an occasion for stylistic virtuosity, as this passage demonstrates: 'Cosimo remained for a long time wandering aimlessly round the woods, weeping, ragged, refusing food. He would sob out loud, as to newborn babes, and the birds which had once fled in flight at the approach of this infallible marksman would now come near him, on the tops of nearby trees or flying over his head, and the swallow called, the goldfinch trilled, the dove cooed, the thrush whistled, the chaffinch chirped and so did the wren; and from their lairs on high issued the squirrels, the owls, the fieldmice, to join their squeals to the chorus, so that my brother moved amidst this cloud of lamentation' (*Our Ancestors*, 247). The catalogue of Cosimo's companions introduces an epic register that confers on the pathetic fallacy a baroque and mannerist modulation. The sophisticated final conceit ('cloud of lamentation') is particularly telling.

The wider significance of the failed synthesis with which the novel closes becomes evident as soon as we focus on the way the narrative articulates the intellectual positions that Cosimo and Viola represent. Calvino makes it quite clear that in many ways Cosimo and Viola embody attitudes and temperaments that are complementary as well as conflicting. Once we resist the temptation to psychologize and recall that Cosimo and Viola are proposals of subjectivity, the characters' love affair can be seen as an attempt to synthesize these two proposals. Turning to 'The Lion,' we can then add that what drives this project is the moral presence informing the narrative as a whole and which, to simplify this discussion, I have referred to as 'Calvino.'

But what precisely is the nature of the synthesis that propels *The Baron* and in the end falters? Here we have to remember *I giovani* and Nino's clumsy attempts to reconcile politics and desire. At first glance, Cosimo seems trapped in the same quandary, and yet much has changed. The mystifying disguises Nino was wearing have been stripped away, with the result that the predicament can now be clearly seen as the expression of a tension within the progressive intelligentsia that Calvino both interpellates and is interpellated by. At stake in *The Baron* is the striving of this social fraction (i.e., the progressive Italian intelligentsia) to both recognize its own socio-historical situatedness and overcome its limitations. Cosimo needs Viola precisely because she represents the aesthetic values he shares and whose seductions cannot be overcome or historicized as long as they remain insulated from socio-political praxis. What *The Baron* attempts is to set in motion a constructive engagement, a true dialectic, between the intellectual tradition that Viola's sensual, baroque, and Catholic sensibility represents and the figure of an intellectual whose ethico-political commitments are nourished by a thoroughly modern pragmatic empiricism. In post-war Italy, when the intellectual elite was struggling to keep pace with the socio-economic transformation of the country, this synthesis could well seem a necessary precondition to the emergence of a new intellectual whose desire would no longer feel alienated and divided between 'political' and 'cultural' allegiances – the dubious antinomy that sealed the fate of *Il Politecnico*.

What makes *The Baron* so interesting in this regard is that on the heels of the 1956 crisis, and in light of Calvino's reaction to it, one might have expected the narrative to emphasize the dangers of the PCI's cultural policy, which wielded a distorted interpretation of Gramsci to justify not only a dubious poetics (as was the case with neorealism) but also an even more problematic political alignment. Cosimo's resolve to maintain a non-aligned position is no doubt central to *The Baron*, and in that sense Calvino sounds a clear warning to a hurried understanding of what it means for an intellectual to be organic to progressive social forces. However, the narrative still identifies the greatest threat to this critical non-alignment as coming not from the incipient 'new' (the organic model of commitment) but from the persisting 'old' (the traditional model of intellectual practice). In other words, it is not Cosimo's ethico-political commitment that threatens the standpoint he must maintain to perform his function as an intellectual, rather, it is his aesthetic sensibility that poses a challenge Cosimo can only in part meet: he will keep his position, but a portion of his desire will be censured and repressed rather than assimilated and sublated. In the end, then, *The Baron* is a parable not only about the imperative of distance but also about the failure of the attempt to dialecticize and move beyond the binary oppositions that characterized the figure of reason in *The Viscount* and marked so deeply the historical conjuncture Calvino was facing.

The image of the intellectual that the novel ultimately provides is that of an eccentric and ascetic (in the Greek sense of exercised, athletic, well-disciplined) figure who must choose marginality and preserve it in order to be able to perform his social function. At the heart of this social function is the search for new cognitive horizons, and for a more fulfiling social praxis. Calvino also makes it quite clear that such a project is meaningful only if sustained by an ethico-political tension toward justice and fairness (albeit, pragmatically defined), and demands a commitment to defying accepted knowledge and testing utopian possibilities.

Yet, in the 1950s, Calvino seemed to think that this program for Italian left-wing intellectuals was bound to falter. The suggestion is not that subjects willing to submit to this harsh discipline could not be found, but rather that the Italian intellectual tradition and the sociopolitical situation conspired to prevent the emergence of a new social synthesis that would provide the material conditions for the emergence of the organic intellectual. Cosimo and Viola's inability to move beyond the vicious cycle of conflict/complementarity is ultimately a sign of Calvino's inability to imagine a way out even when, as in *The Baron*, all his intellectual and emotional resources are deployed. One of the most interesting aspects of this final impasse is its political ambiguity. Does *The Baron* bear witness to the persisting inability of however well-intentioned bourgeois, intellectuals to understand the dynamics of the class struggle and accept their proper role in it? Or is Calvino harking back to his 1940s comment that the duty of the party toward intellectuals is to 'help us to "be" communist' ('aiutarci ad "essere" comunisti'; qtd. in Gambetti 1976, 103), and suggesting that the party had done precious little to promote the emergence of this new consciousness and, if anything, had taken cultural positions that reinforced the form of consciousness of traditional intellectuals? The narrative is not univocal. What can be stated with confidence is that while Calvino's commitment to socialism as an ethico-political project remains as strong as ever, his confidence in seeing that project realized in the short to medium term, as well as in the contribution that intellectuals can make to the process, is waning.[24] Indeed, after having given his best shot and seen it end in an impasse, we may well expect Calvino to be ready for a thorough reassessment of the issues.

The second question that needs to be dealt with is directly related to the issue of genre. We have seen how Calvino reiterates the choice of a non-realist form while at the same time expanding its horizon beyond the sharp but restrictive confines of the black and white binarism typical of an allegorical fable such as *The Viscount*. Calvino needs a cognitively more robust structure, one that can accommodate more complex and nuanced human situations. Realism could appear attractive, and, in the short stories he was writing at the time, Calvino attempted to find a new 'realist' voice that would allow him to leave behind once and for all the experience of *I giovani*.[25] Still, the struggle with the ideological overdetermination of the neo-realist form left little room for the deployment of his imaginative verve, at least until *The Watcher*.

However, precisely in the attempt to give more cognitive breath to the narrative, we can see Calvino moving away from the schematic intellectualism of *The Viscount* and toward the science-fiction model described by Suvin (1979; 1983; 1988) and Angenot (1979), a narrative that posits a departure from verisimilitude as a launching pad for the logically stringent exploration of new possibilities. *The Baron* strikes a strange balance between the allegorical parable of distance and the thought experiment centred on the possibilities that a life in the trees opens for novel human relationships:

The Baron in the Trees turned out very differently from The Cloven Viscount. Rather than a story outside of time, with a barely sketched out setting, thin and emblematic characters, a childlike fairy-tale plot, I was constantly drawn, as I wrote [The Baron], to create a historical 'pastiche,' a repertory of eighteenth-century images, supported by dates and correlations with famous events and people; a landscape and a natural environment that were imaginary, certainly, but also described with precision and nostalgia; a storyline that took care to justify in terms of verisimilitude even the unreality of the initial idea; in sum, I ended up developing a taste for the *novelistic character of the narrative*, in the most traditional sense of the word.[26] (Emphasis added)

Once again, then, we are confronted with an attempt at a synthesis, this time between a variety of generic elements; an attempt that, as we have seen, Calvino considered to have failed: 'shifts in the gradation of fantasy can be found between chapters (and that's a serious defect)' (see note 6). I will argue, on the contrary, that far from being a fault, it is this constant teetering at the edges of the generic divide that is the greatest success of *The Baron*.

The formal tension between the fantastic elements and the concerns for verisimilitude aptly parallels the thematic tension between the utopian impulse and the actual interventions in social reality, a tension that, as we have seen, is essential to the intellectual subject Cosimo proposes. Generic discontinuities, within as well as between episodes, proliferate. For example, the episode describing Cosimo's brief alliance with the cherry-stealing urchins (chapters 4 and 5) is at the verisimilar end of the spectrum, as Calvino provides a great deal of realistic detail, while the episode describing how Cosimo manages to reawaken the French battalion from its torpor (chapter 27) is a typical example of Calvino's fantastic verve. However, the passage describing Cosimo's stratagy for defending Ombrosa from the invading wolves is a mixture of both versimilar and fantastic elements: the traps the villagers set up under Cosimo's supervision are realistically described, while Cosimo's narration of his own encounter with the wolves is thoroughly fantastic – Baron Münchausen's traveller's tales are unmistakably in the background. These discontinuities express divisions within this subject, a lack of unity that in the end emerges not so much as the site of loss but rather as the key to the ability to resist being forced into fixed and definitive subject positions, whether progressive or conservative, in which the fight for social dominance is being articulated. This resistance, however, does not imply a relativistic equidistance or neutrality. Cosimo chooses as his privileged interlocutor those social forces that are considered progressive from a Marxist perspective. The hero is clearly on the side of progress as the Enlightenment defined it, but remains at the margins of the social movement that embodies such

progress. Cosimo wakes the Republican Army not by joining and leading it, but rather by being an irritant. His career as an elected official is
dismissed in a couple of paragraphs.

> They set up a *municipalité*, a *maire*, all in French; my brother was nomi-
> nated to the provisional junta ...
> Cosimo would perch on a carob tree ... and follow the discussions from
> there ... It is an acknowledged fact that revolutionaries are greater
> sticklers for formality than conservatives; they [objected] ... and when the
> Ligurian Republic was set up in place of the oligarchic Republic of Genoa,
> my brother was not elected to the new administration.[27] (*Our Ancestors*,
> 273)

In sum, Cosimo's eccentricities sustain the organic function he fulfils
from the margins, and narratively demand the generic heterogeneity
that *The Baron* provides.

And yet, the longing for a coherent synthesis also colours the novel,
and the time has now come to identify more precisely its source and
significance. There is no doubt that the loss of Viola is portrayed as a
defeat and a failure that definitively deprives the utopian impulse
Cosimo embodies of real purchase. However, this defeat, rather than
resulting in a rejection of the values Cosimo expresses, is depicted as
actually strengthening Cosimo's commitment. The dialectic between
the old and the new did not develop, but the merit of the attempt
remains unblemished as Cosimo passes the baton to the generation that
will follow him. By the end of the novel, Cosimo becomes the storyteller who, from the tree at the centre of the village square, fulfils his
ultimate social function in bequeathing knowledge, aspirations, and
ideals: no shadow of repentance or even regret taints his stories, of
which his hearers never seem to tire. By this time, Viola is an episode,
however important, in a narrative that has lost the desire to make absolute sense. Narrative cohesion does not require that synthesis, it can
live with ambiguities, multiplicity, difference. The act of storytelling
provides an opportunity for making sense that need not dictate one single meaning. The subject Calvino proposes has come to this understanding.

However, this is not the only subject position the narrative contains,
nor, perhaps, even the dominant one. Throughout my analysis of the
novel, I have pointed out how we must constantly read against the
grain of the narrator's biases and prejudices. As we begin the last

chapter of the novel we can have no doubt as to where the nostalgic flavour of the narrative comes from: 'I have no idea what this nineteenth century of ours will bring, starting so badly and getting so much worse. The shadow of the Restoration hangs over Europe; all the innovators – whether Jacobins or Bonapartists – defeated; once more absolutism and Jesuitry has the field; the ideals of youth, the lights, the hopes of our eighteenth century, all are dust' (*Our Ancestors*, 280).

I have often spoken of the limitations that beset the narrator and make it impossible for him to grasp the fuller significance of Cosimo's adventure. And here again, one might well be tempted to see in this pessimistic nostalgia the expression of a subject who has failed to grasp Cosimo's final message. There is something to recommend this interpretation. Coming to the end of his life, Biagio, the narrator, sounds more and more like his father, the Baron Arminio: nostalgia for a world that never was is the common consolation of characters who conform to the demands of the established order. There is even a point of bad faith in Biagio's regretting the return of the order he never challenged. Calvino is rather slyly chastising those intellectuals who in 1956 were only too eager to lament the demise of the socialist dream that they had always contemplated rather from afar! Still, to stop at this level would not do justice to the ambiguities that are a determining characteristic of the narrator as much as of Cosimo. The first suggestion that we should dig deeper comes from the pathos of the passage I have just cited, a pathos that for all its chiaroscuro is clearly not mere pretence. The authorial voice participates in it. Having situated the novel in the context within which it was produced, it becomes easier to understand what vibrates in those lines: Biagio's farewell to the hopes of the Enlightenment echoes Calvino's own farewell to the hopes for social change that the Resistance had raised. The age of Restoration is the age of Scelba, and in 1956 also, in part, the age of Soviet tanks rolling through the streets of Budapest, crushing a movement that had renewed the solidarity between workers, intellectuals, and students, that is, the revolutionary social synthesis that, during the Resistance, had for the first time, if only briefly, appeared realistic, attainable, realizable. What these observations allow us to grasp is the multiplicity within the authorial voice itself, which speaks through different subject positions and with varying degrees of closeness to each of them at different times. The text resonates with these 'closenesses.' At the peak of Cosimo's adventure, they seem on the verge of melding in a choral movement, which is never attained as each voice gradually

collapses upon itself. And I cannot help thinking in this context of Fortini's reflection on the disintegration of the left-wing intelligentsia as a
politically active collective subject in the 1950s: 'Rather than struggle to
understand each other, we thought it better to be right each on our
own' ('Piuttosto di lottare per capirci, preferimmo aver ragione da
soli'; Fortini, *Dieci Inverni*, 1972).

Biagio feels almost desperately alone at the end of the *The Baron*.
Cosimo's legacy is a void he can fill only with a nostalgia whose vehicle, significantly, is writing. But what kind of writing? Cosimo himself
wields the pen extensively, writing treatises, constitutions, bulletins,
articles, and keeping up a correspondence with the leading intellectuals of his time. However, he is never shown writing fiction, which he
reserves for oral delivery. In fact, Cosimo's writings leave no distinct
trace. Having served their immediate purpose, the forgotten pages are
kept in the trees, where they eventually scatter like leaves and return to
the earth as humus for that new generation of saplings. Cosimo's
works, like his stories, refuse mechanical reproduction and stay outside the circuit of commodity circulation. The logic framing this writing is pre-bourgeois, and it is therefore fitting that Cosimo never shows
any interest for that typically bourgeois form, the novel.

It is also fitting that it would fall to Biagio to write Cosimo's story. A
successful manager of the family estate, the narrator has no inhibition
about engaging in profitable commerce: 'But I happened at the period
to make my second journey to Paris in connection with certain con-
tracts in lemons, for many nobles were already taking to commerce
and I among the first' (*Our Ancestors*, 236). That such a subject would
find relief in the production of a narrative that even from the diegetical
point of view is halfway between biography, autobiography, and a collection of stories, which the narrator pieces together and retells, is evidence of the dawning of that private sphere that the novel will soon
colonize. Within this private sphere, the reification and fetishization of
the act of writing is just around the corner: 'That mesh of leaves and
twigs ... was embroidered on nothing, like this thread of ink which I
have let run on for page after page, swarming with cancellations, cor-
rections, doodles, blots and gaps, bursting at times into clear big ber-
ries, coagulating at others into piles of tiny starry seeds, then twisting
away, forking off, surrounding buds of phrases with frameworks of
leaves and clouds, then interweaving again, and so running on and on
and on until it splutters and bursts into a last senseless cluster of
words, ideas, dreams, and so ends' (*Our Ancestors*, 284).

Let us note the ambiguities of this final passage. On the one hand, there is the mesmerizing power of the written word, of its materiality increasingly divorced from the context of communication, a word destined to become a sphinx-like trace ('senseless cluster of words, ideas, dreams'). On the other hand, Biagio's manuscript is full of 'auratic' elements (see Benjamin, *Illuminations*, 217–51): the material circumstances of its composition leave a trace in this highly irregular arabesque, which still has very little to do with the flat regularity of the mechanically reproduced commodity. In short, the materiality of the writing tells a story that accompanies and recontextualizes the narrative (i.e., reintroduces some of the human relations). This is not true prima facie extradiegetically, since *The Baron* as a book comes to us as readers/purchasers in the commodity form that the cultural industry requires. And this is why Calvino has to rely on more subtle stylistic resources (e.g., *mise en abîme*) to resist fetishization.

By raising these issues, then, Calvino is turning on its head one of the questions that was repeatedly asked by post-war writers: not 'is the novel dead?' but 'is it possible to tell stories that are not novels?' that is, is it possible to write without participating in the reification of language that has accompanied the development of the novel as a form. Calvino's polemic is not against the 'classical' realist novel as an aesthetic structure per se, but about the social organization of meaning within which that structure has historically functioned. He is not interested in arguing that the novel is an irremediably compromised form, but rather in exploring how that form can be made to speak against the frame that encircles it. To put it another way, in *The Baron* Calvino is testing the extent to which the novel can be used at a given time and place to deploy the cognitive resources of storytelling. That is the essence of the generic gamble Calvino has taken, a gamble that pays off in *The Baron* because the authorial voice resolutely resists the temptation to resolve the multiplicity of its modulations within a grand synthesis.[28] At this level, we can see an analogy between the seductions of the absolute that Viola represents for Cosimo and the seductions of the 'great novel' that *The Baron* liquidates once and for all for Calvino. In 1956, a grand narrative synthesis is unimaginable except at the price of a wilful blindness to the increasing complexity of a social reality where progress and reaction have lost their univocal referents. *The Baron* succeeds by bearing witness to this crisis and to the energies that it liberates. And Calvino discovers that narrative constitutes the last shore of cognition in an age that acknowledges the subject's loss of sovereignty.

CHAPTER FOUR

The Non-existent Knight: Obstinacy without Illusions

At the end of *The Baron*, the utopian impulse that propelled the narrative of Cosimo's adventures yields to the narrator's pessimism and nostalgia. This final configuration is marked by ambiguity. Having learned to mistrust the narrator's interpretation of events and to read often against the grain of his reflexive discourse, the reader cannot take Biagio's nostalgia as authoritative. The hopes of a more rational and just social order raised by the Enlightenment and the French Revolution may fade in the post-Waterloo age of restoration. And yet, unlike Biagio, the reader knows that the conservative involution sanctioned by the Congress of Vienna would not last for long and that a wave of revolts in 1848 would once again shake Western Europe, setting in motion a process of reform that could no longer be halted. The seeds of the Enlightenment could be kept dormant, but they could not be destroyed.

Taking a closer look at Biagio's nostalgia, it is not difficult to identify the positive element it contains. One of Biagio's key complaints is that he will no longer be able to delegate to Cosimo the demanding task of understanding and intervening in the socio-political arena. In an interesting reversal of Candide's final maxim, Biagio can no longer *cultiver son propre jardin*. His first overt act in the public sphere is none other than the 'bearing witness' that constitutes the fundamental gesture of *The Baron*'s narrator and demonstrates his efforts to achieve a higher level of historical consciousness. That this is a desirable goal the whole narrative implicitly presupposes, and Biagio's nostalgia for the past makes us aware of the difficulty of the task but in no way diminishes its desirability.

This kind of difficult optimism also informs the final act of Cosimo's adventure. Cosimo has not found a way to break out of the binarism of detachment/commitment. At the end of the novel, he seems confined in the trees and in his stubborn eccentricity. And yet, we can also see that his unfailing determination never to touch the ground also represents a kind of success: it suggests that resistance is possible. While the utopia Cosimo envisaged was not, and perhaps could not be, realized within the particular set of historical conditions confronting him, the ethico-political tension he embodied is a lasting and constructive legacy, an enduring value that others can reinterpret, and reinvent within their own socio-historical circumstances. This is precisely the task that Biagio himself so unenthusiastically envisaged at the end of the narrative.

Whether we choose to emphasize the negative or the positive aspect of the situation, our horizon is defined by one unavoidable realization: the attempt to portray a convincing social synthesis, which Calvino has been pursuing since *I giovani*, has once again failed. The prefiguration of an organic relationship between the intellectual and socially progressive collectivities remains a distant goal, since an authentic dialectic between the old values and new commitments fails to develop. The cultural battle theorized by Gramsci becomes a war of attrition. And, in the trenches, the party line is routine dogma that relegates the efforts to imagine more dynamic solidarities to a few more or less tolerated eccentrics. At the end of *The Baron*, Cosimo is at best a prophet whose wisdom remains poorly understood and of little immediate socio-political consequence. Calvino seems to have reached a new impasse.

However, in 1959, two years after the composition of *The Baron* and after the publication of two lengthy short stories in which he continued to struggle with a realist intonation – 'A Plunge in Real Estate,' whose composition was interrupted by *The Baron*, and 'Smog,' both published in 1958 – Calvino returns to the concerns that inspired *The Viscount* and *The Baron* and writes *The Non-existent Knight*. The fact that Calvino felt the need to engage once again the thematic core that he first tackled almost ten years earlier in *I giovani* is indicative of the inner dynamism of the issues Calvino was trying to work through in what ultimately became the fantastic trilogy. What moved Calvino to revisit his fantastic muse? What yet unexplored thematic territory and unexploited generic potential revived Calvino's interest? And what can this renewal of the heraldic vein tell us about the changing socio-political environment Calvino is addressing? These are the questions I would like to consider. Once again, I will begin my discussion by situating *The Knight* within the trilogy and exploring its rearticulation of the role of intellectuals in bringing about social change. I will then examine how this new image of the modern intellectual addresses the changed historical conjuncture within which Calvino was operating.

Agilulfo and Ethical Subjectivity

Calvino hesitated over the order in which the three works of the heraldic trilogy should be presented. In the first Italian edition of the trilogy *Our Ancestors*, *The Knight* appeared first. In the introduction, Calvino explained that: 'In the trilogy, [*The Knight*] can come last as well as first ... because, in relation to the other two stories, it can be considered an introduction more than an epilogue.'[1] In an alternative introductory text to the same edition,[2] Calvino gave an even more suggestive reason for placing *The Knight* first: 'the fact is that, trying to reconstruct a philosophy through the three stories, *The Non-existent Knight*, when placed at the end, reopens all the issues.'[3] In light of these hesitations, it is even more telling that in 1967, on the occasion of the eighth edition of the trilogy, Calvino restored definitively the order of composition (*The Viscount*, *The Baron*, *The Knight*). Perhaps the desire for closure, which the 1960 prefaces manifest, had given way by 1967 to a more positive assessment of the *openness* of the trilogy; Eco's landmark work *Opera aperta*, published in 1962, and the polemics surrounding the neo-avantgarde movement might well have had something to do with Calvino's change of heart.

The Knight, then, is the next stage in the evolution of a problematic that runs through the three works. This problematic, however, does not here achieve a final resolution, a point of rest. On the contrary, it would seem that the last work of the trilogy, far from providing a moment of closure, opens the field up to a radical reconceptualization and reproblematization of the issues explored in the previous novels. In this sense, *The Knight* can be seen to prepare the ground for a distinctly new phase in Calvino's trajectory, a phase characterized by the abandonment of the novel in favour of shorter and shorter narratives grouped in cycles that will gradually acquire the character of stylistic tours de force. Calvino moves on from the concerns that characterized his writings during the 1950s not with a suture but rather with an incision that reopens the whole question.

In order to understand more precisely the way the problematic evolved over the 1950s, let's turn once again to Calvino himself and the 1960 preface:

The Baron in the Trees did not exhaust the problem I set for myself. It's clear that today we live in a world of non-eccentric people, people whose most basic individuality is denied. So much of them is reduced to an abstract sum of fixed behaviours. Today, the problem no longer is losing a part of oneself; it is utter loss, not being at all.

From primitive man, who meshed with the universe and could still be called non-existent insofar as he was undifferentiated from organic matter, we have slowly come to artificial man who, meshing with products and situations, is non-existent because he slides without friction over everything; he no longer has any connection (struggle and, through struggle, harmony) with that which (nature or history) is around him, but only abstractly *functions*.

Little by little, this tangle of thoughts became identified with an image that had been occupying my mind for a while: a walking suit of armor that is empty inside. I tried to write a story about it (in 1959), and it became *The Non-existent Knight*.[4]

Elaborating on Calvino's remarks, I would say that *The Knight* is an attempt to imagine a new subjectivity, a stance that retains the ethico-political dimension of the humanist subject while confronting the *aporias* of Enlightenment rationality. In this sense, *The Knight* can be seen as the necessary complement to the insights of the two preceding works, namely, the impasse of reason (in *The Viscount*) and the fundamental, perhaps insuperable, ethical tension to which the modern subject owes its birth (in *The Baron*). *The Knight* stands at the edge of the cognitive horizon the previous narratives have mapped – a frontier space marked by eminently modern concerns that justify Calvino's otherwise somewhat puzzling statement to the effect that among the three works of the trilogy, *The Knight* is in fact the most contemporary: 'I would say that it is precisely *The Knight*, where references to the present seem more remote, that says something more closely connected to the realities of our time.'[5]

In relation to *The Viscount* and *The Baron*, *The Knight* manifests a continuity in difference that allows the trilogy to function as 'a complete cycle' ('un ciclo compiuto'; *RR*, 1: 1220), a finished (*compiuto*), though not closed, whole. And though each of the three novels is interesting on its own account, setting them side by side unquestionably enriches our understanding of the poetical project they embody. It is therefore essential to examine in detail those stylistic and thematic elements that *The Knight* takes and re-elaborates from its predecessors.

What immediately strikes us as we begin the last work of the trilogy is that we have taken one step back from *The Baron* and returned to a modality of fantastic discourse that is closer to *The Viscount*. A comparison of the respective incipits will suffice to make the point.[6] The opening lines of *The Knight* and *The Viscount* share some key stylistic as well as thematic features. They are both much more impersonal than the opening lines of *The Baron*, even though in *The Viscount* the qualifier 'my uncle' introduces a personal note. Moreover, they both mention wars between Christian and Islamic powers, thus setting off in the reader similar associations (e.g., the chivalric atmosphere). Even the posture of the characters is the same, with both the Viscount and the paladins riding their horses in anticipation of meeting the supreme commander of the Christian forces. Nothing of this atmosphere and tone is to be found in the opening of *The Baron*, which, on the contrary, immediately presents itself as a personal memoir. The 'closeness' to the material that was such a distinctive feature of the narrative in *The Baron* is gone, and we return to a much more distant style of narration. And when the narrator of the story makes her formal appearance at the beginning of chapter 4, Suor Teodora's fullness as a character has the effect of making us keenly aware of the multilayered nature of the narrative discourse and thus of the difference and the distance between the narrated, the narrator, and the authorial voice. While this is certainly not the first time that the reader of the trilogy is confronted with a Brechtian distantiation effect, the technique is used here in an unprecedently explicit manner.[7]

In *The Viscount*, the fable-like simplicity of the narrative contributed to the strict binary logic that governed the denouement and conferred on the novel its distinctive feel as a brilliant intellectual experiment. I have argued that the real protagonist of *The Viscount* is reason itself; and it is by revealing the devices on which his discourse rests that Calvino opens the way for a non-naive reading of the narrative, especially at the end of the novel. In *The Baron*, the spectrum of distance and closeness has many more complex gradients than in *The Viscount*, but once again it is at the end of the narrative that the unveiling effect is to be found. It is in Biagio's meditations about the new responsibilities that his brother's death has thrust upon him that we find a posture that most clearly foreshadows Suor Teodora's interventions.[8] It is in that passage that for the first time in the trilogy the problematic of writing comes directly to the surface. In the context of *The Baron*, I discussed the ambiguity of the text, which hints at the dangers of fetishizing the written word as a surrogate to actual engagement and participation while it attempts to perform a discourse that, in its struggle with the world and with the limitations of a given cognitive horizon, becomes an important intervention in social praxis. Now, in *The Knight*, the act of writing becomes one of the central structural and thematic foci of the narrative as Calvino attempts to work his way out of the ambiguity in Biagio's discourse.

On the basis of these preliminary considerations, we can see how *The Knight* combines crucial stylistic and thematic elements from both of the previous novels in the trilogy, thus pursuing a line of research whose dynamism is not yet spent. But what, then, is specifically new in *The Knight*? Once again we can turn to Calvino's own words for some stimulating suggestions: '[*The Knight*] is also a book written in a period of greater political uncertainty than in 1951 or in 1957; it is more philosophical, and yet this leads to a greater lyrical abandon.'[9] The *differentia specifica* of *The Knight* lies precisely in Calvino's effort to go to the root of the problem with which he has been struggling since *I giovani*, namely, how can an intellectual contribute to the achievement of an authentic social synthesis? The answer *The Viscount* gave was: Enlightenment reason is as much a part of the problem as it is the solution – it splits social reality in the very process of attempting a synthesis. *The Baron* added the cognitive potential of narrative to the equation, but the cohesiveness of storytelling seemed ultimately too fragile to accomplish an enduring synthesis. Learning from these experiences, in *The Knight*, Calvino attempts to tackle the problem in yet another way, by decanting it, as it were, and reducing it to its most essential terms. This involves a double movement: first, a striving for a greater level of abstraction in order to isolate the presuppositions on which the problematic is founded (and this explains the similarities with *The Viscount*, which also used abstraction as a cognitive tool, but to different ends); second, a redescent into narrative where those presuppositions can be put to the test of 'thick description' or, in other words, where the world that those presuppositions entail can be played out, questioned, and eventually surpassed (and this is the link with *The Baron*).

In *The Knight*, the issue of the role of the intellectual in the struggle for progressive social change becomes the much more fundamental issue of how the self, the category of being that classical Western philosophy conceives as the site of moral autonomy and judgment, can exist at all. This radical reduction of the terms of the problem is at the core of *The Knight* and explains why Calvino had to return to a much more allegorical fantastic mode. Agilulfo, the non-existent knight, and Gurdulù, the all-existent squire, are at opposite extremes of the logical spectrum that provides the narrative world with its initial configuration. They are not 'characters' in the usual sense of the term; rather, they exist as names, lexemes, signs, traces, and so on, and it precisely this alternative way of being that poses the philosophical problem Calvino confronts: If it is possible to be the way Agilulfo and Gurdulù are, is there any place left for the humanist self? If yes, how can this place (of selfhood and consciousness) be mapped out and defended from the seductions of those other kinds of being (i.e., Agilufo's and Gurdulù's)? It is not so much that the whole project of the organic relationship of the intellectual to progressive social forces becomes inconceivable in the absence of an answer to these fundamental questions, but rather that the project presupposes an answer to these questions and it is that answer that needs to be challenged and re-examined. To put it another way, the issue for Calvino is not to prove that agency is in fact possible but, rather, to attempt to understand what kind of agency the project of commitment presupposes and in what kind of world that call to agency could be fulfilled.

It is perhaps a bit precious, but nonetheless telling, that the 'non-existent' protagonist named in the title of the novel does not make his entrance until halfway through the first chapter. This authorial wink might have passed unnoticed even among the most attentive readers were it not that this coyness is in stark contrast with the promptness with which the main characters were introduced in the previous novels of the trilogy. Furthermore, this lateness in presenting the knight has a parallel in Agilulfo's evaporation in the second to last chapter of the novel. The fragile ontological status of the character is structurally underlined by these hesitations and absences, which ultimately provide the nodes where the two planes of discourse developed by the novel can join. Agilulfo's late appearance and early departure narrativize the fragility of fictional being, which has no existence beyond the beginning and the end of the story being told: the diegetic vanishing (the 'ending' of Agilulfo) concides, indeed slightly precedes, the extra-diegetic vanishing (the ending of *The Knight*), and as the narrative levels collapse upon each other, we are forced to confront the nature of the text as a multilayered literary construct.

Let us then start from the first layer. How does the ontological tension central to the whole enterprise first manifest itself? Agilulfo is without existence. He does not have a body, the material presence by which we identify human beings. And yet, he functions perfectly well as a paladin: able to wear a suit of armour, Agilulfo can do everything that a paladin needs to be able to do to fulfil the duties and responsibilities of his station. What allows him to perform this feat is, in his own words, his will: "'How [asked Charlemagne] d'you do your job, then, if you don't exist?'" "'By Will power,' said Agilulfo, "and faith in our holy cause!'" (*Our Ancestors*, 289). In a Kantian vein, we could say that, unencumbered by the inertia of the sensorium and its beguiling inclinations, Agilulfo is nothing but pure will, pure practical reason, a transparent gaze upon the material world over which it exercises a near perfect sovereignty. Everything Agilulfo can do he does perfectly. His interventions flow from an absolute coherence and transparency of motives. As long as other consciousnesses do not interfere, a chosen goal is necessarily achieved by Agilulfo as if it were the conclusion dictated by an apodictic axiom. Agilulfo is never wrong and can never be evil, since he knows of only one law (chivalry) and his being is entirely devoted to the application of that law. It is to that law that Agilulfo owes his being: he is the model paladin. Without the law or outside of it Agilulfo not only does not exist but ceases to be altogether. Any transgression against that law is an attack on his very being. It is not surprising, therefore, that Agilulfo is the most zealous paladin in Charlemagne's army; nor is it surprising that his punctiliousness about every single aspect of military life would make his interaction with his more embodied companions difficult: 'Agliulfo Emo Bertrandino of the Guildiverni and of the Others of Corbentraz and Sura, Knight of Selimpia Citeriore and Fez was certainly a model soldier: but disliked by all' (*Our Ancestors*, 290).

The paradox is that the portrayal of this pure practical reason capable of mastering reality without the slightest doubt or hesitation, far from representing an epitome of human freedom, becomes a model of the abolition of moral consciousness and the triumph of necessity. Agilulfo can do whatever he wants, but he has no reason to do anything other than what he has been told befits a paladin. Agilulfo is a pure subject in the sense of being a mere grammatical subject, a mere ability to say 'I' in a sentence, but this 'I' has no depth, no thickness, no history other than a sequence of events (in the sense of one-damn-thing-after-another). Agilulfo repeats the program he has gradually absorbed in Charlemagne's army and all the minute details of everything he has witnessed. He is at best an archive or, better still, a databank where items are organized according to a given and immutable order. In sum,

Agilulfo's being is pure functionality, without hitches and without that surplus of being that we call critical thinking, that same surplus of being that provides the space for choice, agency, and moral tension, which are at the heart of modern notions of subjectivity. As Calvino himself puts it, Agilulfo is the 'organization man' (*RR*, 1: 1362) who can live, breathe, and have his being exclusively within the confines of the institution of which it is the arm.

Opposite to Agilulfo, Calvino sets Gurdulù. Where Agilulfo is pure will, Gurdulù is all nature. Gurdulù's being is at one with everything that exists. The boundary between the 'me' and the 'not-me' is so fragile that the moment Gurdulù fixes his attention on anything he develops such a strong empathy with the thing observed that he attempts to adopt its mode of being: 'He flung the nets in the water, saw a fish just about to enter, and got so much into the part of the fish that he plunged into the water and then into the net himself' (*Our Ancestors*, 302–3); 'When will you understand, Martinzùl [one of Gurdulù's many names], that it's you who is to eat the soup, and not the soup you!' (*Our Ancestors*, 305).

While Agilulfo's determination to be succeeds in outweighing non-existence, Gurdulù's evanescent self-consciousness spreads his being like a thin protean envelope on everything that exists. Both are beyond the sphere where ethico-political choices can occur: Agilulfo cannot conceive of any system other than the one to which he owes his being, while Gurdulù cannot adjudicate between systems and simply adheres to the one with which he is for the moment most immediately in contact. Neither can experience conflict, contradiction, or the effort to resolve them, which constitutes the basis for agency and moral responsibility.

Between these extremes of, on the one hand, being without existence and, on the other, existence to the point of non-being, the narrative develops the vicissitudes of two couples: Rambaldo and Bradamante, Torrismondo and Sofronia. The series of geometrical relays that structure the narrative development is apparent, and in his 1960 preface Calvino describes it explicitly:

With these two characters [Agilulfo and Gurdulù] ... I could not develop a story; they were merely the enunciation of the theme that had to be developed by other characters, in which being and not being would fight within the same person. It is young men who don't yet know that they are; therefore a young man had to be the real protagonist of this story ...

Rambaldo was going to be the moral of practice, experience, history. I needed another young man, Torrismondo, and I made him the moral of the absolute, for whom the confirmation of being had to come from something other than himself ...

For a young man, a woman is what surely *is*; and I made two women: one, Bradamante, love as contrast, as war, that is, the woman of Rambaldo's heart; the other, barely sketched, Sofronia, Love as peace ... the woman of Torrismondo's heart.[10]

Calvino's own comments give me an opportunity to question this well-constructed edifice and show that it is really no more than a basic starting point for the narrative.

No matter what Calvino says, the protagonist of the short novel remains Agilulfo. Rambaldo's and Torrismondo's gradual coming into their own are both overshadowed not only by Agilulfo's struggle to cling to existence but also, and for my purposes more importantly, by Agilulfo's own *Bildung*. It is the story of Agilulfo's own coming into being, which paradoxically ends in his disappearance, that provides the key to the interlocking levels of the narrative and becomes a figure of the vaster problematic Calvino is addressing: the drama of writing when the author comes to terms with his or her unavoidable role as the narrative's ultimate hero.

I have myself argued that in the original configuration Agilulfo and Gurdulù, appear as little more than the boundaries defining a logical space – in Calvino's words, 'an enunciation of the theme' – within which less absolute positions can begin to interact and develop an argument that may in the end supersede the original terms. However, a different fate awaits these two original positions. To evolve from his state of constant confusion and protean instability, Gurdulù needs to emerge into self-consciousness and from there begin to organize the manifold (to use a Kantian expression) in more stable categories. But the precise modality of the passage from universal sympathy to discernment – one could say the anthropological threshold from prehistory to history – is for the moment far from Calvino's concerns. Gurdulù doesn't evolve. Having served the purpose of establishing the thematic axis of the narrative, the character goes on to fulfil two background functions: a rhetorical amplification-by-contrast of Agilulfo's predicament, and a constant reminder of the facticity that the humanist consciousness feels is its 'other.' The sight of Gurdulù causes Rambaldo a Roquentin-like vertigo: 'Rambaldo found this so worrying it made his head go round; not so much with disgust though, as doubt at the possibility of that man in front of him being right and the world being nothing but a vast shapeless mass of soup in which all things dissolved and tinged all else with itself' (*Our Ancestors*, 322).[11]

As we analyse Agilulfo and Gurdulù in more detail, we realize that what differentiates the two characters is not only an opposite thematic polarity but also a structural element. Gurdulù's fluid sense of self, the instability of his perception of such basic categories as inside/outside, me/not-me, and so on, paradoxically provides a remarkably constant rhythm whose maintenance does not require any conscious effort. Scanned by endlessly repeated confusions, Gurdulù's mode of being is nonetheless quite stable. Not so Agilulfo's.

Gurdulù is disorder and abandon to the most fleeting immediate stimuli. Agilulfo is all discipline, coherence, rigorous adherence to a pre-established order. But at the centre of this iron-clad system there is nothing, a vanishing point of being that can only be overcome by constant vigilance, by a truly superhuman effort of will and self-conscious attention. Agilulfo's reliability has no equal among the paladins. He is a tower of organizational strength. And the fortress is built on the void. The slightest inattention would engulf it: Agilulfo's mode of existence is, in the end, exceptionally fragile. And it is precisely in this constant teetering on the edge of the abyss that lies the possibility of a dynamic development.

Agilulfo knows that he does not exist. Intellectual lucidity makes him not only an unrelentingly scrupulous agent of the order he is serving, but also keenly aware of his unique mode of being. Critical of the other paladins, taking pride in the exactitude that sets him apart, Agilulfo nonetheless feels the strain of his effort to be. If he is to keep faith with the thoroughness that is his, he cannot in the end avoid confronting the situation. It is only a slight hesitation that signal Agilulfo's coming to grips with his predicament: 'Agilulfo moved a few steps to mingle in one of those groups, then without any particular reason moved on to another, but did not press inside and no one took notice of him. He stood uncertainly behind one of the knights without taking part in their talk, then moved aside ... Agilulfo, *as if feeling suddenly naked*, made the gesture of crossing his arms and hugging his shoulders' (*Our Ancestors*, 290; emphasis added).

It is of course noteworthy that in this moment of hesitation at the threshold of human solidarity Agilulfo responds as if possessing at least a body image, what might be called an 'auroral' body. Initially, this incipient presence is easily dismissed in the fulfilment of his military duties, but then a stronger sense of his difference comes clearly to the surface: 'Oh corpse, you have what I never had or will have; a carcass. Or rather you have; you are this carcass, that which at times, in moments of despondency, I find myself envying in men who exist ... many things I manage to do better than those who exist, since I lack their usual defects of coarseness, carelessness, incoherence, smell. It's true that someone who exists always has a particular attitude or his own to things, which I never manage to have' (*Our Ancestors*, 324).

Pure practical reason is an ideal that Enlightenment rationality presumes to be above and beyond socio-historical determinations, those very determinations of which the human body can be seen to be the precipitate. As such, pure practical reason can have no individuality. And yet, precisely as the ideal takes on a material form, even the paper-thin form of a character in a novel, its abstract purity is compromised. Agilulfo is at first only a principle, which then gradually grows into denser being as it becomes a character, as the principle no longer functions simply as a conceptual term in a logical argument but is narrativized. It is exactly the presentation of this incarnation of a concept through narrativization that constitutes one of the most singular effects of *The Knight*. The perfect and relentless administrator of army ordinances, Agilulfo begins to feel a lack that brings his incipient individuality a step forward: '[Agilulfo] felt himself a nuisance all round and longed for any contact with his neighbour, even by shouting orders or curses, or grunting swear words like comrades did in a tavern. But instead he mumbled a few incomprehensible words of greeting, shyly, and moved on; going off as if escaping [*scappasse*]' (*Our Ancestors*, 293).

Finally, Agilulfo's profound ambivalence toward the body he cannot have becomes manifest. The sense of superiority he had at first derived from the contemplation of his slumbering fellow paladins gives way to fury: 'Even their wretched bodies [of bats], rat or bird, were tangible and definite, could flutter openmouthed swallowing mosquitoes, while Agilulfo with all his armour was pierced through every chink by gusts of wind, flights of mosquitoes, moon rays. A vague rancour growing inside him suddenly exploded; he drew his sword from his sheath, seized it in both hands and waved it wildly against every low flying bat. No result' (*Our Ancestors*, 293). And when Rambaldo asks him about Bradamante, whose love for Agilulfo is a running joke among the paladins, again Agilulfo explodes in silent anger: 'Agilulfo was holding a sharp two-edged axe. He brandished it, and buried it in the trunk of an oak tree. The axe passed right through the tree and cut it neatly, but the tree did not move from its trunk, so clean had been the blow' (*Our Ancestors*, 326).

Agilulfo does not possess the words to speak this longing, but the drama of his incarnation is well under way. And we should note that the struggle to *become*, rather than simply to *be*, is presented as the struggle to achieve an individuality that is intrinsically related to social solidarities (the companions-in-arms, the lover). Agilulfo is not in search of a radical difference on which to base his singularity – in fact, he already possesses such a difference – but of individuality through relatedness. The distance of this thematic from some contemporary discourses of identity is well worth noting.

Torrismondo's challenge, with which the second part of the novel begins, triggers the next phase in Agilulfo's struggle. The disclosure that the preservation of Sofronia's virginity is at the origin of Agilulfo's career as a paladin (which in his case equates with the achievement of being) is significant. Agilulfo intervened to prevent the most embodied act imaginable, an act that in addition to its paradigmatic sensuousness may also lead to conception and the birth of a new organism. Equally significant is the fact that, in the process of meeting Torrismondo's challenge, Agilulfo will find Sofronia in much the same predicament and will once again prevent her deflowering – her wishes in the matter being rather ambiguous:

'Oh yes ... always you ... you are ...'
'No, protected by this sword, I will accompany you forth from the sultan's domains.'
'Yes ... indeed ... of course.' (*Our Ancestors*, 362)

In sum, from beginning to end, Agilulfo's mission in life seems to be to subjugate the body – the most perfectly subjugated body being precisely one that does not exist![12] In the midst of these adventures, Agilulfo seems to recover his solidity. Even when confronted with Priscilla's lust, he handles himself so adroitly as to preserve his honour while avoiding a challenge to his virility – perhaps a moralist wink suggesting that concupiscence is often best served by simulation.

After all, Agilulfo himself said that 'The only way to understand it [that all the world is not soup, i.e., that clear-sighted discernment is possible] is to fix oneself a clear task.'[13] And with a goal clearly set before him – to find Sofronia, prove her virginity and thus the legitimacy of his titles – Agilulfo's being is at its strongest, as Suor Teodora remarks: 'The only person who can be said definitely to be on the move is Agilulfo, by which I do not mean his horse or armour, but that lonely self-preoccupied impatient something jogging along on horseback inside the armour' (*Our Ancestors*, 358). Once value is determined, practical reason can deploy its method with single-minded assurance.

Still, just as all existential doubts seems to have been laid to rest, when Sofronia is found and his honour on the point of being vindicated, Agilulfo meets his doom. Through an extraordinary series of coincidences and misunderstanding, the virginity of Sofronia is placed momentarily in doubt. With his titles in question, Agilulfo is deprived of the rallying point for his will to be – his very name: '"Nor will you see me again!" said he. "I have no longer a name! Farewell!"' (*Our Ancestors*, 373). And he disappears into the forest. When the full story is told and Agilulfo's claims are restored, Rambaldo runs after him but finds only his empty armour. Agilulfo is gone:

> 'Knight, you have resisted so long by your will power alone, and succeeded in doing all things as if you existed; why suddenly surrender?'
>
> But he did not know in which direction to turn; the armour was empty, not empty like before, but empty of that something going by the name of Agilulfo which was now dissolved like a drop in the sea. (*Our Ancestors*, 375)

The last words in this passage provide us with a clue as to how to give a richer meaning to Agilulfo's disappearance than Rambaldo can articulate. What Agilulfo has lost is his difference, a mode of being that was blocked on the threshold of individuality. He has now rejoined that 'earth's crinkly crust,' as Suor Teodora puts it, where there can be a 'change between the relationship of various qualities distributed over the expanse of uniform matter around, without anything changing in fact [*nulla sostanzialmente si sposti*]' (*Our Ancestors*, 357–8). Deprived of his name, that is, of the law-abiding narrative to which he owes his being and which now is put in doubt, Agilulfo is forced to confront his inability to be other than he has built himself to be. Having no depth of being, unable to rely on the socio-historical sedimentations that make up a body, Agilulfo is a player whose destiny is tied to a single performance. And Agilulfo must die – the baroque quality of the denouement drives home this higher necessity – because the world within which he is confined is dying.

We know from the first pages of the novel that the chivalric world with which we are confronted is old, exhausted, itself stuck in a sterile impasse: 'With knights going into battle loaded with supplementary harness, at the first clash a mess of disparate objects falls to the ground. After that no one can think of fighting, can they? The struggle now is to gather all the things up ... [W]hat is war, after all, but this passing of ever-more dented objects from hand to hand' (*Our Ancestors*, 310). Torrismondo may be accused of a cynical defeatism (to which his adventures will provide the antidote), but his characterization of the war rings remarkably true: 'The war will last [until the end of time], and nobody will win or lose, we'll all sit here face to face for ever. Without one or the other there'd be nothing, and yet both we and they have forgotten by now why we're fighting' (*Our Ancestors*, 332).[14]

With Agilulfo's disappearance, this old world vanishes as the new generation takes over. And yet we must note that in many ways Agilulfo himself has been the midwife of the new. It is through Agilulfo that Torrismondo and Sofronia, as well as Rambaldo and Bradamante, are brought together. The knight, whose greatest deed has been to prevent sexual concourse, becomes in fact instrumental to the coupling of the new generation. The reader cannot help feeling that the strongest legacy from the old generation to the new is truly Agilulfo's, and it is telling that Agilulfo's last act is to bequeath his armour to Rambaldo. That is how Agilulfo's aspiration to be can ultimately take flesh: by helping those who have a body come to fuller being through the solidarity and connectedness of which Torrismondo, Sofronia, the citizens of Curvaldia are the clearest figures.

However, there is another sense in which Agilulfo must vanish. *The Knight* is 'his' story, and as the narrative winds down the conceit that gave him being must unravel as well. The extremely involved way in which the plot comes to its resting point only underlines the formal necessity of ending, like the endless finale of certain romantic symphonies. And here is the place where Agilulfo's role as switching device among the different levels of the narrative emerges most clearly. This is also the place where generic considerations become most immediately helpful in disclosing the cognitive issues Calvino is attempting to negotiate.

Agilulfo's evaporation at the end of *The Knight* catapults us into the (para)narrative discourse that Suor Teodora has been conducting from the incipit of chapter 4 and that frames all subsequent chapters, with the notable exception of chapters 10 and 11, when the narrative cannot brook interruptions as it sprints down the last stretch to tie up all the loose ends before the final coup de théâtre, in Suor Teodora's own words, 'Those last pages I found myself writing away at breakneck speed' (*Our Ancestors*, 380). On this (para)narrative level Agilulfo appears as one of the characters in the story that Suor Teodora is painstakingly writing. Within Suor Teodora's world the ontological status of the narrative is at first uncertain: 'I'm writing in a convent, from old papers unearthed or talk heard in our parlour here or a few rare accounts by people who were actually present' (*Our Ancestors*, 308), and the twinkle in the eye in the phrase 'people who were actually present' should not escape the attentive reader! It seems that Suor Teodora's penitential exercise is governed less by a preoccupation with the factual accuracy of the 'ancient ... chronicle' (*Our Ancestors*, 357), as the story is called, than by the effort to contemplate and illustrate the universal truths that underlie the confusing appearances of the world: 'my assiduous penance of seeking words and all my meditations on ultimate truths' (*Our Ancestors*, 357). It is this meditation on the essence of things that ultimately leads Suor Teodora to a critique of the act of writing that cannot reproduce appearances – 'To tell it as I would like this blank page would have to bristle with reddish rocks' (*Our Ancestors*, 356) – and yet can be faithful to essences: 'Everything moves on this bare page with no sigh, no change on its surface, as after all everything moves and nothing changes on the earth's crinkly crust; for there is but one single expanse of the same material, as there is with the sheet on which I write' (*Our Ancestors*, 357–8).

The hiatus between the contemplation of truth and its representation in language is bridged by the sign functioning as a cognitive map:

> To help tell my tale it would be better if I drew a map, the gentle country-side of France ... Then with arrows and crosses and numbers I could plot the journey of one or other of our heroes. Here, for instance, with a rapid line in spite of a few twists, I can make Agilulfo land in England and direct him towards the convent where Sofronia has lived retired for fifteen years.
>
> He arrives and finds the convent a mass of ruins. (*Our Ancestors*, 358–9)

Within this universe of writing, characters are nothing but 'some such very faint pucker on the surface as can be got by pricking paper from below with a pin' (*Our Ancestors*, 357). And yet this ephemeral 'being' rejoins the ephemerality that is the 'truth' of human 'being':

'and this pucker would always have to be impregnated with the general matter of the world and this itself constitutes its sense and beauty and sorrow, its true attrition and movement' (*Our Ancestors*, 357).

In the final analysis, then, Suor Teodora's reflections bring us back to the paradoxes of being that provide the underlying thematic of Agilulfo's story. Just as Agilulfo's lack of existence does not prevent him from being the most compelling presence among the paladins, so, paradoxically, the traces left by the human subject's effort to be are ultimately no more substantial than the traces left by a nib on a sheet of paper. In this light, the final coup de théâtre acquires its full meaning.[15] The two levels of the narrative collapse upon each other as we discover that Suor Teodora 'is' Bradamante. The world of the narrator is consubstantial with the world narrated; the difference between the two lies in the discursive registers through which that world is evoked. We now see that Suor Teodora is no less a device than Bradamante, and we also realize that the nodal point between the two registers is Agilulfo: what propels the story is Bradamante (Suor Teodora)'s impossible desire to possess and awaken the flesh of the non-existent paladin; and what propels the reflections about writing is Suor Teodora (Bradamante)'s desire to grasp cognitively the being that Agilulfo so (im)perfectly embodies. And in the final chapter of the novel these two desires merge in Bradamante=Suor Teodora's acceptance of Rambaldo as the heir of Agilulfo's legacy: 'When I came to shut myself in here I was desperate with love for Agilulfo, now I burn for the young and passionate Rambaldo' (*Our Ancestors*, 381).[16] The ascetic spell cast by the abstract ideal of a perfect rational ordering of the world is broken and replaced by a renewed and thus more deeply felt sympathy with the generous flow of young blood. That is the lesson that, paradoxically, the penitential practice of writing has taught Suor Teodora= Bradamante. At the end of the novel the dichotomy between the imaginative elan that sustains the storytelling and the reflective posture that inspires the (para)narrative discourse is enthusiastically overcome. The basic modernist 'art vs life' binarism is sublated by the dialectical movement through which writing engages adventure just as adventure engages writing: 'This is why my pen at a certain point began running on so. I rushed to meet him; I knew he would not be long in coming. A page is good only when we turn it and find life surging along and confusing every passage in the book. The pen rushes on urged by the same joy that makes me course the open road [*correre le strade*]. A chapter started when one doesn't know which tale to tell is like a corner turned on leaving a convent, when one might come face to face with a dragon, a Saracen gang, an enchanted isle or a new love' (*Our Ancestors*, 381).

Of course, as the last few phrases remind us ('a dragon, a Saracen gang, an enchanted isle'), this synthesis is a *fictional* one. The lyricism of the novel's envoy further emphasizes the artifice of the narrative resolution: 'From describing the past, from the present which seized my hand in its excited grasps, here I am, oh future, now mounting the crupper of thy horse. What new pennants wilt thou unfurl before me from towers of cities not yet founded? What rivers of devastation set flowing over castles and gardens I have loved? What unforeseeable golden ages art thou preparing, ill-mastered, indomitable harbinger of treasures dearly paid for, my kingdom to be conquered, the future' (*Our Ancestors*, 381–2).

La boucle est bouclée: the narrative does not simply stop, it is emphatically closed. Once again a profusion of stylistic means (the coup de théâtre, the high-flown lyrical envoy) are brought to bear, marking the end; the effect is a resounding finale to match the elaborate conclusion of Agilulfo's adventure. And it is precisely this insistence on closure, the excessive theatricality of the final configuration, that foregrounds the artifice of the narrative and raises the question of its wider significance. Suor Teodora=Bradamante may well have overcome her alienated state of narrator/subject and narrated/object and found a new subjective synthesis in the desire for the richly embodied life that Rambaldo offers, but the much-ostended machinery through which this synthesis is achieved reminds the reader that this is not a simple parable with a straightforward moral, but rather a sophisticated and multilayered fictional text. And as we move on to the level of allegory and reference, we should prepare ourselves for a further twist disclosing distinctly new interpretive possibilities.

Pessimism of the Intellect, Optimism of the Will

A few observations comparing the three novels in Calvino's heraldic trilogy will provide some guidance as to where we should focus our analysis of the allegorical and referential dimension of *The Knight*. In particular, we are now in a position to identify a few of the salient characteristics of the type of fantastic narrative Calvino is deploying in *Our Ancestors*. First, the narratives proceed from the literalization of a thematically central metaphor (Milanini 1990): the divided self in *The*

Viscount, the dialectic of distance and engagement in *The Baron*, and the struggle to achieve fullness of being in *The Knight*. Second, a key stylistic constant is the ostension of the text's literary quality, which reminds the reader of the cognitive performance the text is eliciting. I am referring here not only to the numerous explicit and implicit literary allusions, which are the most evident, and ultimately less interesting, indicators of literariness, but also to the great variety of literary devices Calvino is able to deploy and contrast to great effect: from the essay-like geometry of the argumentation in *The Viscount*, through the profusion of generic modulations in *The Baron*, to the display and eventual collapse of superimposed narrative levels in *The Knight*. Third, the filtering of the narrative through the sensibility of a narrator who is also a participant in the events narrated: the Viscount Medardo's nephew; Biagio, the Baron's brother; and, in *The Knight*, Suor Teodora=Bradamante. It is specifically in relation to this third constant that emerges what is for my purposes the most distinctive aspect of *The Knight*.

The figure of the narrator becomes more and more significant, thematically and structurally, through the trilogy. In *The Viscount*, the Viscount's nephew lends to the narrative a resourceful matter-of-factness that is an ideal background against which to set off the ideological strictures of the Viscount's bad and good halves. What marks this narrator for most of the novel is a young boy's light-hearted savvy, which harks back, albeit in a much brighter and less dramatic key, to Pin, the street-smart and yet vulnerable protagonist of *The Path* and one of the most engaging boy-narrators to be found in the works of Calvino. It is only at the very end of *The Viscount* that a note of melancholy and nostalgia colours the narrator's discourse and we suddenly discover a reflective, adult sensibility as the nephew's storytelling function is explicitly thematized.

Biagio, in *The Baron*, is from the very beginning a more complex figure. The reflective and storytelling registers through which Biagio tells his brother's story raise the issue of his incomplete grasp of the world that his own discourse evokes. Biagio himself invites us to read against the grain of his own cognitive grid, by professing on a variety of occasions his inability to comprehend the full significance of his brother's conduct. In short, the narrator's storytelling function is very much in the foreground of the whole novel, which even ends with a brief, somewhat lyrical, and unprecedented meditation on the act of writing. Still, Biagio has much to share with the narrator of *The Viscount*. Calvino's predilection for presenting the world through the eyes of a young boy still predominates in *The Baron*. More than half of the novel is devoted to Cosimo's adventures as a youth, and even later Cosimo's originality lends itself to a presentation in a stubbornly youthful key. While depressed resignation, one of the most obvious markers of maturity, colours Biagio's reflective register, the storytelling register of Biagio's discourse is infected by Cosimo's exuberance, whose antecedents are not only the narrator of *The Viscount* but also, once again, the archetypical Pin. Furthermore, Biagio, much like the Viscount's nephew, participates in the events narrated but he remains essentially in the background, his 'common' and sometimes 'good' sense providing a clear contrast to Cosimo's eccentricities. Even though the storytelling function of the narrator is increasingly the object of direct commentary, the narrator's persona is still that of the witness.

Not so in *The Knight*. In the last work of the trilogy the storytelling function is no longer simply thematized but rather expressly and distinctly problematized. And we should note the striking thematic linking: at the end of *The Viscount* storytelling emerges as a theme, which is then taken up and developed in *The Baron*; at the end of *The Baron* the practice of writing makes its appearance as a motif, which then becomes one of the central concerns of *The Knight*. This linking further confirms the legitimacy of considering the trilogy a fictional cycle.

The significance of this shift from thematization to problematization is signalled by a change in the gender and age of the narrator: the young-boy perspective is finally abandoned in favour of that of a grown woman who has clearly been around the block a few times. Her disclaimer makes the point in a humorous and typically Calvinian way: 'I must crave indulgence: we country girls, however noble, have always led retired lives in remote castles and convents; apart from religious ceremonies, triduums, novenas, gardening, harvesting, vintaging, whippings, slavery, incest, fires, hangings, invasions, sacking, rape and pestilence, we have had no experience. What can a poor nun know of the world?' (*Our Ancestors*, 308). Also, until the coup de théâtre that marks the end of the novel, we are led to believe that the narrator played no role in the event described: the storyteller as witness is replaced by the storyteller as provider of meaning. In other words, the narrator can no longer hide behind the pretence of transparently reporting the events narrated (albeit with commentary, as in Biagio's case). Rather, Suor Teodora, whose late medieval sensibility is preoccupied by the dialectic between appearances and the substance of things, has to confront squarely the problematic function of writing: how can the sign be made true to the substance of its referent when the universe of discourse seems to be the furthest removed from the universe of human action? This is the difficult enterprise that constitutes Suor Teodora's penitential labour, an enterprise that is not casually entrusted to a female character in so far as it involves a narrative of *delivering into being*. In the end Agilulfo's determination to be is paradoxically fulfilled by his evaporation and the adoption of Rambaldo as heir, which is its corollary; in the same vein, the narrator achieves a new synthesis of being when the split between Suor Teodora and Bradamante is finally healed (as in *The Viscount* but here rather more convincingly).

In *The Knight*, the direct problematization of the relationship between the narrator and her material allows Calvino to deploy the resources of allegory in an especially focused manner. Suor Teodora's critique of writing provides the vehicle to directly address the cluster of issues whose development I have been tracing since my discussion of *I giovani*. In the course of her meditation on the substance of things – the cognitive end to which her writing penance is a means – Suor Teodora finally comes to the conclusion that there is no solution of continuity between life and writing: both are, or can be, modalities of engagement or, for that matter, evasion. This does not mean that the difference between these modalities are erased, but rather that the crux of the problem is to set in motion a constructive dialectic between them. The end of the novel suggests, as we have seen, that Suor Teodora=Bradamante has succeeded in achieving such a dynamic synthesis. Does this mean that at the allegorical level Calvino is confidently positing the resolution of the tension between the cultural and the political role of the intellectual?

The answer to this question is, as usual, rather complex. And since we are once again approaching the interaction between fiction and history, it is useful to begin our discussion by widening our horizon and considering how Calvino positioned himself within the social fraction that he considered his primary interlocutor. From this point of view the document that immediately commands attention is the essay 'The Sea of Objectivity,' originally published in the second issue of *Il Menabò* in 1960, but written by Calvino in October 1959, that is to say, just after the completion of the first draft of *The Knight*, composed between March and September of the same year. In this essay, the most influential ever to spring from his pen, Calvino sets out his poetical program with great lucidity and unusual fervour:

> [In Pasolini's novels], we begin to wade through ... a human jam spread on the squalid edges of the city: but at some point there is the friction of a thought, a feeling, an emerging consciousness ...
>
> From the literature of objectivity to the literature of consciousness ... Today, the notion of the complexity of the whole, the notion of a swarming, packed, variegated, labyrinthine, stratified reality has become of necessity complementary to the world view that relies on simplification, on a schematization of the real. But what we would like to see emerge from both these ways of understanding reality is still the non-acceptance of the given situation, an active and conscious reflex, the will to disagree, an obstinacy without illusion.[17]

It is easy to see a continuity in the evolution of Calvino's position. The emphasis on the ethical dimension of writing, which marked 'The Lion,' remains. In that essay, Calvino spoke of the necessity for writers to take responsibility for the moral presence, the *proposal of subjectivity*, which a narrative inevitably contains; in 'The Sea,' he reiterates that ethical stance against the tendency to elude that responsibility by surrendering to the objectivity of the given, of things that possess their own inexorable, non-human logic: 'The surrender to objectivity ... appears in a period in which man loses confidence in his ability to direct the course of things ... because he realizes that *things go on by themselves*' (emphasis added).[18] While acknowledging the crisis of the revolutionary ideals that nourished the moral tension for which he is arguing – 'The tension towards an ideal, that's what has worn out ...; it is the crises of the revolutionary spirit. Revolutionary is the person who does not accept natural and historical givens and wants to change them'[19] – Calvino insists on the reciprocal relation between cognition and ethical commitment: 'if the logic [*la ragione*] of the universe triumphs over that of man, it is the end of human doing, of history. The glimmering logic of the universe is enlightening when it sheds light on the limited and obstinate story of man; but when it takes the place of that human story, it is a return to the indistinct original crucible.'[20] In short, the universe becomes comprehensible only against an ethical horizon, and it is precisely that relationship between responsible action and the emergence of a human world that literature must keep bringing into focus.

However, while the emphasis on the ethical function of literature is a constant theme in Calvino's poetical discourse, the accent has significantly shifted. In 1959, Calvino's tone has an urgency that it did not have in 1955. And the reason for the shift can be quickly identified. In 'The Lion,' Calvino had been speaking to, and as a member of, a left-wing intelligentsia whose main preoccupation was still, as we have seen, the battle for realism. Against a simplistic view of what this realism might be, Calvino had raised the issue of the moral presence or the proposal of subjectivity informing the literary work. Only by taking this aspect of the work into account, Calvino had gone on to argue, could the Gramscian problematic of the role of intellectuals and their organic relation to the proletariat be cogently addressed, and a more sophisticated and non-reductive notion of realism and commitment elaborated. Calvino's argument had been more about means than ends. The need to recapture, after the years of clerico-Fascism, the progressive spirit of the Resistance had been taken for granted, and so had the leading role of the PCI, which had managed to keep that spirit alive in spite of the heavy ideological toll exacted by the Cold War and Stalinism. Calvino had articulated a clarification within a fairly well-defined political horizon.

Four years later, this was no longer the case. We have already discussed the traumatic effect on left-wing intellectuals of the Twentieth Congress of the CPSU in 1956 and, even more, of the Soviet invasion of Hungary later in the same year. It is significant that Ajello's 1979 book *Intellettuali e Pci: 1944–1958* ends with a chapter entitled 'Hungary Is Still With Us.' Calvino was one of those intellectuals who returned their party membership card though, unlike some, he qualified his dissent by confirming his commitment to socialism. In fact, Calvino remained on good terms with the party throughout his life, first as a fellow-traveller and then as a sympathetic observer.

In 1959, then, though clearly still within the PCI's sphere of influence, Calvino was outside the party, a new situation that he shared with the many members of the left-wing intelligentsia who left the PCI in 1956–7 after years of militancy. This meant that the political horizon of Calvino and of many of his primary readers (particularly of the essay) substantially changed. And this change reflected in many way the changes in the wider political conjuncture. By 1959, Togliatti's PCI had clearly weathered the crisis of 1956. The results of the 1958 election showed the PCI holding its own and even gaining some ground in spite of the significant reduction in the number of card-carrying members. On the other hand, under Nenni's leadership a revitalized and combative PSI was beginning its long march toward the Christian Democrats, who were discovering the merits of a prudent reformism as well as of a more muscular and dynamic state intervention in the economy; the foundations of the centre-left alliance that would govern Italy for the next three decades were being laid. From the PCI's point of view, the most immediate challenge became to avoid political isolation, a particularly unpromising position in a country that was slowly, unevenly, and yet steadily on the way to neo-capitalist affluence. With the international revival of social democracy and the establishment of the welfare state – both slow to reach Italy – the socio-political equation was changing significantly, and the PCI came under increasing pressure to revise and update its platform to take into account the social, political, and economic evolution of the country.

In 1959 the need for this renewal of the left was still only dimly felt by most. However, there was a perceptible restlessness within the left-wing intelligentsia. Undoubtedly, this restlessness had its roots in the 1956 crisis and the loss of a clearly defined political horizon occasioned by that crisis, but it also went further. It was not only that the options appeared less inevitable precisely as the political axis moved, however marginally, to the left. It was also that once the Stalinist anathema no longer prevented a serious appraisal of the character of bourgeois democracies, Marxist intellectuals were forced to confront the reality of a new kind of capitalism: strong economic growth accompanied by a lively and dynamic cultural production, which belied the long-cherished image of a moribund bourgeois world. In this light, the Vittorinian program of a vast cultural renewal that would not set strict ideological preconditions was bound to regain currency. It is significant that 1959 marked the demise of Pasolini's *Officina*, a journal still firmly anchored in the Italian historicist tradition – the De Santis-Croce-Gramsci line – and the launch of *Il Menabò*, Vittorini's last major editorial enterprise. Chosen by Vittorini to share editorial duties for the journal, Calvino found in the *Menabò* experiment a kind of consecration that established him as one of the major voices of the left-wing intelligentsia. It is in this journal that Calvino's most famous and influential essays ('The Sea' and 'The Labyrinth') appeared between 1959 and 1962. As we have seen, his polemic with Fortini on the pages of *Il Menabò* signalled the end of a by then fragile consensus among left-wing intellectuals.

One of the keys to 'The Sea' is to consider it as the articulation (which will be elaborated further in 'The Labyrinth') of the basis on which Calvino agreed to participate in Vittorini's enterprise. The urgency that, as we have noted, clearly distinguishes 'The Sea' from 'The Lion' becomes then symptomatic of the apprehension with which Calvino approached the new decade.

The loss of a firm political point of reference and the much diminished hopes in the early realization of an authentically progressive political project lend to Calvino's ethical stance a new peremptoriness. The image that emerges from the essay is that of a writer beset by the double temptation of surrendering to the absurdity of things or to the cataloguing power of reason. The stakes are much higher here than in 'The Lion.' The effort is no longer to correct a reductive poetics and vindicate the validity of a fuller range of literary experiences. Rather, Calvino is attempting to rescue consciousness itself, the human dimension of the literary experience, its cognitive significance. The discussion is most emphatically about ends as well as means. Indeed, the main thrust of the essay is to point to the inescapable link between means and ends, and suggest that the surrender to objectivity is, among other things, a surrender to means, an evasion of the challenge to define human ends, a challenge that a more than merely decorative/ evasive literature must confront. In the context of the socio-political conjuncture of 1959, we can see how this message would hit home among a left-wing intelligentsia who, after many years of dogmatic slumber, was awakening to the complexities of neo-capitalism and slowly coming into contact with the many attractive and dangerous instruments developed, mostly overseas, by the new human sciences. Calvino's insistence on the ethico-political dimension of literature, on a humble and yet all the more stringent humanism based on the dialectic between cognition and commitment (one could say cognitive commitment and committed cognition), supplied a criterion to distinguish between co-optation and resistance, between intellectuals who still fought to write critically and those who surrendered to ideologically determined givens.

It is interesting to complement these observations with Calvino's statement in an unpublished introduction to the first 1960 edition of the trilogy:

The 1950s and 1960s are like a thick wall. Looking at them from the outside, they have not been ungenerous and our comfort has increased. But in reality they have been tough years, with alternating phases of teeth-

clenching, waves of hope, descents into pessimism and cynicism, shells
that we built for ourselves. We all lost something of ourselves, whether a
little or a lot. What matters is what we have been able to salvage, for us
and for others. On my part, it is through these three stories that I believe I
have saved something of what was *on the other side* ...

[T]he three novels collected in this volume were born of a need I felt
each time to express an active drive, optimistic in its way *without lying*.[21]

What was beyond the thick wall of the 1950s? The Resistance, of
course, and the hopes of radical social progress, the 'Wind of the
North,' which lost its impetus in the labyrinths of realpolitik. And yet,
at the beginning of the new decade, Calvino seemed to feel that a page
had been turned; a historical scansion coincides with the completion of
his heraldic cycle. The parallel with Suor Teodora=Bradamante at the
end of *The Knight* is compelling and allows us to explore a final level of
significance for Calvino's allegory.

What if, remembering Flaubert's famous dictum, we attribute to
Calvino 'Suor Teodora=Bradamante c'est moi!'? What if we then take
into account the concerns Calvino expressed in 'The Sea'? We have
already noted in passing that Suor Teodora=Bradamante's writing is
presented in *The Knight* as an act of penance. This penitential activity is
not so much an atonement for past sins as a means to deepen the peni-
tent's grasp of the substance of things. The morality that underpins
this type of discourse is an active one; proper repentance is achieved
not through grieving for sins committed but rather by learning from
past experience, working out the issues that experience has raised.
Though dressed in pre-Reformation Catholic habit, this is essentially
an Enlightenment morality.

Once we realize that Suor Teodora is also Bradamante, the nature of
the narrator's assignment becomes even clearer. By telling Agilulfo's
story, Suor Teodora has been commanded to work through her infatua-
tion with him; or, lifting the allegorical veil, Suor Teodora is the figure
of the intellectual fascinated with the dream of complete integration
within a powerful organizational structure. In this sense Agilulfo represents, as Calvino himself put it, the 'organization man' who has
absorbed the directives coming from outside and above, and is utterly
and inevitably devoted to their implementation (as well as their justification as a propagandist). Agilulfo is the type of intellectual envisaged
more or less explicitly by Zhdanovian theory and practice. In a more
argumentative and polemical vein, we could add that this is also the

type of intellectual that a misguided and Stalinist reinterpretation of Gramsci's notion of the organic intellectual could yield.

One of the great merits of *The Knight* is precisely to make intelligible the attraction of this proposal of subjectivity, as well as its inhumanity and inherent fragility. Agilulfo's impeccable conduct, his unshakable commitment to duty, his ability to sublate the contradiction between freedom and necessity, thus effortlessly realizing the dream of Enlightenment rationality – this is the dream that Suor Teodora=Bradamante has to exorcise and that, through the narrator, Calvino is himself confronting.[22] It is the dream of surrendering one's critical function and becoming the organizer of consensus, the manager of cultural hegemony. This is the seductive pledge that the PCI's cultural policy held out to intellectuals, a pledge, however, that neo-capitalism on the counterattack will not hesitate to make its own with incomparably greater resources. Because, after all, while the PCI could only promise future fulfilment, the DC and its allies were now prepared to offer immediate privileges to a whole army of Agilulfos. In this context, the cultural battle would from now on no longer be fought between traditional and organic intellectuals but rather between intellectuals with different and varied allegiances. Within this fragmented world, Agilulfo's single-mindedness can only be maintained at the cost of blindness. It can no longer seduce as an ideal, and Suor Teodora=Bradamante/Calvino have to get over a nostalgia for an anachronistic dream/nightmare of total cohesion, integration, and mastery.

There is a second exorcism that Suor Teodora=Bradamante/Calvino are conducting through Agilulfo. The final collapse of the two levels of the narrative, that is, the reflections about writing and Agilulfo's story, brings to the forefront a fundamental paradox: the artfulness of the act of writing is emphasized precisely as the narrative pretends to dissolve into life. The narrator claims the narrative as her own, and yet in so doing destroys the illusion of her own status as anything other than a narrative device. The attempt of a narrating instance to speak in his or her own name is inevitably destined to fail in the endless regress of narrative mirrors. Thus, the optimism of the envoy becomes a predicate of the fictional universe. The allegorical folding of the narrative upon itself brings the level of reference explicitly 'inside' the text, and yet the ostensive artfulness of the procedure not only invites cognitive distance but also taints the narrative solution with a sort of excessive wilfulness (reminding us of the ending of *The Viscount*). At the end of the *The Knight*, we confront one of the paradoxes of the fantastic genre

Calvino has been developing throughout the trilogy: fantastic distantiation allows for a cognitively rewarding simplification of issues and
themes, but also seems to inevitably compromise the final 'bite' of the
narrative, its ability to reach the real. This is a serious limitation when
we consider that Calvino warns us in 'The Sea' about the danger of
denying literature the function not only of helping us grasp the world
(cognition) but also guide our interventions in the world (ethics). The
simplification of reality afforded by allegory no longer seems equal to
its key task, which has now become that of grasping and intervening in
an increasingly complex, irreducibly multiple social world. Already in
The Baron, Calvino had pushed the limits of the form by exploring a
wide range of generic modulations in different episodes. The result
was a type of fantastic mode that was always extremely literary and
inflected now and again by generic elements borrowed from the
adventure novel, the Gothic tale, the fable, and so on. Though to a
lesser extent than in *The Baron*, this was also characteristic of *The Viscount*. In *The Knight* this range of modulation largely disappears. The
last novel of the trilogy is unusually uniform in style. Calvino does not
let his pen be tempted into sudden generic excursions. And this is a
clue to the nature of the second exorcism *The Knight* is attempting to
perform.

The singularly focused and controlled style of the narrative echoes
Agilulfo's single-mindedness, thus pointing to a further facet of the
character's significance. We can now grasp the kinship between the
type of subjectivity that Agilulfo proposes and the narrating subject
with that Suor Teodora and, through her, Calvino are struggling. Agilulfo's discipline, his determination to (re)order the messy reality that
he confronts, have much in common with the writer's task as Suor
Teodora understands it. Her penance consists in meditating on the
vanity of appearances so as to retrieve the providential order that
underpins them. Faced day after day with the white page, Suor
Teodora cannot but feel a profound affinity for the knight whose very
being was the constant striving to fill an empty suit of armour. And
just as Agilulfo occupies his free moments with military drills that
remind him of his raison d'être, so Suor Teodora begins each new
chapter with a meditation on the task lying before her, such as on writing and its functions, on the difficulty of the task, and so on. Only
through this somewhat laborious propaedeutics can Suor Teodora
overcome the anxiety of the white page.

For Calvino, Agilulfo and Suor Teodora are two sides of the same coin or, rather, two manifestations of the same fundamental anxiety of exhaustion and powerlessness. The obsession with the ordering power of ideology, which can become a barren schematism or a false comfort, is paralleled by the obsession with the nature of writing, which can function as a last shore for a depleted imagination. These have to be exorcised by (re)discovering the element of surprise, the epiphanic moment of storytelling. In *The Knight*, this epiphanic moment is the final unveiling, which suddenly reconfigures the narrative and opens up the various levels of interpretation we have examined. While at the compositional level the unveiling, or recognition, of the identity of Suor Teodora as Bradamante is merely a clever stylistic device (indeed one of the most venerable ones) providing closure, at the allegorical level this is a key moment of insight where, as it were, Calvino (re)cognizes Suor Teodora as Bradamante and finally exorcises both the fascination with order that Bradamante's attraction for Agilulfo represents and the fixation on the act of writing that threatened to absorb and replace his storytelling verve. On this level, Suor Teodora=Bradamante's return to a life of action can be read as a desire to return to a less explicitly self-reflexive style of narrative.

What emerges at the end of the trilogy is a longing for a new departure. The fantastic/chivalric vein developed over the 1950s is showing signs of involution. Calvino can sustain it only with an extreme effort of concentration and by explicitly narrativizing the difficulties of such an endeavour. Calvino's characteristic imaginative flair seems cramped in *The Knight*, and only a few episodes remind us of the freshness of *The Baron* (e.g., Rambaldo's spying of Bradamante's bath in the river). Even in relation to *The Viscount*, *The Knight* lacks the youthful confidence that lent a sharp brilliance to the schematizations of his earlier work. *The Knight* bears witness to a disquiet mixed with anticipation at the discovery of the increasing complexity of the modern world. The heroic period of the Resistance and, in a different way, of the Cold War is definitively over. The ethico-political horizon is much changed and more troubling, though possibly more open. For the left-wing intellectual, the most urgent task no longer seems to commit, to dare stand up and be counted, but rather to chart the treacherous waters of the neo-capitalist revival while keeping alive the ethico-political tension that informed the post-war period. On the literary scene, the time is ripe for new developments that will soon manifest themselves. The neo-avant-garde movement is beginning to take shape and will replace neo-realism, whose protracted agony is approaching its end, as a polemical point of reference for Calvino. The generic system we have been dealing with is crumbling and a new one is emerging. Calvino will have to find a new answer to the challenge of writing. The trepidation with which the narrator quits the convent at the end of *The Knight* to plunge again into the stream of life resonates with Calvino's own trepidation as he approaches this new challenge.

CHAPTER FIVE

The Watcher: The Intellectual in the Labyrinth

In the previous chapter I argued that *The Knight* confronts in a more focused and direct manner the larger theoretical issues that the previous works of the trilogy raise either explicitly or implicitly. At the thematic level, the problematic of the social role of the progressive intellectual becomes a meditation on the being of the writer, and more particularly on the tripartite relation between the writer as ethical subject, the social world within which such a subject is located, and the cognitive potential of writing as engagement/intervention in that world. At the structural level, the architecture of *The Knight* explicitly confronts the reader with the task of negotiating a plurality of narrative planes. The fantastic strategy developed and deployed in *The Viscount* and *The Baron* is laid bare in *The Knight* and finally unravelled in the coup de théâtre that closes the novel. While *The Knight* does not provide a definitive resolution but rather opens up the field for a reconceptualization of the issues that have preoccupied Calvino during the 1950s, the work does mark the completion of a cycle. In this context, it may seem surprising that I propose to step over this convenient boundary and conclude my discussion of this phase in Calvino's trajectory as a writer with *The Watcher*, a work published in 1963, that is, well into the 1960s, and whose tone and style could hardly represent a more dramatic departure from the fictional universe of the trilogy.

There are, however, a number of excellent reasons for considering *The Watcher* a sort of coda to the trilogy, and indeed a novel whose import cannot be fully appreciated except in relation to the trilogy. The first of these reasons is that, as the dates on the last page of the work indicate (1953–63) and an interview Andrea Barbato of *L'Espresso* confirms, Calvino worked on *The Watcher* over much the same period during which he wrote the last two works of the trilogy, though a good portion of the actual writing was probably done as late as in 1962:

> The first idea for this story came to me precisely on 7 June 1953. I was at the Cottolengo for about ten minutes during the elections. No, I was not a scrutineer, I was the PCI's candidate ... And it was then that the idea for the story came to me, indeed, the general outline was already almost complete as I have written it now ... The opportunity to become scrutineer at the Cottolengo arose during the administrative elections of 1961. I spent almost two days at the Cottolengo and I was also among the scrutineers who went to collect votes in the wards ... In sum: before I was short of images, now the images I had were too strong. I had to wait for them to recede ... and I had to allow my reflections to mature more and more, as well as the meanings that radiated from them.[1]

The overlapping composition dates remind us that the works Calvino produced in the 1950s are often seen as constituting two parallel lines of development: on one side there are the fantastic narratives of *Our Ancestors* and, on the other, the (neo)realist novellas 'A Plunge in Real Estate' (1956–7) and 'Smog' (1958). Milanini (1990) groups these two works with *The Watcher* to create what he terms 'the trilogy of speculative realism' ('la trilogia del realismo speculativo'), clearly a foil to the heraldic trilogy and its speculative fantastic. While Milanini's proposal does possess a certain geometrical elegance, I believe it is more useful and rewarding to consider Calvino's trajectory in the 1950s as involving not so much two parallel developments as a single movement with the fantastic trilogy at its centre and at its edges the realist texts. Among these, *I giovani* and *The Watcher* are of strategic importance to Calvino's evolution, though they are not necessarily the most aesthetically successful. We have seen already how *I giovani* provides an ideal introduction to the thematic and aesthetic concerns that are central to *The Viscount*. I will now argue that *The Watcher* has the symmetrically obverse function in relation to *The Knight*.

It is in itself remarkable that two neo-realist attempts (vastly different in style and merit, no doubt) frame the discovery and exhaustion of Calvino's heraldic vein. In writing *I giovani*, Calvino confronted the limitations of a then triumphant neo-realist poetic, while in writing *The Watcher* he settled his accounts with the concerns and the generic solutions explored in the trilogy, the vitality of which seemed spent.

The Watcher does not pursue the search for new generic solutions, but is rather the expression of Calvino's desire to distance himself and critically assess the achievements and failures of a phase in his development as a writer and an intellectual, a phase that is now concluded. The interest of the work lies, for my purposes, primarily in the complex sedimentations that this reckoning process stirs up.

As Falcetto notes in his excellent annotations to *The Watcher*, there is ample evidence to support the assertion that in the early 1960s Calvino found himself in transition. The issue was not, as at the time of *I giovani*, how to follow up on a successful first novel, but rather how to extend the range of an established personal voice: 'After four years of narrative silence, or just about ("I perhaps don't write anymore and manage to live well nonetheless," one reads in a letter to Natalia Ginzburg ...), which followed the period of intense activity between the *Italian Folktales* and *The Non-existent Knight*, Calvino reappears in bookstores with "his most pensive story." This is what the inside cover of the first edition of *The Watcher* recites ... It is in fact a "book of question marks," which in a way does not really interrupt that silence ("In this book I only give some news about my silence").'[2]

These comments seem somewhat at odds with other declarations made by Calvino in an interview published in *Il Giorno* of 6 May 1963. In this interview, Calvino situates *The Watcher* within a much larger project: a narrative cycle about mid-century Italy that would pursue a reflexive and realist intonation. The project was intended as a polemical response to the shallow optimism of the early 1960s – the cultural counterpart of the economic boom and the advent of consumer society. 'Smog' and 'The Plunge' are cited as also belonging to this cycle, and it is in part following up on this suggestion that Milanini developed his classification. In the end, Falcetto maintains that '*The Watcher* remains essentially a *plural* text' ('*la Giornata* resta essenzialmente un testo *plurale*') (*RR*, 2: 1312), citing in support a passage from the 1963 interview: '[*The Watcher* is] at the same time a kind of reportage ... and a pamphlet ... and even a philosophical meditation ... but above all, it is the protagonist's own meditation upon himself (as a Communist intellectual), a kind of *Pilgrim's Progress* of a historicist who wants to salvage the grounds for intervening in history, as well as other kinds of grounds, barely guessed at during that day, about the secret depths of the human person.'[3]

Confronted with this plethora of authorial suggestions, one is compelled to remark that Calvino is being unusually loquacious about a book that is supposed merely to give 'some news of his silence'! Undoubtedly, as Falcetto notes, 'in the text ... one finds the sediment of a multiplicity of discursive valences' ('nel testo ... si sedimentano molteplici valenze discorsive') (*RR*, 2: 1312). But this comment begs the question: What is the nature of this sediment? How can we organize in a meaningful way the multiplicity of the text? In this way, *The Watcher* brings explicitly to the fore the issue of choosing an interpretive perspective, a key that will allow us to do more with the text than simply reconnoitre its suggestions. This is the nature of the challenge the work presents to a reader who wants to do justice to its merits.

Once situated within Calvino's trajectory (as well as within the wider historical context), the novel acquires a complexity that the author has perhaps insufficiently mastered or resolved poetically (the dialogue with the reader is laborious, at time almost painful), but which can tell us a great deal about the transition between two cultural moments. This is the route taken by more recent criticism that has rediscovered this work, with some Italian critics even considering it (mistakenly, in my opinion) Calvino's masterpiece. Between the original muted critical reception and the more recent encomia, I intend to chart a rather different course. First, I will consider *The Watcher* as less significantly related to the group of works within which Calvino wanted it to function than to the chivalric trilogy, and in particular to the issues raised by *The Knight*, that concludes the heraldic cycle. Second, I will attempt to relativize the gravity that all critics attribute to the work, which I believe is based on an insufficient appreciation for the distance between Amerigo and the narrating voice (cf. 'Jamais l'autopotrait n'a été aussi précis et aussi poussé' in Leroy 1991, 16), and which has so far prevented critics from appreciating the dark humour, at times verging on sarcasm, that lends to *The Watcher* a distinctly Calvinian quality. And finally, I will assess the significance of *The Watcher* as the connecting evolutionary link between Calvino's modern period and his subsequent postmodern production (from *Cosmicomics* onward).

The Language of Paralysis

The Watcher opens with a description of a rainy day in Turin, a city whose potential for dreariness is proverbial. Amerigo Ormea, the novel's protagonist, sets off for the polling station where he will be the PCI's scrutineer. What most strikes the reader in these first pages of the novel is the unprecedented dominance of the reflexive register, and the claustrophobic atmosphere it evokes and mimics. The 'squirrel of the pen' (in Pavese's felicitous formulation), the writer who taught us in the trilogy but also in his more realist short stories and novellas to expect narratives full of movement and adventure, the critic who just before his death intended to open his lecture series at Harvard University with a spirited defence of his lifelong commitment to 'lightness' and 'quickness' in writing, Calvino confronts us with a style that is as leaden as the landscape it describes. Amerigo's walk through the wet and deserted city streets is rendered with a detachment that says a great deal about the narrator's view of the protagonist and clearly distinguishes the passage from what might at first seem to be its antecedents. In *Marcovaldo*, for example, even the most neo-realist cityscapes are transfigured by the narrator's overt sympathy for the naive protagonist, as well as by the introduction of a wondrous element to relieve and qualify the evocation of a modern urban wasteland. As the same time, the smog in the homonymous short story, which is Calvino's most sustained previous attempt to wring a powerful literary image from a modern industrial city, has a fantastic and uncanny dimension now totally absent from the first pages of *The Watcher*.

And it only gets worse. Amerigo, we soon find out, is stationed at the Cottolengo, a venerable institution for the mentally and physically handicapped that immediately evokes the image of some vague, horrifying, misshapen form of mind-body, a vertigo where horror and repulsion mix at the boundary between categories of life forms: human, animal, vegetable. As the protagonist finds with some difficulty his way to the asylum, his meanderings are paralleled by a labourious meandering syntax: there seems to be no solution of continuity between the dreary landscape, Amerigo's prosaic consciousness, and Calvino's convoluted style. The narrative drags on in this fashion for about five pages before finally grinding to a virtual halt in a definition of the term 'communist.' Here a single sentence gradually accretes to a page and a half, as it gets entangled in a Gordian knot of digressions, qualifications, reconsiderations, as well as a number of parenthetical interjections by the narrator.

Bonura (*Invito alla lettura di Italo Calvino*) points out quite rightly that *The Watcher*'s opening smacks of provocation. Calvino is ostentatiously adopting the grimly detached authorial stance recommended by the naturalist and neo-realist poetics, which by 1963 were totally discredited. If we add to this consideration the fact that this belated defence of realism is coming from the author of a trilogy that challenged the poetic of neo-realism when it was dominant, then the provocation becomes even more blatant, as well as interesting.

And yet, we should be careful here. We should remember that *The Watcher* was written over an entire decade. Therefore, the provocation is likely to be more widely aimed, and more complex, than it might at first appear. Bonura sees Calvino's polemics as being aimed primarily at the neo-avant-garde movement, which is finally liquidating neo-realism in the early 1960s: 'These were the years of the neo-avant-garde, of its major triumphs and its attacks against the traditional novel, the novel, to be quite clear about it, which continued undaunted to propose naturalistic stories or stories about one's inner world [*intimiste*], with characters that had a well-defined psychology ... In the end, it was essentially naturalism and its techniques that were being subjected to the critical volleys of the neo-avant-garde: *The Watcher* seems a provocation.'[4]

We may well agree that Calvino is flagrantly parading a realist strategy, but there may be more to Calvino's irony than Bonura is willing to grant.[5] After all, to what extent does it make sense to consider *The Watcher* an attempt to repropose, polemically or not, aesthetic canons that Calvino had always questioned theoretically and struggled with (for the most part unsuccessfully) in his realist narratives? This question is to my mind central to the interpretation of the novel. If we take *The Watcher* to be the culmination of Calvino's long-unassuaged desire for 'the-true-realist-novel-reflecting-the-problems-of-Italian-society' (to use his own ironical description in 1980 of *I giovani*), then it is hard to escape the conclusion, shared by a majority of critics, that the work is a failure. It attempts to be a historical novel in the Lukácsian sense, but it succeeds only in being a portrait of the rather tedious contradictions of an all-too-bourgeois consciousness in communist uniform, certainly not a 'world-historical individual' (or is it?). At the very best we could say with Pautasso that 'Indeed, one has the impression of being brought face to face with the dramatic statement of a profound crisis that affects the narrative structures themselves, and of witnessing the utmost effort to overcome such a crisis. And that's not all, the narrator seems to have reached a threshold beyond which there seems to lie only the impossibility of telling; in other words, silence.'[6]

This interpretation is suggestive and certainly speaks to one aspect of the narrative, namely, the polemics against the boisterous loquacity of the neo-avant-garde. However, this view, like Bonura's, is too narrow and has a crucial weakness: it collapses without explanation or justification two distinctly different narrative voices, that of the protagonist and that of the narrator. On repeated and key occasions the latter distances itself explicitly from the former, as we shall see, inviting the reader to pay close attention to the difference between passages that reproduce Amerigo's thoughts and passages that introduce, sometimes surreptitiously, the narrator's own comments on those thoughts. In fact, through the narrator's interjections, the reader actually gains considerable distance from the protagonist's predicament, a distance from which one can see well beyond the narrow horizon of the protagonist's consciousness (just as in *The Baron* we could see beyond the limits of Biagio's ideology). The tendency to ignore this fundamental structural element and the ironic spaces that it opens is, unfortunately, widely shared, with the result that the novel is universally taken much more apocalyptically than I think is warranted.

What if, on the contrary, we took the lesson of the trilogy more seriously? What if we read in the laborious deployment of psychological realism a polemic not only against the shallow exuberance of the late neo-avant-garde but also against the complacent left-wing intelligentsia, which suddenly has to face the fragility of its commitments? My suggestion is that we should read *The Watcher* not simply and not primarily as the record of a Pascalian vertigo in the face of nature's darker labyrinth (the troubling creatures populating the Cottolengo), but rather as a grim parody of the intellectual trapped in the quicksand of an increasingly dreary rhetoric and fatuous pragmatism.

This reinterpretation of *The Watcher* moves from some interesting suggestions in Calvino's declarations about the genesis of the work. In particular, we should note the rather startling comments by the author about his actual experiences as a scrutineer in 1961:

> I spent almost two days at the Cottolengo ... As a result, I became utterly unable to write for many months: the images that I had in my eyes, of poor creatures unable to understand, speak, move, for whom the comedy of a vote by proxy through the priest or nun was staged, were so infernal that they could have inspired only an extremely violent pamphlet, a manifesto against the Christian Democrats, a series of anathemas against a party the power of which is supported by votes ... obtained in this way. In sum ... the images I now had were too strong. I had to wait for them to recede, to fade a little in my memory; and I had to allow my reflections to mature more and more, as well as the meanings that radiated from them.[7]

The biographical interest of this passage (we get here a rare glimpse at Calvino as the indignant political activist) has a hermeneutical dimension.

Calvino states that he could not work on *The Watcher* for many months as a result of his actual experience. He had to let the images simmer and mature before he could weave them into the narrative on which he had already been working for many years. Eight-year-old materials suddenly became too new, too immediate to be metabolized into narrative – an interesting dynamic that shows how for Calvino the act of writing was an intrinsic part of the ongoing effort to better grasp his experiences, that is, writing as an essentially cognitive act (and we are reminded here of the constellation Suor Teodora=Bradamante/ Calvino in *The Knight*).

In the context of *The Watcher*, it is rather surprising to see the extent to which the narrative elaboration seems to have sublimated the affective quality of the experiential material. If one reads *The Watcher* as another neo-realist attempt, no trace is left of political indignation, which seems to have been completely introjected and turned into a somewhat masochistic and certainly claustrophobic interior monologue about such abstract notions as the essence of human nature, the value of values, and so on. The protagonist of *The Watcher* displays none of the shock, anger, and frustration that characterized Calvino's own response. One would have to conclude that, on reflection, Calvino completely discounted those affects and denied their cognitive significance, preferring the dreary ratiocinations for which Amerigo becomes the vehicle. But it is hard to accept that Calvino is succumbing to the mode of denial of which Amerigo is the exemplar. Even the protagonist's name suggests a bitter irony. Amerigo vs Italo, the anti-Calvino, the type of intellectual Calvino sees as his contrary and antagonist. The other Amerigo, Vespucci, gave his name to the new continent but did not discover it, and in Italian the expression *hai scoperto l'America!* is a common sarcasm directed at people who think they have discovered something new, deep, and profound when in fact they have found something obvious.

However, if we begin to pay attention to the satirical potential of the novel, the alleged evacuation of affect appears in a rather different light. Affects have not disappeared; instead, they have been internalized, or, to use a technical term, introjected, and thus undergone a personal re-elaboration. Calvino did not want to write a political pamphlet; he wanted to grapple narratively with the experience in order to develop a better understanding of the kind of world that made those images possible, perhaps looking for ways to imagine a world in which those images would acquire a completely different meaning, would be different images. In more concrete terms, simply to use the narrative to denounce the Christian Democrats for shamelessly abusing the democratic process was easy but, cognitively, neither interesting nor useful; it would be more interesting and useful to explore the limits of that process and question the standards of humanity it presupposes. And yet, why did Calvino choose realism this time to confront the situation in a cognitively rich and rewarding way? The answer to this question is at the heart of my reading of *The Watcher* and, predictably, rather complex, which forces us to consider in more detail the context within which *The Watcher* acquires its full significance.

We should begin by noting that the realism of the text dates back to the original sketches and was never put in question by Calvino (see Falcetto's observations about the manuscript of *The Watcher* in *RR*, 2: 1315–17). However, the final draft tones down the exploration of the protagonist's psychology in favour of a more detached narrative posture. In particular, the deletion of a passage expanding on the notion of human love first introduced by Amerigo in the much-discussed chapter 12 (the episode narrates the Sunday visit of a father to his mentally disabled son), and a few similar editorial interventions mentioned in Falcetto's notes to the critical edition of *The Watcher* (*RR*, 2), have the effect of accentuating the gap between the narrator and the protagonist. Insofar as the former no longer functions as a validating conduit for the latter's reflections, the scope to question Amerigo's authoritativeness as a provider of meaning significantly increases.

We can now see more clearly that the novel started out as one of the long short stories Calvino worked on contemporaneously with the chivalric trilogy. In this sense Calvino's later indications that the novel should be situated within a cycle of narratives about mid-century Italy seem legitimate though significantly incomplete. The fact is that much water will have passed under the bridge in the ten years that it took Calvino to complete the narrative, and the neo-realistic intonation will be reoriented to accommodate a new range of polemical reverberations. The text receives the sediment of some of the most dramatic experiences in Calvino's life and works, and we should be particularly sensitive to changes in inflection that may signal a significant reshaping of the original project. After all, *The Watcher* was completed and published well after the other works within the 'mid-century Italy cycle' (five years after the publication of 'Smog' and six years after 'The Plunge,' which more closely resembles *The Watcher*). Furthermore, after the publication of *The Watcher*, Calvino never again spoke of such a cycle, which suggests that the alleged project functioned as a sort of default category for works that bore some structural similarities but, most of all, could not be easily situated within a more clearly demarcated group. The unusually complicated editorial history of 'The Plunge' and 'Smog' provides further evidence of this: 'The Plunge' was first published in a journal, then in *Racconti*, and finally in a single volume (though the abridged version kept its place in the subsequent edition of *Racconti*); 'Smog' was also first published in a journal and then in *Racconti*, then in a single volume with 'The Argentine Ant' – a work which was written between 1949 and 1952, that is, prior to *The Viscount*, and which has nothing to do with 'mid-century Italy' – and then, finally, always coupled with 'The Ant,' in the 1970 collection of short stories entitled *Difficult Loves*. All of this shows that we should not associate too closely *The Watcher* with other realist texts.

From this perspective, the manuscript evidence that psychology has been toned down in an attempt to distance the narrator from the protagonist seems to me much more significant than Calvino's attempt to organize his fictional works in neat categories that tend to conceal the vicissitudes of composition and publication. Indeed, the accentuation in the final draft of *The Watcher* of the distance between the narrator's voice and the protagonist's interior monologue makes it possible to establish a quite different lineage for this difficult work. In doing so, I am assisted by Milanini's perceptive remarks in his introduction to the second volume of *Romanzi e racconti* – remarks that complement his earlier classification:

> In the 1963 volume, there is ... an explicit meditation on the failures of uto-pian rationality. Already the second chapter underscores the involution of international communism, and laments the return of the old separation of those who govern from those who are governed. On the one hand, [the narrative] exalts the elan of nascent democracies, while, on the other, it denounces the bureaucratic necrosis affecting parties and states that had given a voice to that elan. What re-emerges, then, in pages that prove to be at times surprisingly solemn, is a series of issues that are discussed in a completely different register in works such as 'Becalmed in the Antilles,' *The Baron in the Trees* or *The Non-existent Knight*.[8]

I do not share this analysis in toto; in particular, I will argue that it is not so much the failings of utopian rationality that are at stake but rather an abdication of the utopian moment in favour of a dreary ordinary administration à la Togliatti.[9] Nonetheless, Milanini's observations do provide us with the clue for a thorough rereading of *The Watcher*. Such a rereading pays careful attention to the novel's crucial and, at times, bitter parodistic edge. The interesting polemic that *The Watcher* contains is not the obvious and, considering the circumstances, fairly muted one against the electoral practices of the DC. Rather, it is a subterranean and much more painful argument against the type of communist intellectual Togliatti's PCI helped to create. The real scandal the novel portrays is not so much the electoral fraud perpetuated by cynical politicians and unscrupulous religious orders for whom the supposedly divine end amply justifies any available earthly means. Instead, the real scandal is that, faced with such an abuse of trust, indeed an abuse of love (and it is in contrast to this violation of a fundamental human bond that chapter 11 acquires its full significance), Amerigo remains paralysed and adopts an almost decadent meditative stance, one that has nothing in common with the indignation Calvino himself experienced. Is this the point of arrival of that realpolitik which made Amerigo and many other left-wing intellectuals like him swallow the PCI's line on the invasion of Hungary or, in cultural matters, on Pasternak?[10] At the stylistic level, the polemic is not only against the formalist excesses of the neo-avant-garde but also, and, perhaps, primarily, against a languishing neo-realism that has lost the ability to speak out against the corrupt and corrupting Cold War realpolitik and neo-capitalist order. In reflecting on the meaning of the experience that *The Watcher* narrativizes, Calvino's indignation has shifted its object: the target of the satire is the left-wing intelligentsia whose impotence Calvino recognized only too well.

Hamlet and the Minotaur

I have already cited the opening of *The Watcher* and remarked how its dreary realism seems almost a provocation from an author who had few qualms about defying the then dominant neo-realist canons in his fantastic trilogy. However, we now suspect that the provocation is a double one. It strikes a blow at the voluble formalism of the neo-avant-garde (Gruppo '63), whose ascendancy a meeting in Palermo had just celebrated; it also strikes a more subtle but no less damaging blow at a poetics (i.e., the neo-realist one) that suddenly finds itself mired in a hopelessly defensive position.

Indeed, the extreme circumspection with which, in the first chapters of *The Watcher*, the narrator describes the situation and the protagonist's psychology is not only exceptionally un-Calvinian, but it is also tinged by an irony that gradually acquires a bitter edge. Would any reader (particularly when the book first came out) doubt for a moment that Amerigo is a member of the PCI? And the long first paragraph of chapter 2, in which the narrator finally reveals the 'secret,' only compounds the pervasive irony since it provides elaborate reasons for not doing exactly what is being done, that is, naming the left-wing party to which Amerigo belongs and the institution in which the polling station is located: 'Se si usano dei termini generici come "partito di sinistra," "istituto religioso," non è perché non si vogliano chiamare le cose con il loro nome, ma perché anche dichiarando d'emblé che il partito di Amerigo Ormea era il partito comunista e che il seggio elettorale era situato all'interno del famoso "Cottolengo" di Torino, il passo avanti che si fa sulla via dell'esattezza è più apparente che reale' (*RR*, 2: 7).[11]

The narrator's observations are not without merit in themselves, but they are formulated in a manner that mimics an affected and pedantic intellectual discourse. It is true that naming a party that has been demonized by the conservative press and an institution that has a prominent and dark place in the popular imagination will immediately trigger in each reader a number of associations – associations that may have little to do with the reality of either the party or the institution. Still, this is a rather obvious point, and above all it is an inevitable consequence of how natural languages function. The semantic field, or, as Eco would say, the encyclopedic entry for a word, contains all of these associations, and it will be the task of the narrative to gradually suggest to the reader which one of all those possibilities the given text actually calls to the foreground. This self-conscious lingering on the inevitable does nothing to further the process of selection, that is, the process of cognition, but rather delays it further.

Constant postponement soon emerges as the logic that guides the narrative discourse, at least in its initial configuration. The clearest example of this procedure is the notorious attempt at a definition of the term 'communist' at the end of chapter 2. The definition occupies, as I have noted, more than a page and a half of text organized in a single paragraph within which the flux of coordinate and subordinate clauses is interrupted by as many as nine parenthetical passages voicing more direct interventions by the narrating voice. This structure is so exceptional that Calvino himself felt compelled to comment on it: 'To explain what *Communist* means I had to use an extremely long paragraph in that all the meanings were articulated in a syntactical structure that maintained both logic and complexity.'[12] And once again Calvino delivers himself of a statement that is perfectly reasonable but not very helpful in getting at the root of the passage.

The most interesting characteristic of this laborious meditation on what the protagonist understands himself as saying when he uses the term 'communist' is that it disguises in an ostended syntactical complexity a string of more and more obvious commonplaces. The trite and superficial nature of these statements is revealed by the narrator's parenthetical interpolations, which constitute a running critical commentary on Amerigo's discourse. It is worth noting that in his first intervention the narrator evokes the image of a sponge: 'nel percorso che, per designazione del suo partito, egli compiva in quest'alba umida come una spugna' (*RR*, 2: 9).[13] And a sponge, with all its labyrinthine recesses, as well as its capacity to absorb and, if pressed, release the substances circulating in its immediate environment, seems to be the most appropriate metaphor for Amerigo, whose discourse sounds like a rather unimaginative recapitulation of accepted wisdom and becomes increasingly pedestrian as the period wears on. Let's examine it more closely.

The reference to himself as 'un ultimo anonimo erede del razionalismo settecentesco ... nella città che tenne Giannone in ceppi' (*RR*, 2: 9),[14] with which Amerigo's argument begins, is, in fact, not altogether trite, though the formulation displays a pedantic rhetorical emphasis (in the phrase 'città che tenne Giannone in ceppi,' note the use of the simple past 'tenne' and the inversion of the more usual word order for the last two complements) and a type of erudition that were the surest identifiers of the traditional, old-style, petty-bourgeois Italian intellectual. So much for class consciousness. In the next parenthetical passage the narrator's voice begins the process of clearly establishing its distance from Amerigo: 'allora era attraverso "le contraddizioni interne della borghesia" o "l'autocoscienza della classe in crisi" che la lotta di classe era arrivata a smuovere anche l'ex borghese Amerigo' (*RR*, 2: 10).[15] The parodistic, even satirical, edge is here undeniable. The narrator puts within quotation marks phrases that seem to be taken from a communist catechism, thus refusing to validate the ready-made answers Amerigo seems to accept. Further, and more pointedly, the narrator's description of Amerigo as an 'ex-bourgeois' cannot but sound sarcastic; the only result of the momentous historical changes is to put a little prefix in front of what Amerigo was (and in fact continues to be). Is the traditional intellectual truly changed simply by refurbishing his vocabulary with a few Marxist phrases and obtaining a PCI membership card? Amerigo remains in every respect a bourgeois, and, in fact, his consciousness becomes an exemplar of the petty-bourgeois intellectual precisely when his attempt to grasp the meaning of the word 'communist' becomes a pretext to parade erudition, rhetorical dexterity, oversubtle psychologism, and Jesuitical hair-splitting.

From this point on the structure of the argument follows a very simple rhetorical device: the oxymoron. Amerigo is attracted by 'questo gioco di cui molte regole parevano fissate e imperscrutabili e oscure ma molte si aveva il senso di partecipare a stabilire';[16] he is both a pessimist ('ogni volta che vince s'accorge d'aver perso' ['everytime it wins, realizes it has lost']) and an optimist ('crede d'aver vinto ogni volta che perde' ['which thinks it has won each time it loses']); he is a sceptic but opposes scepticism: 'perché chi parte in guerra contro lo scetticismo non può essere scettico sulla sua vittoria' ('because a man who sets out to make war on skepticism cannot be skeptical about his victory'; all these brief quotations are from the long paragraph in RR, 2: 9–11; The Watcher 8–9) – not to mention that he is still supposed to believe that 'ogni cosa che fai potrà servire' ('every little bit helps'; RR, 2: 6; The Watcher, 4). The upshot of all of this is: '[L]'aver capito finalmente quel che non ci voleva poi tanto a capire: che questo è solo un angolo dell'immenso mondo e che le cose si decidono, non diciamo altrove perché altrove è dappertutto, ma su una scala più vasta (e anche in questo c'erano ragioni di pessimismo e ragioni d'ottimismo, ma le prime venivano alla mente più spontanee)' (RR, 2: 11).[17]

This constant alternation of a term with its opposite is designed to evoke dialectical thinking and its potential dead ends. However, an attentive reading of the text – a reading mindful of the critique of the aporias of reason already carried out in The Viscount – cannot but conclude that Calvino is caricaturing dialectical thinking, and that the butt of the joke is the protagonist himself, as well as anyone else who might take the caricature for the real thing. Here, then, we begin to see that the object of the critique is not, as Milanini (1990) suggests, the dialectical movement of utopian rationality, but rather the kind of thinking that a certain type of left-wing intellectual will pass off as dialectical, when it is just a lazy stringing of oxymorons. Once we reread the passage in a satirical register, we realize that Amerigo's vacillation from one concept to its opposite is both quite funny and infuriating (in this we finally rediscover a truly Calvinian vein).

The protagonist's superficiality is underscored by another parenthetical passage, a few pages further on, when the narrator catches Amerigo in a positive mood (of brief duration): 'già Amerigo arrivava a sentirsi soddisfatto, come se tutto ormai andasse per il meglio (indipendentemente dalle oscure prospettive delle elezioni, indipendentemente dal fatto che le urne si trovavano dentro un ospizio, dove non avevano potuto né tenersi comizi, né manifesti essere affissi, né vendersi giornali)' (RR, 2: 14).[18] Hardly more than a trifle, such as the orderly setting up of the polling station, is enough for Amerigo to feel that the democratic process is functioning against the odds. The mentality that Amerigo embodies becomes clearer. For the protagonist of The Watcher, 'good form' is extremely reassuring. In fact, he will find a way to avoid backing up his fellow socialist at the polling station (the young woman wearing an orange sweater) because her objections break the purely formal solidarity that the process of setting the stage for the farcical electoral exercise has created. Once again, Amerigo emerges as a bon bourgeois, typically reluctant to disrupt social conventions, and the narrator does not let the occasion pass without a stinging satirical comment: 'E, con l'estremismo, riusciva a giustificare l'abulia e l'accidia, metteva subito a posto la sua coscienza: se di fronte a un'impostura come questa egli restava fermo e zitto, come paralizzato, era perché in queste cose o tutto o niente, o si faceva tabula rasa o si accettava' (RR, 2: 29).[19]

The narrator also makes sure that the reader understands how Amerigo's acedia is not simply a personal trait, an individual weakness of only anecdotal interest and little socio-political significance.[20] Indeed, the protagonist of The Watcher is exhibiting an attitude that is deeply rooted in, and typical of, the mentality promoted by the party itself, a mentality marked above all by a self-serving and ultimately complacent sense of superiority:

E Amerigo si chiudeva come un riccio, in una opposizione che era più vicina a uno sdegno aristocratico che alla calorosa elementare partigianeria popolare ... si buttava allora coi suoi pensieri nella direzione d'un possibilismo tanto agile da permettergli di vedere con gli occhi stessi dell'avversario le cose che dianzi l'avevano sdegnato, per poi ritornare a sperimentare con più freddezza le ragioni della sua critica e tentare un giudizio finalmente sereno. Anche qui agiva in lui – più che uno spirito di tolleranza e adesione verso il prossimo – il bisogno di sentirsi superiore, capace di pensare tutto il pensabile ... come dovrebb'essere prerogativa del vero spirito liberale.

In quegli anni in Italia il partito comunista s'era assunto, tra molti altri compiti, anche quello d'un ideale, mai esistito, partito liberale. E così il petto d'un singolo comunista poteva albergare due persone insieme: un rivoluzionario intransigente e un liberale olimpico. (*RR*, 2: 29)[21]

In the first sentence of this passage, two expressions should catch our attention. The 'sdegno aristocratico' ('aristocratic hauteur') that the narrator mentions evokes in this context a clearly identifiable political stance, as well as the prestigious intellectual who was its most ardent proponent during Mussolini's regime, namely, Benedetto Croce. In the immediate post-war period, Croce was severely criticized by progressive intellectuals precisely for his aristocratic dismissal of Fascism as an accident of history, an attitude that led him to maintain a lofty distance from the regime while discouraging any concrete attempt to restore democracy;[22] the 'culture of consolation' that Vittorini attacked in his famous 1946 editorial for *Il Politecnico* is precisely the Olympian culture Croce represented. The express reference, in the last sentence of the quotation, to an ideal liberal party and a 'liberale olimpico' ('Olympian liberal') makes the point crystal clear: Croce was a senator for the PLI until his death in 1952.[23]

Once we have identified who the Olympian liberal is, we can return to the first sentence. Following the dialectic of Amerigo's argumentation, we should now ask what the opposite of this Olympian, aristocratic stance is. The answer is clear and telling: '[la] calorosa elementare *partigianeria popolare*' ('the warm, elementary *partisanship of the people*'; emphasis added). We cannot read this without noting that for a left-wing Italian intellectual in general, and all the more so for Calvino, who fought in the Resistance, the term I have italicized is loaded: *partigiani* are those who fought against the Nazi-Fascist forces from 1943 to 1945. The reader's attention is drawn to the word 'partisanship' by the fact that in common Italian usage terms such as *faziosità* or some locution with *di parte* are more likely to be used in such a context to express the idea of partisanship. We should also note that the more common alternative terms have a negative connotation that would seem more in keeping with Amerigo's attitude. By contrast, the use of the less usual substantive stands out and manifests the narrator's judgment of Amerigo. 'Partisanship' evokes the Resistance and with it a time when the struggle for social progress was not bogged down in self-serving meditations about the merits of the opponent's position. 'Partisanship' is the attitude of the people (*popolare*), whom the petty-bourgeois intellectual (communist or not) disdains from the height of its Olympian standpoint. The rhetoric might have changed, but the basic structure of the relationship still obtains.

The compass of the narrator's condemnation of Amerigo becomes evident in the second paragraph of the citation, where the link between the position articulated by the character and the PCI's aspiration is made explicit. In the end, the protagonist of *The Watcher* emerges as a latter-day representative of the historicist tradition (in chapter 9, the narrator will explicitly speak of 'lo storicista, in Amerigo'),[24] of which the PCI claimed to be the legitimate heir – the famous De Sanctis-Croce-Gramsci line.[25]

At this point, the polemical edge finds an outlet in thinly veiled sarcasm. Not only does Amerigo choose a Crocean stance over revolutionary partisanship, but he does so by pretending to maintain the tension between the two. The surrender to the intellectual tradition of the class enemy is couched in a pseudo-dialectic that only makes the bad faith of the manoeuvre more apparent. There is no real synthesis, only contraposition; worse, the purely discursive synthesis is rhetorical and abstract, a prime example of bourgeois idealism. Through subtle stylistic accentuations, Calvino's satire infiltrates the narrative and undermines Amerigo's pomposity: 'E così il *petto* d'un singolo comunista poteva albergare due persone insieme: un rivoluzonario intransigente e un liberale olimpico' (cited earlier in note 21; emphasis added) and 'nel *petto* di un singolo militante, quel che il comunista perdeva di ricchezza interiore uniformandosi al *compatto blocco di ghisa*, il liberale ... [acquistava] in *sfaccettature* e *iridescenze*' (*RR*, 2: 29–30; emphasis added).[26]

The parameters of the narrative situation are now set, and we witness Amerigo giving free reign to his musings about such issues as 'una beatitudine esiste?' ['does blessedness exist?']; *RR*, 2: 34, which are the epitome of false consciousness, especially in a character whose sensibility is rigorously secular. Even in their context, these navel-gazing excesses sound funny at first, and ultimately more pathetic than tragic. At times, the narrator seems to efface himself and adhere to the movement of Amerigo's imagination, and yet there is a false note that prevents empathy. A surplus of repressed tension, a mannerist bad taste distances the reader: 'Portavano una monaca in barella. Era una giovane. Stranamente era una bella donna. Tutta vestita come fosse morta, il viso, colorito, appariva composto come nei quadri di chiesa ... [Amerigo] Guardò la fotografia [della monaca]; ebbe spavento. Era, con gli stessi lineamenti, un viso d'annegata al fondo d'un pozzo, che gridava con gli occhi, trascinata giù nel buio. Capì che tutto in lei era rifiuto e divincolamento: anche il giacere immobile e malata' (*RR*, 2: 35).[27] The result is that even Amerigo's more honest attempts to gain a foothold in the inconclusive plethora of meanings sound distinctly precious, pathetic, and, ultimately, risible: 'Non sapeva cosa avrebbe voluto; capiva solo quant'era distante, lui come tutti, dal vivere come va vissuto quello che cercava di vivere' (*RR*, 2: 35).[28]

Then, as Amerigo seems to reach a new low of pusillanimity when he resorts to another string of pretentious commonplaces (this time about Hegel) to justify his non-relationship with Lia, suddenly the narrative administers a shock: Lia is pregnant. Amerigo's response is typical – he plunges once again into ratiocinations: 'Cosa poteva esser cambiato in lei? Poca cosa: qualcosa che ancora non era e che quindi si poteva ricacciare nel nulla (da che punto in poi un essere è davvero un essere?), una potenzialità biologica, cieca (da che punto un essere umano è umano?) un qualcosa che solo una deliberata volontà di farlo essere umano poteva far entrare tra le presenze umane' (*RR*, 2: 58–9).[29] What is shocking about the attitude displayed in the passage is not the rather blatant reference to abortion (which in 1963 Italy was not only illegal but still pretty much a taboo subject, no less within the PCI than the DC), but the callous and vulgar egotism that Amerigo voices (note the impersonal phrase 'si poteva ricacciare nel nulla' ['could be thrust back into nothingness'], which erases all the parties involved). This egotism is disguised once again in a reasoning that is Jesuitical in the extreme, as well as profoundly abstract and bourgeois. Amerigo is looking for a definition of essence while totally ignoring even the most basic concrete aspects of the situation: How does Lia feel about becoming a mother? How would being a father change his life? Are they both ready to make the changes necessary to raise a human being? What are their responsibilities to each other and to the community? These are the material realities that a Marxist analysis would thematize explicitly. Once again, and in the most blatant manner yet, the narrative demonstrates that being a communist has had no perceptible impact on Amerigo's approach to reality. The questions he asks are the same that would be raised by an old-fashioned liberal or, for that matter, a Catholic, the difference being that Amerigo would then be able to dispose of the issue by appealing to Church doctrine or tradition.

In the chapter that immediately follows the revelation about Lia, the issue of parenthood is confronted again. This is the most famous episode of *The Watcher*. The narrative brings us to a ward populated by seriously deformed, fish-like sentient beings whom one would hesitate to call human; at the heart of the labyrinth, our diminished and middle-aged Hamlet is finally facing the boundary between man, beast, and plant. In this disenchanted world, sacred horror turns into vertigo; and, paradoxically, Amerigo cannot retreat into a sense of superiority. The narrative registers the struggle to address the real: 'Il grido acuto proveniva da una minuscola faccia rossa, tutta occhi e bocca aperta in un fermo riso, d'un ragazzo a letto, in camicia bianca, seduto, ossia che spuntava col busto dall'imboccatura del letto come una pianta viene su da un vaso, come un gambo di pianta che finiva (non c'era segno di braccia) in quella testa come un pesce, e questo ragazzo-pianta-pesce' (*RR*, 2: 61).[30]

When the real finally breaks through the net of Amerigo's false consciousness, we find ourselves in a surreal environment. Critics have been too quick to associate this episode with a vision of hell, when in fact the atmosphere evoked is more like that of a strange and grotesque fable (Calvino's Gothic vein, perceptively identified by Cecchi in 1951, makes a sudden appearance in this dreary realist landscape). There may be suffering, but there is no guilt and no punishment here, unless one projects onto the scene a more-or-less explicitly religious perspective. The dominant colour is a blinding white, painful but not infernal.

Among these strange beings is a father visiting his mentally disabled son. The image of the man and the boy is all tension and struggle: 'Il figlio era lungo di membra e di faccia, peloso in viso e attonito, forse mezzo impedito da una paralisi. Il padre era un campagnolo vestito anche lui a festa, e in qualche modo, specie nella lunghezza del viso e delle mani, assomigliava al figlio. Non negli occhi: il figlio aveva l'occhio animale e disarmato, mentre quello del padre era socchiuso e sospettoso, come nei vecchi agricoltori. Erano voltati di sbieco, sulle loro seggiole ai due lati del letto, in modo da guardarsi fissi in viso' (*RR*, 2: 63).[31] There is no Olympian peace here. Before them, the protagonist's discursive effluvium is finally checked and disciplined into a few epigrammatic comments: 'Ecco, pensò Amerigo, quei due, così come sono, sono reciprocamente necessari. E pensò: ecco, questo modo d'essere è l'amore. E poi: l'umano arriva dove arriva l'amore; non ha confini se non quelli che gli diamo' (*RR*, 2: 69).[32]

What is most striking about these formulations is not their profundity (though not banal, the statements are not strikingly original), but rather the respectful restraint Amerigo exhibits here for the first time. For once, the protagonist does not fly into Byzantine discursive elaborations but seems to pay attention to what he is witnessing. The father and the son do not function as a mere pretext for some self-serving reflection, rather, their difference is allowed to come through and mark the observing consciousness. The staccato style to which the narrator resorts further underlines the caesura this passage constitutes.

After this brief epiphany, the narrative unfolds rapidly, as if the thread of the discursive cocoon had at long last been found. Amerigo's acedia has receded; he no longer hesitates to intervene in order to prevent abuses that he can see, and he no longer needs to define these abuses in abstract terms:

> Dal momento in cui s'era *sentito meno estraneo a quegli infelici*, anche il rigore della sua mansione politica gli era divenuto meno estraneo. Si sarebbe detto che in quella prima corsia la ragnatela delle contraddizioni oggettive che lo teneva avviluppato in una specie di rassegnazione al peggio si fosse rotta, e adesso si sentiva lucido, come se ormai tutto gli fosse chiaro, e comprendesse cosa si doveva esigere dalla società e cosa invece non era dalla società che si poteva esigere, ma bisognava arrivarci di persona, se no niente.
>
> Si sa come sono quei momenti in cui pare d'aver capito tutto: magari un momento dopo si cerca di definire quel che si è capito e tutto scappa. (*RR*, 2: 70; emphasis added)[33]

Amerigo has (re)discovered the social horizon, the bond of human solidarity that confers meaning on, and assures concrete purchase to, human praxis, political or otherwise. From this point of departure, Amerigo can begin to build a new understanding of his relationship with Lia. The task, however, will not be easy. Amerigo is not suddenly redeemed, a new man after the epiphanic moment. His brief insight and new resolve are still mired in long-established patterns of thought. The interminable paragraph that follows the passage I have cited above demonstrates that a self-indulgent sensibility is bound to re-emerge and cannot be fought off simply by plunging into an equally self-indulgent activism (Amerigo's call to Lia ends in failure). At the

end of the novel, a lingering either/or mentality still prevents the protagonist of *The Watcher* from perceiving the difference between a spuri-
ous complexity that serves as an alibi to inertia, and the authentic and
irreducible complexity of the real, which calls for a delicate and difficult balance of thoughtfulness and determination. The parody softens
but does not disappear as Amerigo's forecasts about the result and
meaning of the elections are explicitly contradicted by the narrator.
And in the final image, Amerigo is still at the window, observing a
strangely idyllic scene in which he has no part. The most that can be
said is that Amerigo has caught a glimpse of a distant horizon, of possibilities that are yet to be explored.

Exorcizing the Labyrinth's Lure

Considering Amerigo's trajectory from the vantage point provided by
the trilogy, *The Watcher* emerges as a sort of recapitulation of the main
issues raised by the previous novels: the crisis of reason (*The Viscount*);
the difficulty of dialectically relating active participation in, and reflective estrangement from, social processes (*The Baron*); and the constant
effort to use narrative to comprehend the human bond of solidarity,
without which the individual ceases to be a human subject in the only
meaningful sense of the word, that is, as the site of an ethico-political
tension (*The Knight*). The questions that I would like to ask now are
two: First, where does the need to recapitulate (and recapitulate in this
particular manner) come from? Second, what does this recapitulation
add to our understanding of Calvino's contribution as a witness of,
and participant in, the cultural moment that the trilogy, as I have
argued, addresses?

    The answer to the first question is easily given. Calvino's long
silence – he did not publish a major work of fiction between 1959 and
1963 – largely coincides with a widely acknowledged historical
caesura, the nature of which I have canvassed at some length in chapter 1. It was not only Calvino individually but also the country as a
whole that was going through a period of transition.

    It is quite tempting to see an analogy between Amerigo's exhausting
intellectual musings and the endless negotiations that would at long
last give birth at the end of 1963 to the centre-left coalition led by the
DC's left-leaning leader Moro. And there is a sense in which the analogy is perfectly legitimate. Calvino was responding to the socio-
cultural atmosphere that characterized the early 1960s in Italy. This

atmosphere was dominated by a growing awareness of the tensions created by Italy's economic boom. The massive capitalist development which propelled Italy into the select club of the most highly industrialized Western nations had undoubtedly brought prosperity to an increasing number of people, but had also aggravated (sometimes created) vast social imbalances that, if not corrected or managed in some way, might well lead to social conflict on an unprecedented scale, and even social chaos. It was this realization that drove the advocates of planning, of a greater and more organic state intervention to guide economic development. This Keynesian approach represented a significant departure not only from the rigid liberist economics espoused by Einaudi, De Gasperi's Minister of Finance in the immediate post-war years, but also from the chaotic expansion of the state-run sector of the economy that took place under Fanfani's leadership during the second half of the 1950s.

This progressive, interventionist line was struggling against two opposite forces. First, the traditional left, increasingly on the defensive, saw in the contradictions of the new capitalist expansion a sign of impending catastrophe, and rejected as a mystification any attempt to see development as also providing opportunities for a greater democratization of Italian society. Second, a new shallow self-satisfaction with the material benefits of the economic boom, and with the American way of life it promised, was becoming pervasive among the expanding middle class.

The need for a thoughtful, even sober, recapitulation of the experiences of the 1950s could have been the best antidote against the ecstatic consumerism that would pervade the country until the mid-1960s, when the *angst* characteristic of the bourgeois 'morning after' set in. This was the most immediately topical subject to which Calvino explicitly referred when he stated that *The Watcher* was 'a polemics against the odd belle époque we are living' ('in polemica con la strana belle époque che stiamo vivendo'; qtd. in *RR*, 2: 1312). However, we must not forget that Calvino's primary interlocutors were not only the younger intellectuals who were translating this new optimism into an anti-dialectical and neo-positivist thinking (cf. Cases 1958) much in evidence within the neo-avant-garde. Calvino was also and, as I have argued, primarily addressing those leftist intellectuals who were not yet willing to jump on the new bandwagon. For these, the most crucial issue was not to denounce a vulgar nouveau riche optimism (though this is also a useful task), but rather to grasp why and how an intellectual left that seemed to have gained the upper hand since 1945 was suddenly feeling overtaken by events and defenceless in the face of the neo-capitalist reshaping of cultural processes.

How did Calvino negotiate these new impulses, and in particular the polar opposites of an increasingly optimistic neo-avant-garde that was positioning itself to manage the culture industry and a traditional left that seemed unable to constructively address the conjuncture? It should be noted that Calvino's discourse always valued a type of optimism: not the confident assurance of an impending collapse of capitalism, which was one of the elements of the neo-realist poetics, but that passion for adventure and curiosity about the world of which the trilogy is a memorable expression. Was Calvino changing his tune in *The Watcher*?

It would not be hard to find a justification for such a change. The dominant discourse had changed. One of the main functions of the trilogy had been to expose the ponderous commonplaces of literary neo-realism and open new spaces for an imaginative meditation on the social and progressive role of the intellectual. Now the neo-avant-garde (or at least one of the main currents within it) was trying to sweep away the whole notion of a politically committed intellectual in favour of free linguistic experimentation. Calvino might well have wanted to remind his interlocutors that he had criticized neo-realism not for its aims but for its failure to achieve them; the project of using literature to reach social reality remained valid. As the explicit polemic with Angelo Guglielmi (a leading member of Gruppo '63) will make clear, Calvino was eager to distance himself from a movement toward which, at least for the moment, he had reservations no less serious than, though obviously different from, the ones he had had a decade earlier toward neo-realism.

However, we should also remember that 'The Labyrinth,' the essay by Calvino that occasioned the debate with Guglielmi, also contained a sharp polemic against what I will term the apocalyptic position (along the line of Adorno and Horkheimer's *Dialectic of Enlightenment*), which was at the opposite extreme of the views embodied by neo-avant-garde critics such as Guglielmi and Renato Barilli. One of the earliest and most coherent interpreters of this standpoint, which was further splintering the once relatively compact left-wing intelligentsia, was Franco Fortini. In his important essay 'Clever as Doves,' the main target of the attack was Vittorini's neo-positivism, but Fortini's article ultimately rejoined a distinctly Adornian horizon that condemned a priori as shallow and self-serving any attempt to find something progressive and potentially valuable in the dramatic advance of neo-capitalism.[34] A brief citation will suffice to give a sense of Fortini's intent and tone: 'Today, every literary expression that portrays enslavement in such a way as to make immediately possible the illusion of freedom serves an illusory freedom ... Today, I believe it is up to the coherent Marxist and socialist to mock the noble anguish with which capitalist reformism tries to hide its substantial optimism, the persuasion of having succeeded in assuring progress and democracy to our country.'[35] In his rejoinder, Calvino did not mince words either: 'To those who ask themselves every instant: "But am I not playing capitalism's game?" I prefer those who tackle all the problems of transforming the world with the confidence that what is best serves the best. After all, in this same number the text by Fortini is a document of how a revolutionary tension, if sustained only by a passion for theory and not for practical human action (and for the things that are the instruments and products of that action), turns out to be a choice of nothing.'[36]

In the final analysis, therefore, Calvino's position was considerably nuanced: polemics against the shallow optimism of a middle class gaining access to levels of consumption until then reserved for a small élite, polemics against that element within the neo-avant-garde movement that seemed to surrender too easily to the seductions of the neo-capitalist cultural supermarket, and polemics against the asceticism of those who would reject everything neo-capitalism was bringing about as at best a false hope and at worse a deadly trap. But what, then, did Calvino propose?

In the passage from 'The Labyrinth' that I have quoted above, Calvino makes it clear that he does not have a ready-made grand theory. Rather, he opts for a day-to-day struggle to better grasp the transformations brought about by the new conjuncture. This better understanding can then be mobilized to exploit the opportunities for progressive change that the socio-economic transformations may offer, thus keeping alive the ethico-political commitment to a more just social order. Is this position consistent with my analysis of *The Watcher*? Better still, does *The Watcher* push Calvino's analysis further, thus vindicating the validity of the lesson about the cognitive value of narrative learned in *The Baron* and *The Knight*?

We have already seen that there is an obvious connection between Calvino's critique of the happy consumerism Italian society was experiencing in the early 1960s and the choice to write a novel about a sombre, uneventful, dreary election day in a forbidding institution. A reading of *The Watcher* that understands the text merely as a polemical return to a (neo)realist poetics would point out that in addition to ridiculing the new bourgeoisie's desire for carefree entertainment (these are the golden years of Italian *canzonette* – easy-on-the-ear, sugary love songs), Calvino's polemic has a literary target, namely, those within the neo-avant-garde movement who seek to sunder the link between aesthetic production and political action. This is undoubtedly true, as far as it goes, but it doesn't go far enough. Specifically, one of the difficulties with such an analysis is that, once we go beyond the gesture of choosing a topic and a formal apparatus that the new generation of writers and critics considered hopelessly outmoded, there is very little in *The Watcher* to support the view that the narrative contains a sustained engagement with the neo-avant-garde's aesthetics. To put it more bluntly, Calvino's criticism of the linguistic experimentations propounded by the intellectuals of the neo-avant-garde is of a negative character: rather than actually engage in a dialogue with (or diatribe against) the new literary theories, he simply ignores them.

Once we go beyond the basic realistic/non-realistic divide, the text has more affinities with the novelistic experiments of a Svevo (but without Svevo's humour and insight into the complexities of bourgeois psychology) or a Gadda (but without Gadda's linguistic range and fierce pessimism about human nature) than with the canons of post-war neo-realism. This has a great deal to do with the uneasiness that even favourable critics have exhibited toward the work; judged by their standards of realism, *The Watcher* comes up short and looks like a failed effort (with the exception of a few passages) to move beyond the confines of another little bourgeois drama with a political backdrop.

However, as soon as we recognize the keen edge of parody that constantly undercuts even the most apparently solemn passages, we realize that Calvino's ultimate target was a type of left-wing 1950s intellectual who ought to have been the conscience of a frivolous middle-class and the nemesis of the neo-avant-garde dandies, but who turned out to be the precursor of both.

The more interesting interaction between *The Watcher* and 'The Labyrinth' now becomes clear. The essay contains a pointed reply to Fortini, who had rejected any compromise with the economic and social reality brought about by post-war capitalism. This extremist position is directly addressed also in *The Watcher* and criticized when Amerigo justifies his reluctance to intervene to prevent electoral fraud 'perché in queste cose o tutto o niente, o si faceva tabula rasa of si accettava' ('because in such situations it was all or nothing, either you accepted them or else: tabula rasa'; *RR*, 2: 29; *The Watcher*, 25). Yet, we should be careful here. Amerigo is not the champion of a negative dialectic and his constant wavering has nothing to share, ultimately, with the iron discipline proposed by someone like Fortini. Calvino's argument is not that nihilism yields an Amerigo, but, and much more subtly, that the Fortinian position plays into the hand of the Amerigos. In other words, this type of nihilism can become the justification for the increasingly unprincipled pragmatism that *The Watcher* argues is the real problem for leftist intellectuals faced with the transformations of neo-capitalism.[37]

Then, suddenly, we realize that the butt of the satire is none other than Calvino himself (and in this context the nexus between 'Amerigo' and 'Italo' re-emerges). Amerigo is not the 'other' but rather the 'enemy within' (only in this sense one can legitimately talk of autobiographical elements). The satire is also a painful exorcism. It is here that much of the difficulty of *The Watcher* lies. The sharp edge of the narrative is turned against itself: Amerigo's stance is not merely described – it is performed in a procedure strongly reminiscent of *The Knight*. But while in the last work of the trilogy the fantastic register allowed Calvino to perform Agilulfo's hollowness through a seductive magical object (the empty armour), in *The Watcher* the author has no such option and can only perform Amerigo's dreary subjectivity by presenting it in all its dreariness. The realistic register does not allow any easy escape. Discipline and rigour are the fundamental characteristics of Calvino's realistic intonation. They also constitute the most effective antidote to Amerigo's perversion of reason and affect, just as the power of the fantastic was the most effective antidote to the excess of rigour and discipline that plagued *The Knight*.

In the final analysis, *The Watcher* is sustained by a determination to examine and finally exorcise the type of intellectual that Calvino had tried to be: a member of the PCI, a fair-minded observer and participant in the political and cultural fray of the preceding fifteen years. Amerigo represents the left-wing intelligentsia to which Calvino saw himself as belonging and which is now splintering under the pressures of neo-capitalism. Amerigo is the intellectual who idealizes the Resistance as a turning point in the history of the country and in his own personal history, and who sees his conversion to communism (the explication of which occupies directly and indirectly so much of the text) as the almost natural issue of a moral and intellectual tradition rooted in the Enlightenment and its notion of human progress. For this intellectual, the commitment to socialism is first and foremost an ethical response in the face of injustice rather than a well-defined political project grounded in an analysis of the capitalist system, within which, one should add, this intellectual is (at least for the moment) relatively well taken care of (Amerigo is distinctly middle class). But this ethical élan is wearing thin.

While the novel is set in 1953, Amerigo's comments make it quite clear that the intellectual climate is post-1956, as evidenced by references to 'l'ombra grigia dello Stato burocratico' ('the gray shadow of the bureaucratic State') and 'l'antica separazione tra amministratori e amministrati' ('the old gap between the managers and the managed'; *RR*, 2: 16; *The Watcher*, 13), and the following remarks: 'Non viene per ogni organismo il momento in cui subentra la normale amministrazione, il tran-tran? (Anche per il comunismo – non poteva non domandarsi Amerigo – anche per il comunismo sarebbe avvenuto? e stava già avvenendo?)' (*RR*, 2: 17).[38] The affinity between these statements and the concerns expressed more directly and flippantly in the 1957 short story 'Becalmed in the Antilles' (a thinly veiled satirical allegory of Togliatti's immobilism vis-à-vis the Soviet Union) is obvious. Even clearer, however, is the fact that Amerigo addresses these concerns in a manner that reflects the defensive wait-and-see approach Calvino satirized in the earlier narrative. Reflecting on any problem becomes in Amerigo a further ground for an intellectual 'spinning of the wheels,' the effect of which is inaction. Borrowing a couple of metaphors from the novel itself, I will suggest that Amerigo's consciousness possesses the strange swamp-like ability to swallow up any object and make it an integral part of its accumulated inertia. And this inertia is the only resistance that Amerigo is able to oppose to the dynamism of neo-capitalist development.

It is through the protagonist's characterization that Calvino delivers his critique. He is warning the Italian intelligentsia that the PCI has fostered the intellectual complacency of which Amerigo is the exemplar. Indeed, the party leveraged such a complacency to weather the crisis of 1956. It achieved this by refusing to budge substantially from its socio-political analysis of the conjuncture since the 1940s, thus forcing party intellectuals to stand firm on increasingly untenable positions. It is only in the early 1960s that a significant *aggiornamento* got under way.[39] In cultural terms, the insistence on realism (and on a realism rigidly defined in ideological terms, as the 1958 debate on Pasternak demonstrates), with its corollary refusal to entertain a more nuanced approach to the relation between the text and the world, laid the foundations for a reaction such as that of the Gruppo '63. However, when it came to recruiting intellectuals in the name of peace or to denouncing U.S. imperialism, the party struck an ecumenical tone (the 'we are the real heirs of the liberal tradition' type of rhetoric) that allowed intellectuals to believe that the more rigid positions were in fact dictated by pragmatic and tactical considerations.

This constant fluctuation between what had to be said because it was politically opportune or even necessary, and what could be thought and spoken about privately, fostered a confusion of which Amerigo provides an excellent picture. Togliatti's tacticism had a cost, and Calvino points to the type of consciousness that it tended to foster. The habit of quiet submission to party discipline resulted in a lack of personal commitment and initiative, which entailed a surrender, on the one hand, to ordinary administration and, on the other, to the inscrutable complexity of the modern world: 'la rivoluzione s'era fatta disciplina, preparazione a dirigere, trattative da potenza a potenza anche dove non si aveva il potere (attraeva dunque anche Amerigo questo gioco di cui molte regole parevano fissate e imperscrutabili e oscure ma molte si aveva il senso di partecipare a stabilirle)' (*RR*, 2: 10).[40] The sharp irony of such phrases as 'trattative da potenza a potenza anche dove non si aveva il potere' ('bargaining among powers even where the party wasn't in power') – this reminds one of the notoriously oxymoronic bent of Italian political discourse, e.g., Moro's notorious 'parallel convergences' – must be noted, particularly since the historical referent was still 'warm': the 1956 Soviet invasion of Hungary and the arguments the PCI had provided to support it. And as the sociopolitical situation became increasingly complex and capitalism demonstrated a vitality that belied the optimistic prophecies about its imminent collapse, 'inscrutability' was bound to increase. How long would it take before the type of intellectual Amerigo portrayed would quietly and rather comfortably settle down in the mesmerizing neocapitalist labyrinth?

For the moment, however, Amerigo does not quite succumb to the lure of the labyrinth. In the end, he seems to regain his footing somewhat, though we are left with the suggestion that the path ahead is long and hard. One wonders why, finally, *The Watcher* does not pass sterner judgment on Amerigo. Why is the sharpness of the parody ultimately attenuated, though by no means forgotten (as we have seen, the narrator comes right out and explicitly denies the validity of certain of Amerigo's final assertions)? What surfaces again here is Calvino's commitment to avoiding the easy answer. Amerigo represents for Calvino a type that needs to be exposed and fought against precisely because it is too close for comfort. Amerigo is a caricature, a caricature that exorcises a stance that is not without its seductiveness. To reduce each problem to an intellectual challenge, to reduce writing to the articulation of such challenge and, possibly, of its equally intellectual (i.e., in this context, abstract) solution, these are temptations that Calvino recognizes to be part of his cultural heritage, a heritage that commitment failed to confront fully, and against which he is aware of constantly having to struggle not only as an individual but as a member of the Italian intelligentsia. *The Watcher* is also an attempt to remind himself and his interlocutors of this reality.

The link between *The Watcher* and *The Knight* now becomes apparent. As in the case of *The Watcher*, one of key functions of the last work of the trilogy was to accomplish an exorcism. Through Suor Teodora= Bradamante, Calvino works through the seductions of Agilulfo, the perfectly efficient organization man who has no being beyond the dictates of the ideology that guides him. Agilulfo is all action, pure purposiveness, an optimal efficiency of means to achieve an unquestioned and unquestionable end. This ideal of total control is the siren song that the narrator (and, with him, the writer) has to confront and overcome. One of the marvels of *The Knight* is that Calvino succeeds in presenting the hollowness and fundamental inhumanity of this ideal without sacrificing any of its appeal.

In *The Watcher*, it is the contrary position to the one presented by Agilulfo that has to be exorcised. Amerigo is all speculation and very little action, at least, for most of the book. There is in fact a telling irony in the relation between his name (that of a famous explorer who gave his name to a new continent) and the title Amerigo has in the novel (which is also part of the novel's title): 'scrutatore,' a term that, apart from its technical meaning of 'scrutineer,' refers to the act of seeing in its most speculative sense.[41]

In sum, Amerigo is an armchair explorer. Yet, lest we jump to conclusions too quickly, let us not forget that it is to this type of exploration that any writer necessarily invites us. And therein indeed lies the seduction, the temptation to forget the world, as it were, and explore imaginary landscapes without disagreeable intrusions from actual experience. The fact that this position is presented in a realistic narrative provides a comment on how imaginary any fictional narrative, whether realistic or not, necessarily is given its nature as a linguistic construct, and this adds a new dimension to the reflections on the nature of writing that we encountered at the end of *The Baron* and *The Viscount*. In this context, however, what also emerges is a comment about how imaginary (in the negative sense of reductive and even consolatory) so-called realistic narratives can be, particularly when realism ceases to be an authentic interest in the real and becomes just another literary canon (i.e., a mere form).

The narrator's interventions and the constant distancing of the reader from the rather consolatory web of words the protagonist spins (or, to be more accurate, we should say the protagonist *is*) turn *The Watcher* as a whole into anything but a consolatory work. On the contrary, the novel contains a complex and painstaking exfoliation of a mode of thinking and being that turns the tools of understanding against themselves and cognition itself. When reflection becomes a clever way to keep reality at bay and narrative a means to inertia, then the intellectual ceases to be a sign of contradiction and can function only as an administrator of the culture industry. Calvino finally rescues Amerigo from this fate, but the counterproject is not an easy one to define. It is not, obviously, Agilulfo – a return to a hollow militantism. Rather, it is a confrontation with the complexity of the real, without self-indulgence, keeping a firm hold on the intuition of human solidarity, which ultimately grounds, above and beyond Enlightenment rationality, the ethico-political impulse to know the world and act in it. In this way *The Watcher* rejoins 'The Labyrinth' and makes clear that Calvino remains, at least at the end of this phase in his trajectory, firmly anchored in what has been called the emancipatory project of modernity.

Conclusion: Literature as an Ethical Project

In 1962, Calvino met Esther Judith Singer. Two years later they married. Their daughter, Abigail, was born in 1965, and in 1967 the whole family moved to Paris, where Italo and Esther had first met. Calvino's life had taken a new turn. Artistically, Calvino abandoned the novel and the realist mode of the *The Watcher*. The collection of science fiction short stories he published under the title *Cosmicomics* in 1965 overbrimmed with vitality and cleverness, inaugurating a phase that would bring Calvino international acclaim as one of the leading representatives (with Borges, Perec, and Pynchon, among others) of a transnational current of postmodern writing. At first sight, it would seem that the experiences of the 1950s had been left definitively behind. This is the position implicitly taken by many critics, though when the issue is directly confronted most recognize that a deeper continuity underpins the surface discontinuity in Calvino's opus. Indeed, a sensitive reading of Calvino's later works reveals that the questions raised and left unanswered by his early novels and stories continued to trouble the author and inform his literary production. Unfortunately, this argument cannot be developed here – it would require a book of its own, and one that would significantly enrich the current assessment of Calvino's achievement. However, more important for our present purposes is to take a step back from the analysis of the works we have examined and reflect upon the overall trajectory they disclose. What, ultimately, is the legacy of the 1950s for Calvino? What horizon does it open for future developments? The answer to these questions will require us to think more deeply about the larger significance of Calvino's experiences and broach some larger theoretical issues about the nature of literature that so far have remained in the background.

What Is Literature Good For?

One of the most important essays written by Calvino in the 1970s ends with the following paragraph:

> Now, right at the end of my talk, it occurs to me that I have been speaking throughout of 'levels of reality,' whereas the topic of this conference reads 'The Levels of Reality.' Perhaps the fundamental point of my talk is exactly this: literature does not recognize Reality as such but only *levels*. Whether there is such a thing as Reality, of which the various levels are only partial aspects, or whether there are only the levels, is something that literature cannot decide. Literature recognizes the *reality of the levels*, and this is a reality (or 'Reality') that it knows all the better, perhaps, for not having come to understand it by other cognitive processes. And that is already a great deal. (*The Uses of Literature*, 120–1)

In many ways this whole study traces the emergence and gradual refinement of the thesis this passage develops in a typically self-deprecating Calvinian style.

Literature is what allows us to understand and explore the reality of the layers that make up our experience. In *I giovani*, the work in which the neo-realist poetic is most strenuously pursued, Calvino still seemed to think that there was one fundamental layer from which all the others derived a precise position and meaning. This layer was social reality, understood in Marxist terms as the place where the individual overcomes alienation and recovers a sense of wholeness through engagement in social praxis. Harmony within oneself is the mirror of solidarity with other human beings, with whom one shares the struggle to live freely, creatively, meaningfully. But this dream of cohesion, brotherhood, and clarity failed miserably in *I giovani*, leading Calvino to confront in *The Viscount* a thoroughly modern predicament: the divided self. The levels begin to multiply: there are fissures, and soon there will be diversity, wherever one looks. Enlightenment reason splits its objects in the very attempt to grasp their function and significance. When the world appears increasingly under the aspect of multiplicity, the dialectical synthesis becomes elusive.

Energized by the success of *The Viscount* and still looking for a solution to fragmentation, Calvino explores the power of narrative: perhaps storytelling can reconstruct a world, bring coherence to multiplicity without eliminating diversity. That is the hypothesis of *The Baron*, a hypothesis that seems on the verge of being successfully worked out as we witness the ability of storytelling to speak a polyphony of voices (Biagio, Cosimo, Viola), voices that get through in spite of the narrator's own limitations. However, this solution is too abstract and in the end unsatisfactory. At the conclusion of *The Baron*, we realize with Calvino that there is one more, crucial layer we have not yet confronted: the level of writing itself, the dynamic interrelation between the text and the narrator, between the author and the reader, between the fictitious and the real. *The Knight* places this problematic at the centre of the narrative. The writer becomes explicitly a character in a text that operates at many levels, all of which are meaningfully related to each other. Still, the synthesis of Calvino/Suor Teodora=Bradamante appears ultimately as a discursive sleight of hand. It convinces only in the fantastic realm of the trilogy and in fact underscores the distance between the fiction and a social reality that seems irredeemably fragmented.

The Watcher attempts to impart a new rigour and lucidity to the lessons of the trilogy, with the result that the configuration Calvino presents in his 1978 speech, cited above, finally emerges. At first, Amerigo gets lost in the multiplicity of levels, and even tries to enjoy the maze. But in the end he understands that his function is to bear witness to multiplicity more than to resolve it in some abstract way. Amerigo discovers the function of literature. Not the only one, but that which constitutes literature's unique contribution, its most authentic cognitive compass. After the heady days of neo-realism, this can only seem a humble, diminished role. Amerigo has no good news to bring to the proletariat or to any other social class. He cannot even be sure himself about the choices he has made; rather, he has to confront the fact that the struggle to be human is never over and that justice, solidarity, and all that we value as human beings must be understood better and fought for day by day. The key function of literature, then, is to remind us of this perpetual, inalienable task. And here is where the other side of the equation begins to emerge.

What Calvino does not explicitly mention in his 1978 speech is what can sustain the project he outlines for literature. Note how his argument is couched in impersonal terms. No human subject appears in the passage. Literature is personalized and becomes itself the agent of knowledge while the human horizon is barely adumbrated by the reflexive/impersonal *si* ('s'arrivi a conoscerla'). Why such precautions?

In the 1960s and 1970s, Calvino encountered, and for a while fell under the spell of, Parisian semoiticians and semiologists whose battle cry was the death of the subject/author. One of the results of this encounter was an accentuation of the playful and cerebral elements in Calvino's style, and the attenuation of the overt reflection on the social and political role of the intellectual – the central theme, as we have seen, in the group of works we have examined. However, the crucial point sometimes missed by postmodern readings of Calvino's work (readings that, not surprisingly, tend to steer clear of the trilogy and *The Watcher*) is this: what I have termed Calvino's ethico-political tension remains fundamental to the author's style.

Why is it important to understand the 'reality of the levels'? Why is it important to grasp what literature can and cannot do? Why is it important to defend the value of literature? These questions continue to underpin Calvino's discourse in the 1970s and 1980s, and the answers they beg bring us irresistibly back to the trilogy of essays in which Calvino first defined his poetics: 'The Lion,' 'The Sea,' and 'The Labyrinth.' Behind and beyond the brilliant semiotic games of works such as *Invisible Cities* and *If on a Winter's Night a Traveller*, or even *The Castle of Crossed Destinies*, the question of whom one writes for and why continues to provide the engine that propels the narrative above the level of mere amusement. This layer, which lies beneath the constant attention to the most topical and fashionable theoretical debates about literature, can be reached and mined for the contribution it makes to the enduring value of Calvino's opus only in the light of the works we have discussed. Only then does the subterranean but persistent utopian dimension of Calvino's fiction becomes apparent.

Over the years, as the political skies darkened – the 1970s are sometimes termed the 'years of lead' – Calvino would become more and more reluctant to articulate explicitly the possibilities that the simultaneous coexistence of multiple levels of reality creates – possibilities for new beginnings, for creative challenges to the ideological regimes that perpetuate the existing order of things. The focus would be on the fact that literature cannot bring the good news to the world (as Vittorini sometimes seemed to think), and yet Calvino would always come back to the notion that literature cannot forget history and its own conditions of production within a particular social and political situtation. Literature can and, implicitly, must take stock of the complexity of the real so that we can continue our struggle to *become human*. That is the legacy of the 1950s, a legacy Calvino will never reject.

Calvino and the Parable of Contemporaneity

One of the goals of this study has been to renew interest in the early works of Calvino as a means to restore a more balanced view of his achievement. By returning to his formative years as an intellectual, we discover how deeply Calvino was marked by the 1950s and the profoundly modern concerns that pervaded the Italian cultural scene during that decade. As a writer, he must be understood as belonging to the cerebral and moralist tradition of European novelists, of which Stendhal is the nineteenth-century master. This is also one of the important points of contact between Calvino and a writer such as Thomas Pynchon, who belongs to a very different literary tradition and has an almost antithetical style and yet whose preoccupations are remarkably elucidated by a comparison with Calvino's. And this leads me to the final point I would like to make here: I have highlighted the legacy of the 1950s to Calvino, but we should take a moment to consider Calvino's legacy to us.

Calvino's trajectory in the 1950s helps us define the cultural dynamic of contemporary Italy because it set the tone not only for his increasingly successful career but also for a whole generation of Italian intellectuals. His intellectual lucidity and his ear for what mattered most in a particular cultural moment first emerged in the years of confident, almost triumphant, neo-realism. Then Calvino made the first of a long series of 'scandalous' generic choices and found his most convincing voice in a fantastic trilogy that anticipates by more than a decade the critique of the neo-realist interpretation of the Gramscian project for intellectuals. And while a novel such as Pratolini's *Metello* (1955) – hailed by some as the great realist work of the decade – is remembered today mostly because of the polemics surrounding it, Calvino's trilogy has acquired a well-deserved reputation as one of the most significant achievements of post-war Italian literature. When neo-realism finally collapsed and became almost a dirty word, Calvino produced *The Watcher*, a realist novel that, as we have seen, has steadily grown in appeal as an exemplification of the struggle against the crisis of reason (dialectical and other), which was one of the dominant cultural issues at the end of the last century and still occupies socially minded intellectuals today, at the rather dismal dawn of the new millennium.

Calvino's stubborn non-conformity was not the result of a desire to stand out from the crowd at all costs – nothing could be further from

Calvino's sensibility than the 'protagonism' that would mark, for example, the neo-avant-garde movement (cf. Romano [1977], who coined the term 'stregoni della fantacultura' ('wizards of a phantom culture'). Rather, it was the result of a steadfastly developed poetics that became increasingly explicit as the years went by and which cast the fate of literature with that of cognition. Therein lies the sense of seriousness and even urgency that marks Calvino's efforts: the task of literature is to help us know our world in a humane and ethical way, a task that beckons us today all the more urgently as we witness the degradation of the planet and the degeneration beyond any level hitherto imaginable of political discourse. In sum, Calvino emerges as the ideal witness of a pivotal period in Italian and indeed world history: the transition from Fordist capitalism to a much debated but yet to be fully defined and understood new conjuncture (neo-capitalism, late capitalism, global capitalism, post-industrial society, etc.) – our conjuncture.

And finally, a more specifically literary issue resurfaces, the issue that provided the initial impulse for this book: my interest in non-realist narrative genres. In the heading to this section of my conclusion, I have called Calvino's trajectory a 'parable,' playfully allowing interferences from the French *parabole*, and the Italian *parabola*, which mean both 'parable' and 'parabola' – a path through space, a horizon that also tells a story and has a moral. The question that Calvino's use of the fantastic raises is precisely this: in a world where the effort to grasp the totality of human experience is increasingly abandoned and even ridiculed; where global capitalism dictates that reality be equated with corporate interests, or, to use more literary vocabulary, where the corporate grand narrative is granted the status of reality; and where social antagonism itself has been turned into a profit-making enterprise – is there any room left in this world for the intellectual and literature? If so (and the answer is anything but clear), how can the Sisyphean task of keeping pace with an increasingly complex human experience be fulfilled? By raising these issues, I am not suggesting that Calvino possesses the answers, only that his trajectory has something of critical importance to teach us. Calvino is asking us to reflect on the nature and possibilities of parable, and to consider the implications for both narrative and real life of eliminating parable from the cultural horizon. What happens when fables are no longer true, or no longer know how to tell the truth? What happens when storytelling ceases to provide us with a human compass for the world?

Notes

Introduction

1 Throughout this book I have adopted the following conventions when citing from works in Italian. If the work has been translated into English, I cite from the English translation and refer the reader to the title and page number in that edition, which is included in the bibliography. If the work has not been translated into English, I provide my own translation and refer the reader to the title and page number in the Italian edition, which is also included in the bibliography. In these cases, the Italian original is placed, depending on length, in parentheses after the English citation or in a note. The one exception to this convention is my discussion of *The Watcher* (*La giornata d'uno scrutatore*) in chapter 5, which is based on a very close reading of the style, diction, and syntax of the Italian text. In this case I cite the English text in parentheses after the Italian citation or in a note, depending on its length. I have also abbreviated some of the titles of the works by Calvino discussed in this book as follows:

The Path to the Nest of Spiders [*Il sentiero dei nidi di ragno*] – *The Path*
I giovani del Po – *I giovani*
The Cloven Viscount [*Il visconte dimezzato*] – *The Viscount*
The Baron in the Trees [*Il barone rampante*] – *The Baron*
The Non-existent Knight [*Il cavaliere inesistente*] – *The Knight*
Una pietra sopra – *Una pietra*
Eremita a Parigi – *Eremita*
Romanzi e racconti – *RR*, followed by the volume number
'The Argentine Ant' ['La formica argentina'] – 'The Ant'
'A Plunge in Real Estate' ['La speculazione edilizia'] – 'A Plunge'
'The Lion's Marrow' ['Il midollo del leone'] – 'The Lion'

'The Sea of Objectivity ['Il mare dell'oggettività'] – 'The Sea'
'The Challenge of the Labyrinth ['La sfida al labirinto'] – 'The Labyrinth'

Chapter 1 Italy at the Crossroads

1 See, generally, Cravieri (1995); De Felice (1983); Asor Rosa (1975); and, for a literary perspective, Luperini (1981).
2 '[N]on so se mi sarei deciso a impegnarmi totalmente su quella strada: c'era in me un fondo troppo forte di gusti individuali, d'indifferenza e di spirito critico per sacrificare tutto questo a una fede collettiva. Soltanto la guerra ha risolto la situazione, travolgendo certi ostacoli, sgombrando il terreno da molti comodi ripari e mettendomi brutalmente a contatto con un mondo inconciliabile ... A un certo momento gli intellettuali devono essere capaci *di trasferire la loro esperienza sul terreno dell'utilità comune,* ciascuno deve sapere prendere il suo posto in una organizzazione di combattimento ... Quanto a me, ti assicuro che l'idea di andare a fare il partigiano in questa stagione mi diverte pochissimo; non ho mai apprezzato come ora i pregi della vita civile e ho coscienza di essere un ottimo traduttore e un buon diplomatico, ma secondo ogni probabilità un mediocre partigiano. Tuttavia è l'unica possibilità aperta e l'accolgo' (Pintor in Milanini 1980, 36–8; emphasis added).
3 Calvino's own article 'La letteratura italiana sulla Resistenza' (rpt. in Milanini 1980, 91–7) manifested this attitude. The poetics of neo-realism will be discussed in more detail in the next chapter as a prelude to the analysis of *I giovani,* the novel in which, as we shall see, Calvino tries to apply the conventions of neo-realism.
4 The word 'culture' is notoriously intractable in all languages I know, and Vittorini's use of it is particularly imprecise. To facilitate a correct comprehension of the discussion that follows, I warn the reader that in Italian *cultura* has a more marked tendency to mean formalized 'high' culture than in the English 'culture' (so that, for example, Vittorini's *ricerca culturale* refers to something like intellectual and scholarly research much more than to the social anthropology the English 'cultural research' strongly suggests).
5 'Ocuparsi del pane e del lavoro è ancora occuparsi "dell'anima." Mentre non volere occuparsi che "dell' anima" lasciando a "Cesare" di occuparsi come gli fa comodo del pane e del lavoro, è limitarsi ad avere una funzione intellettuale e dar modo a "Cesare" (o a Donegani, a Pirelli, a Valletta) di avere una funzione di dominio "sull'anima" dell'uomo' (rpt. in Forti and Pautasso 1975, 56).
6 'E tu [Vigorelli] dici che noi riveliamo, per questa frase, una mentalità reto-

rica. Hai avuto tu una persona cara che ti sia caduta nella lotta di questi anni? Io ne ho avute tre che mi erano carissime: Giaime Pintor ... Giorgio Labò ... ed Eugenio Curiel ... Io ho lavorato assieme a tutti e tre, e con tutti e tre si è spesso parlato di una *nuova cultura* che avremmo dovuto cercare, di un *Politecnico* che avremmo dovuto fare. Così quel caduto della fotografia si chiama per me Giaime Pintor, si chiama Giorgio Labò, si chiama Eugenio Curiel; ed ha un nome vero per chiunque abbia avuto un compagno morto nella lotta' (rpt. in Forti and Pautasso 1975, 60).

7 The reader may be reminded of the polemics sparked by Vittorini's Resistance novel *Uomini e no*, and in particular by the very ambiguous figure of its protagonist Enne 2.

8 'Ecco, per esempio, secondo me è intellettualismo giudicare "rivoluzionario" e "utile" uno scrittore come Hemingway, le cui doti non vanno al di là d'una sensibilità da "frammento," da "elzeviro," e "rivoluzionario" e "utile" un romanzo come *Per chi suona la campana* che rappresenta la riprova estrema dell'incapacità di Hemingway a comprendere e a giudicare (cioè poi a *narrare*) qualcosa che vada al di là d'un suo quadro di sensazioni elementari e immediate: egoistiche. Ed è, per esempio, intellettualismo giudicare "rivoluzionario," "utile," un vecchio e superficiale *reportage* giornalistico sulla rivoluzione di Ottobre qual'è *Dieci giorni che sconvolsero il mondo* di Reed' (Alicata 1946, 116).

9 'L'indirizzo annunciato non veniva seguito con coerenza, veniva anzi sostituito, a poco a poco, da qualcosa di diverso, da una strana tendenza a una specie di "cultura" enciclopedica, dove una ricerca astratta del nuovo, del diverso, del sorprendente, prendeva il posto della scelta e dell'indagine coerenti con un obiettivo, e la notizia, l'informazione (volevo dire, con brutto termine giornalistico, la "varietà") sopraffaceva il pensiero' (rpt. in Forti and Pautasso 1975, 118).

10 'Humanist' is a very slippery term. I am referring here to the ideological reflexes engendered by the already mentioned Italian humanist tradition, a tradition frozen in the celebration of its glorious past (the classical heritage plus the triad Dante-Petrarch-Boccaccio) and, less adoringly, of the Risorgimento.

11 'Il ruolo stesso degli intellettuali assumeva un carattere diverso e costruttivo. Erano gli intellettuali a essere considerati i soggetti dell'organizzazione culturale e della politica di alleanze, diventavano essi gli artefici, in quanto uomini di cutura, della politica culturale comunista: il partito, quindi, doveva misurarsi sul loro terreno far sí che essi stessi divenissero produttori di cultura e di cultura qualificata' (Vittoria 1992, 33).

12 I am relying on Romanò's 'Analyses' which appeared regularly in *Officina*

between 1955 and 1957. For the instalment here in question see *Officina* 6 (1956): 238–45.

13 The reference here is to Italian hermeticism (e.g., Eugenio Montale), which could be considered the most sustained and important Italian contribution to high modernism.

14 Pasolini's intervention in the debate on the role of criticism sponsored in 1960 by *Nuovi Argomenti* addressed specifically the issue of the relationship between Spitzer's stylistics and Marxism.

15 A very significant portion of the pages of the journal was reserved for the poetry produced by the group and some collaborators, as well as some prose by Calvino, Gadda, Volponi, and a few others.

16 I am using the term 'management' to render the Italian concept of 'organizzazione' because it seems to me that it expresses accurately the new managerial role assigned to the intellectual in modern developed society.

17 'I limiti di *Officina* ... li starei per definire dialettici. Sono i sintomi di una dialettica della *disorganicità* che è stata tentata ed è fallita proprio perché si è misurata ... con la *sintesi* politico-culturale e non con la radice dell'analisi di classe ... C'è *l'errore* della mancata analisi di classe della società e della cultura capitalistica, con strumenti marxiani che permettessero di definire l'economia politica dell'intellettuale e *della produzione* (non solo *funzione*) *intellettuale*, il modo di produzione capitalistico della cultura, dei rapporti sociali, in cui si produce cultura e letteratura' (Migliori 1979, 89; emphasis added).

18 'Dall'inizio degli anni Cinquanta, insomma, si sviluppò nella politica culturale del PCI un discorso unitario che, per tappe successive e spesso contraddittorie, attraverso la spaccatura del 1956, e con l'influenza e la guida determinanti di Togliatti, arrivò alle concezioni dei primi anni Sessanta e alle elaborazioni del IX e soprattutto del X Congresso. Quando cioè, si affermò a chiare lettere che se al partito spetta il compito di "organizzare intorno a sé le forze della cultura che affrontano in modo progressivo i problemi che derivano dalla vita della società," non gli spetta però quello di "proporre soluzioni dei problemi della ricerca scientifica e artistica" o di "sentenziare a proposito della validità scientifica o artistica di questa o quella soluzione," che era una chiara e netta sconfessione dello zdanovismo' (Vittoria 1992, xxv).

19 'Quando l'esperienza dei *Gettoni* potè dirsi conclusa ... egli [Vittorini] sentì il bisogno d'una pubblicazione dove la discussione critica avesse più spazio, accanto alla presentazione di testi nuovi. Propose a Einaudi qualcosa che fosse tra una rivista e una collana, cioè numeri-volumi che uscissero senza una periodicità fissa, con interventi critici ma senza la struttura

tradizionale delle riviste e abbastanza ampi da contenere brevi romanzi e raccolte di poesie. Numeri non strettamente monografici ma ciascuno centrato su uno o due temi generali' (qtd. in Marchi 1973, 10).

20 'Oltre che dei *Gettoni*, *Il Menabò* prese anche una parte di eredità della bolognese *Officina*. Vittorini era dall'inizio molto legato a Roversi e Leonetti; e in seguito Leonetti ebbe una partecipazione di rilievo alla impostazione dei numeri centrali del *Menabò*. Sia pure dall'esterno, un contributo di primo piano venne tanto da Pier Paolo Pasolini quanto da Franco Fortini' (qtd. in Marchi 1973, 10–11).

21 'La verità industriale risiede nella catena di effetti che il mondo delle fabbriche mette in moto. E lo scrittore, tratti o no della vita di fabbrica, sarà a livello industriale solo nella misura in cui il suo sguardo e il suo giudizio si siano compenetrati di questa verità e delle istanze (istanze di appropriazione, istanze di trasformazione ulteriore) ch'essa contiene' (Vittorini, *Il Menabò* 4: 100).

22 'Si vuole illuminare il rapporto fra oggetto e utente, fra oggetto e produttore. Ma questo non dovrebbe oscurare l'eziologia umana degli oggetti stessi' (Fortini, *Il Menabò* 5: 30).

23 'Non si vuole solo privilegiare l'immediatezza ma, si direbbe, concludere che, sostituita dalle categorie di Vecchio e di Nuovo, la storia non esiste; che cioè esistono lacune nei rapporti di cause e che nessuno dovrebbe chiedersi – pena la condanna alla morte dell'anima, coiè alla *ideologia* – di che esista l'industria moderna, chi la muova, chi la produca, a chi giovi' (Fortini, *Il Menabò* 5: 33–4).

24 'Oggi qualsiasi espressione letteraria che rappresenti una servitù in modo da rendere immediatamente possibile l'illusione di una libertà, serve una libertà illusoria ... Credo tocchi al marxista, al socialista coerente schernire oggi le nobili angosce di che il riformismo capitalistico cerca nascondere il suo sostanzioso ottimismo, la persuasione di avercela fatta ad assicurare al nostro paese progresso e democrazia' (Fortini, *Il Menabò* 5: 44).

25 'A chi si chiede ogni momento: "Ma non farò il gioco del capitalismo?" preferisco chi affronta tutti i problemi di trasformazione del mondo con la fiducia che ciò che è meglio serve per il meglio. Del resto, in questo stesso numero lo scritto di Fortini è un documento di come una tensione rivoluzionaria, se alimentata solo dalla passione per la teoria e non per l'operare pratico umano (e per le cose che di questo operare sono strumento e prodotto), si risolve nella scelta del nulla' (*Una pietra*, 88).

26 '[Joyce] si aliena nella situazione assumendone i modi, ma portando questi modi ad evidenza, rendendoseli consapevoli come modi formativi, esce dalla situazione e la domina. Esce dall'alienazione estraniando nella

struttura narrativa la situazione in cui si è alienato' (Eco, *Il Menabò* 5: 227).

27 'E' l'arte che per far presa sul mondo vi si cala assumendone dall'interno le condizioni di crisi, usando per descriverlo lo stesso linguaggio alienato in cui questo mondo si esprime: ma portandolo a condizione di chiarezza, *ostentandolo* come forma del discorso, lo spoglia della sua qualità di condizione alienanteci, e ci rende capaci di demistificarlo. Di qui può avere inizio una operazione successiva' (Eco, *Il Menabò* 5: 228).

28 'E' il mondo della natura modificata, delle opere costruite, dei rapporti che noi avevamo posto e che ora ritroviamo fuori di noi ... Ora questo mondo che noi abbiamo creato, contiene in sé, oltre il rischio di ridurre noi a strumento di se stesso, gli elementi in base ai quali stabilire i parametri di una nuova misura umana' (Eco, *Il Menabò* 5: 230).

Chapter 2 Italo Calvino: From Neo-realism to the Fantastic

1 Lucia Re's important and useful book, *Calvino and the Age of Neorealism*, is very much in the background of my own analysis of Calvino's relationship to neo-realism. However, our approaches are quite different. Re centres her impressively wide-ranging discussion on the early years of Italian neo-realism and its intellectual roots in the European debates about realism in the 1930s. She also concentrates her attention on Calvino's first novel, *The Path*, and early short stories. My emphasis, on the other hand, is more on later neo-realism, the specifically Italian cultural dynamic of the 1940s and 1950s, and the works that Calvino wrote as the contradictions within the neo-realist poetics became apparent. Perhaps because of our different foci, our assessments of the artistic importance of *The Path* also diverge.

2 My discussion in this section is informed by Romano Luperini's extensive and superb two-volume study *Il novecento*, as well as Re's discussion, mentioned in the previous note.

3 Sartre (1979) would develop this point in the 1960s and 1970s.

4 It is interesting to note that the first non-foreign best-sellers were Cassola's *La ragazza di Bube* and Lampedusa's *Il gattopardo*, published in the late 1950s, that is, when neo-realism, having lost its revolutionary pretensions, disclosed all its aesthetic conservatism, of which these two works, in spite of their merits, are a good example.

5 'Con esso [*I giovani*] volevo finalmente esprimere in forma narrativa anche quella parte di interessi e d'esperienza che sono finora riuscito solo a far vivere in qualche pagina di carattere saggistico: cioè la città, la civiltà industriale, gli operai; e insieme quella parte della realtà e dei miei interessi (da

cui invece m'è sempre stato più facile trarre simboli narrativi) che è natura, avventura, ardua ricerca d'una felicità naturale oggi. *Miravo a dare un'immagine d'integrazione umana*; invece mi venne un libro insolitamente grigio, in cui la pienezza della vita, benché molto se ne parli, si sente poco' (*RR*, 3: 1342; emphasis added).

6 '– Non capisco bene quello che dici ... – [Bastia] cominciò, lentamente.

«Certo, non può capirmi. Perché ho voluto parlargli?» pensava Nino.

'– ... Io voialtri giovani non posso seguirvi tanto, – continuava Bastia – ho la mia età, sono d'altri tempi, ho avuto un'altra vita, tutta diversa dalla vostra ...'

«Ecco la solita storia ...» pensò Nino.

E Bastia: – Tornassi a nascere, mah! rifarei da capo quello che ho fatto ... non c'era altro da fare. Certo il mondo è grande ... la vita d'un uomo è fatta di tante cose ...'

Nino drizzò le orecchie.

'– ... Noi siam gente che non vuole rinunziare a niente ...'

«Ecco quel che volevo dire,» pensò Nino.

'– ... ma quando ci troviamo in ballo, che vuoi fare? ... Tante cose che ci piacevano si perdono per strada, e si va avanti lo stesso ... Mah ... Voi siete giovani ... Vedrete tante cose che noi non vedremo ...'

«Lo so, – pensava Nino, – ma io dico ...».

'– ... Certo sarebbe meglio non perdere niente per strada ... non dimenticare niente ... e nemmeno i desideri ...'

«Capisce, capisce tutto, il vecchio! Accidenti se capisce!». Nino era tutto ansioso.

'– Mah ... Cose che pensavo quand'ero in prigione, i primi tempi ... Ero appena un po' più vecchio di te ... Cinque anni ci sono stato ...'

Non era solito a tirar fuori i suoi ricordi, Bastia; e nemmeno a fare dei discorsi tanto lunghi: quindi stette zitto. E adesso era tutto concluso. Ma non l'aveva disapprovato per il tono di quel discorso, non se n'era neppure stupito. Tutto andava avanti come prima.

Si salutarono, Bastia rimontò in bicicletta e pedalò via, Nino gli aveva stretto la mano macchinalmente ed era rimasto fermo sull'orlo del marciapiedi' (*RR*, 3: 1120).

7 'I pesci non si domandano mai: "Cos'è il fine?" Vivono da pesci, e basta. Hanno ragione. Io cerco di fare come loro: cioè di vivere da uomo come loro vivono da pesci. Non è facile come sembra, ma è l'unica via, credimi' (*RR*, 3: 1037).

8 'E' tutto una cosa "di testa," fredda, costruita in simboli inadeguati. E' un saggio su una problematica che riconosco come mia, ma espressa in *formule*

narrative che non sono mie, e in cui io mi muovo a disagio. Non lo pubblicherò in volume' (*RR,* 3: 1341; emphasis added).

9 These few examples give an idea of the range of subjects just mentioned: a series of articles 'from our special correspondent' on the 1947 World Youth Festival in Prague; 'Freud and Marxism' ('Freud e il marxismo'), 19 November 1946; 'Let's give the joy of childhood to these four-year-old men: One hundred little Neapolitans in the North' ('A questi uomini di quattr'anni diamo la gioia dell'infanzia: Cento piccoli napoletani nel Nord'), 22 May 1947; 'Delegates from Viet-Nam among the workers of Turin: Fighters against imperialism' ('I delegati del Viet-Nam tra i lavoratori di Torino: Combattenti contro l'imperialismo,') 11 November 1948. Cf. also Ferretti's (1989) interesting study of Calvino's non-fictional production.

10 'L'ambizione giovanile da cui ho preso le mosse è stata quella del progetto di costruzione d'una nuova letteratura che a sua volta servisse alla costruzione d'una nuova società ...

Il personaggio che prende la parola in questo libro (e che in parte s'identifica, in parte si distacca dal me stesso rappresentato in altre serie di scritti e di atti) entra in scena negli Anni Cinquanta cercando d'investirsi d'una personale caratterizzazione nel ruolo che allora teneva la ribalta: *l'intellettuale impegnato'* (*Una pietra,* vii–viii).

11 'Con queste tre storie [*The Cloven Viscount, The Baron in the Trees,* and *The Non-existent Knight*] ho voluto ritrovare – e far circolare nella realtà, tenere viva – quella tensione individuale e collettiva insieme, esistenziale e razionale, autobiografica e storica, lirica ed epica, che è stata d'una stagione della letteratura mondiale e anche italiana; l'unica via possibile di restarvi fedele' (*RR,* 1: 1222).

12 'Dimidiato, mutilato, incompleto, nemico a se stesso è l'uomo contemporaneo; Marx lo disse *alienato,* Freud *represso;* uno stato d'antica armonia è perduto, a una nuova completezza s'aspira. Il nocciolo ideologico-morale che volevo coscientemente dare alla storia era questo. Ma più che lavorare ad approfondirlo sul piano filosofico, ho badato a dare al racconto uno scheletro che funzionasse come un ben connesso meccanismo, e carne e sangue di libere associazioni d'immaginazione lirica' (*RR,* 1: 1211).

13 Milanini (1990) was the first to note that the three novels of the chivalric trilogy are all based on an image that literalizes a popular metaphor.

14 It has been noted that one of the sources of *The Viscount* is chapter 10 of *Don Quixote:* 'It is a balsam the recipe of which I have in my memory, and whoever possesses it need not fear death nor consider any wound mortal. Therefore when I have made and given it to you, you have naught else to do when in any battle you see me cleft in twain (as often happens) but

deftly to take up the part of the body that has fallen to the ground with the greatest nicety before the blood congeals and put it up again on the half that remains in the saddle, taking great pains to fit it exactly in the right place. Then you must give me just two sips to drink of the balsam I have just mentioned, and you will see me become as sound as an apple' (*Don Quixote* [New York: Penguin-Signet Classics, 1964] 113).

15 'Eravamo nel cuore della guerra fredda, nell'aria era una tensione, un dilaniamento sordo che non si manifestavano in immagini visibili ma dominavano i nostri animi. Ed ecco che scrivendo una storia completamente fantastica, mi trovavo senz'accorgermene a esprimere non solo la sofferenza di quel particolare momento ma anche la spinta a uscirne; cioè non accettavo passivamente la realtà negativa ma riuscivo a riimmettervi il movimento, la spacconeria, la crudezza, l'economia di stile, l'ottimismo spietato che erano stati della letteratura della Resistenza' (*RR*, 1: 1210).

16 This does not mean that *The Viscount* could not be enjoyed by other audiences as well, such as young adults, for whom Einaudi prepared in collaboration with Calvino a special edition of the chivalric trilogy.

Chapter 3 *The Baron in the Trees*

1 The distinction I am drawing here between the 'reflective register' and the 'storytelling register' is reminiscent of the famous five codes Barthes elaborated in *S/Z* (1970). In particular, the reader may be tempted to assimilate my 'reflective register' with *le code herméneutique: la voix de la Vérité*, and the 'storytelling register' with *le code proaïrétique: la voix de l'empirisme*. While there is a family resemblance between my articulation and that of Barthes, it is important to note that the whole point of my discussion is to describe the dynamic interaction between these two codes and, more specifically, the gaps, contradictions, and tensions they create as the reader performs the cognitive operations that the text mediates. It is precisely this view of language as a dialogical mediation of social relationships, rather than as a self-contained mechanism, that distinguishes my approach from that of Barthes.

2 'Per *Il barone rampante* avevo il problema di correggere la mia spinta troppo forte a identificarmi col protagonista, e qui misi in opera il ben noto dispositivo Serenus Zeitblom; cioè fin dalle prime battute mandai avanti come "io" un personaggio di carattere antitetico a Cosimo, un fratello posato e pieno di buon senso' (*RR*, 1: 1218).

3 The difference between the Italian 'solidarietà' and its English translation 'sympathy' seems unjustified and obscures the political message. This is an

example of how Colquhoun's translations tend to evacuate the crucial political commentary that Calvino's work contains.

4 Biagio is 'old' by the time he narrates Cosimo's story but he tends to revert to childhood as he tells it, as if in sympathy with his subject (the complex focalization of the narrating voice as well as of the authorial voice are an important aspect of the novel and will be discussed later in this chapter).

5 'Credo che nella mia opera si possano trovare non due anime e poetiche, ma molte. *Il visconte dimezzato* e *Il barone rampante* sono due racconti fantastici, ma d'una diversa gradazione di fantasia. E in ognuno dei due libri (specie nel *Barone*) tra un capitolo e l'altro si possono trovare (grave difetto) degli scarti all'interno di questa gradazione' (*RR*, 1: 1331).

6 The reasons for my disagreement with this particular aspect of Calvino's statement will become clear later in this section.

7 I have quoted earlier the letter in which Calvino expresses to Vittorini his apprehensions about *The Viscount* being seen as little more than a stylistic divertissement.

8 These passages demonstrate how Colquhoun's original translation attempts to 'clean up' the Italian text, unfortunately.

9 'Ecco che il protagonista, il barone Cosimo di Rondò, uscendo dalla cornice burlesca della vicenda, mi si veniva configurando in un ritratto morale, con connotati culturali ben precisi; le ricerche dei miei amici storici, sugli illuministi e giacobini italiani, diventavano un prezioso stimolo per la fantasia. Anche il personaggio femminile (Viola) entrava nel gioco delle prospettive etiche e culturali: *a contrasto con la determinatezza illuminista, la spinta barocca e poi romantica verso il tutto che rischia sempre di diventare spinta distruttiva, corsa verso il nulla*' (*RR*, 1: 1214–15; emphasis added).

10 '*Il barone rampante* ... appare nel 1957, n. 79 dei *Coralli* Einaudi ... In calce al volume sono indicati i termini della composizione: 10 dicembre 1956–26 febbraio 1957. Una stesura piuttosto rapida, quindi, quasi un felice, spumeggiante interludio ... che interrompe la faticosa gestazione della "Speculazione edilizia"' (*RR*, 1: 1329).

11 'Anche qui [in *The Baron* and *The Vicount*] la data di composizione illumina sullo stato d'animo. E' un'epoca di ripensamento del ruolo che possiamo avere nel movimento storico, mentre nuove speranze e nuove amarezze si alternano. Nonostante tutto, i tempi portano verso il meglio; si tratta di trovare il giusto rapporto tra la coscienza individuale e il corso della storia' (*RR*, 1: 1213).

12 'Ma quando Kruscev denunciò Stalin dinnanzi al comitato centrale e poi dinnanzi al Congresso del partito, pensammo: ecco, la pace fiorisce, ora i

frutti del socialismo arriveranno, quell'oppressione, quell'angoscia segreta che sentivamo [us, the Italian Communists], scompare ...

Al posto dei vecchi stalinisti andavano comunisti che avevano sofferto la galera e l'accantonamento da ogni funzione. Noi vedevamo in tutto ciò la conferma delle nostre speranze, un rinnovamento concreto, una svolta di portata storica ...'

Fu per me una serata decisiva ... Aveva [Gianni Rocca, editor in chief of *l'Unità*] la voce rotta di pianto. Ci disse: i carri armati stanno entrando a Budapest, si combatte per le strade. Guardai Amendola [at the time the second in command within the PCI]. Eravamo tutti e tre come colpiti da una mazzata. Poi Amendola mormorò: "Togliatti [then the PCI's leader] dice che ci sono momenti nella storia in cui bisogna essere schierati o da una parte o dall'altra ..."

Io non volli lasciare il partito in un momento di particolare difficoltà, ma ormai la mia decisione era presa. Me ne andai senza clamore nell'estate del '57' (*Eremita*, 231–2).

In fact, Calvino made a fair bit of noise as he quit the party. He criticized the PCI's cultural policy from the pages of *Il contemporaneo*; he attacked Alicata at a meeting of the PCI's central commission on culture, during which Calvino tabled a non-confidence motion against the party's cultural leadership; he asked his cell at Einaudi to formally denounce the reporting by *l'Unità* on the Hungarian revolt (*RR*, 1: lxxiv). The publication of his thinly disguised allegory of the PCI's lack of dynamism ('La gran bonaccia delle Antille,' *Città aperta* 25 July 1957: 3; *L'Espresso* 25 August 1957: 5) was another rather public sign of dissent. And finally came his letter of resignation published in *l'Unità* 7 August 1957: 2. Still, he managed not to burn all his bridges with the PCI and *l'Unità*, which would always observe Calvino's intellectual itinerary with respect if not with approval.

13 This law would have given a 'majority premium' (extra seats) to the coalition, which obtained more than 50 per cent of the popular vote. The effect would have been to marginalize opposition parties (essentially the left) for the sake of greater political stability. To the surprise of many, the DC and its allies narrowly failed to win more than 50 per cent of the vote; the law then lapsed and was not reintroduced.

14 These lectures were published posthumously, first in Italian as: *Lezioni americane: Sei proposte per il prossimo millennio* (Milano: Garzanti, 1988), and then in English as *Six Memos for the Next Millennium*, trans. Patrick Creagh (London: Cape, 1992).

15 For the fullest account of this debate see O. Parlangeli, ed., *La nuova ques-*

tione della lingua (Brescia: Paideia, 1971). Calvino's comments were singled out for a specific and lively reply by Pasolini.

16 'Noi pure siamo tra quelli che credono in *una letteratura che sia presenza attiva nella storia*, in una letteratura come educazione, di grado e di qualità insostituibile ... La letteratura deve rivolgersi a quegli uomini, deve – mentre impara da loro – insegnar loro, servire a loro, e può servire solo in una cosa: aiutandoli a essere sempre più intelligenti, sensibili, moralmente forti. *Le cose che la letteratura può ricercare e insegnare sono poche ma insostituibili*: il modo di guardare il prossimo e se stessi, di porre in relazione fatti personali e fatti generali, di attribuire valore a piccole cose o a grandi, di considerare i propri limiti e vizi e gli altrui, di trovare le proporzioni della vita, e il posto dell'amore in essa, e la sua forza e il suo ritmo, ed il posto della morte, il modo di pensarci o non pensarci ... Il resto lo si vada a imparare altrove, dalla scienza, dalla storia, dalla vita, come noi tutti dobbiamo continuamente andare ad impararlo' (*Una pietra*, 13–14; emphasis added).

17 That for Calvino the emphasis on a narrowly defined realism had become an obsession in the post-war period and was on the verge of becoming a blinding fetish can be gathered by the subtle but nonetheless poignant jab at Lukács: 'It would seem that in Italy the fact of being an intellectual is considered a misfortune, an irredeemably negative condition, which does not inspire powerful allegories such as Kafka's and Joyce's, but remains a dull and narrow torment ... Perhaps Lukás, who is so concerned about "the intellectual physiognomy of the character," would not take an interest in this kind of literature [in which the intellectual remains an abstract figure], and yet this literature would undoubtedly provide a rich field for investigations such as his' ('Si direbbe che in Italia il fatto d'essere un intellettuale sia sentito come un guaio, come una condizione negativa senza riscatto, che neppure ispira allegorie potenti come quelle di Kafka o di Joyce, ma resta un rodimento sordo e limitato ... Forse il Lukács che tanto si preoccupa della "fisionomia intellettuale del personaggio," non proverà interesse per una letteratura così poco caratterizzata in questo senso, ma pure essa costituirebbe certo un campo assai ricco per indagini come le sue'; *Una pietra*, 7).

18 After Vittorini's death, Calvino would alone edit the last number of *Il Menabò*, which appeared in 1967 and was entirely devoted to Vittorini's crucial contribution to cultural debates in post-war Italy.

19 'Perché, tra le possibilità che s'aprono alla letteratura d'agire sulla storia, questa è la più sua, forse la sola che non sia illusoria: capire a quale tipo d'uomo essa storia col suo molteplice, contraddittorio lavorio sta preparando il campo di battaglia, e dettarne la sensibilità, lo scatto morale ...
È chiaro che questo tipo d'uomo che un'opera o un'intera epoca letteraria

presuppone, sottintende, o meglio propone, inventa, può anche non essere uno di quei personaggi a tutto tondo che sono prerogativa del romanzo o del teatro, ma vive altresì e forse soprattutto in quella *presenza morale*, in quel protagonista non meno individuato che hanno pure le poesie liriche o le prose dei moralisti, quel vero protagonista che anche in tanti romanzieri, a cominciare dal Manzoni e dal Verga maggiore, non s'identifica con nessuno dei personaggi' (*Una pietra*, 3; emphasis added).

20 '[L]o scrittore, quasi fosse geloso del dirigente politico ... cerca di ripetere le cose che il dirigente politico fa ... e s'illude di dar lezioni ... Questa illusione di scrittori e soprattutto di critici ha le sue radici nella tradizione di pensiero della vecchia socialdemocrazia, nella sua identificazione della predicazione con la pratica, della educazione con la rivoluzione' (*Una pietra*, 13).

21 Sartre's influence on Calvino has been studied by Milanini (1990), Petroni ('La discesa agli inferi,' 1991), and Bertoni (1993) who, however, have not focused on the concept of bad faith, which might have influenced Calvino's assessment of the predicament of the modern intellectual.

22 'Ritornare a una più calma considerazione del posto delle idee e della ragione nell'opera creativa vorrà dire la fine d'una situazione per cui l'io dello scrittore è sentito come una specie di maledizione, di condanna. E questo avverrà forse solo il giorno in cui l'intellettuale si accetterà come tale, si sentirà integrato nella società, parte funzionale d'essa, senza più dover sfuggirsi o sfuggirla, camuffarsi o castigarsi ...

[L]a nostra forza non potrà essere sete di trascendenza, non dramma interiore, alla presenza d'un dramma esteriore così imponente; la nostra forza può essere solo la esperienza di questo dramma, e quella *estrema freddezza di giudizio*, quella *volontà tranquilla di difendere la propria natura* di cui Pintor appunto ci diede un esempio così limpido' (*Una pietra*, 16).

23 The first edition of *The Baron* bore the dates of composition 10 December 1956–26 February 1957 (*RR*, 1: 1329).

24 A brief citation from chapter 9 of *The Path* will suffice to show how much water has passed under the bridge: 'Perhaps the Soviet Union is already an untroubled country. Perhaps there is no human misery there anymore. Will he ever be untroubled, himself, Kim? Perhaps one day we will all be untroubled, and we won't understand anymore many things because we'll understand everything' ('L'Unione Sovietica forse è già un paese sereno. Forse non c'è più miseria umana, laggiù. Sarà mai sereno, lui, Kim? Forse un giorno si arriverà ad essere tutti sereni, e non capiremo più tante cose perché capiremo tutto'; *RR*, 1: 108). We might also note that this passage was censored in the 1956 Colquhoun translation, which is still in use.

25 I am thinking here of 'A Plunge in Real Estate,' a text with which Calvino struggled both before and after the composition of *The Baron*.

26 '*Il barone rampante* mi venne dunque molto diverso dal *Visconte dimezzato*. Invece d'un racconto fuori dal tempo, dallo scenario appena accennato, dai personaggi filiformi ed emblematici, dall'intreccio di favoletta per i bambini, ero continuamente attratto, nello scrivere, a fare un *pastiche* storico, un repertorio d'immagini settecentesche, suffragato di date e correlazioni con avvenimenti e personaggi famosi; un paesaggio e una natura, immaginari sì, ma descritti con precisione e nostalgia; una vicenda che si preoccupava di rendere giustificabile e verisimile persino l'irrealtà della trovata iniziale; insomma, avevo finito per prendere gusto al romanzo, nel senso più tradizionale della parola' (*RR*, 1: 1215; emphasis added).

27 Inexplicably, Colquhoun translates 'trovarono da ridire' as 'they found Cosimo laughable.' I am providing a more reasonable version: 'they [objected].'

28 The question of whether Bakhtin's notion of 'polyphony' (Bakhtin 1981) still constitutes a synthesis in extremis cannot be broached here. However, it should be fairly clear that in Calvino's text the problem does not lie in a kind of encyclopedic accumulation of voices, but rather in the ultimately irreconcilable discontinuities between the various voices and generic modulations encompassed by the narrative.

Chapter 4 *The Non-existent Knight*

1 '[*Il cavaliere*] nella trilogia può occupare l'ultimo posto quanto il primo ... perché, rispetto agli altri due racconti, può essere considerato più un'introduzione che un epilogo' (*RR*, 1: 1216).

2 This text was first published in 1991 (volume 1 of *RR*). The fragment reads like a very early draft of the introduction that was eventually published with the 1960 edition. The somewhat informal tone of this text in no way diminishes the value of Calvino's remarks.

3 'Il fatto è che, cercando di ricostruire una filosofia attraverso le tre storie, *Il cavaliere inesistente* messo alla fine mi riapre tutti i problemi' (*RR*, 1: 1220).

4 '*Il barone rampante* non esauriva il problema che mi ero posto. È chiaro che oggi viviamo in un mondo di non eccentrici, di persone cui la più semplice individualità è negata, tanto sono ridotte a una astratta somma di comportamenti prestabiliti. Il problema oggi non è ormai più della perdita d'una parte di se stessi, è della perdita totale, del non esserci per nulla.

'Dall'uomo primitivo che, essendo tutt'uno con l'universo, poteva essere detto ancora inesistente perché indifferenziato dalla materia organica,

siamo lentamente arrivati all'uomo artificiale che, essendo tutt'uno coi pro-
dotti e con le situazioni, è inesistente perché non fa più attrito con nulla,
non ha più rapporto (lotta e attraverso la lotta armonia) con ciò che (natura
o storia) gli sta intorno, ma solo astrattamente *funziona*.

'Questo nodo di riflessioni s'era andato per me a poco a poco identifi-
cando con un'immagine che da tempo mi occupava la mente: un'armatura
che cammina e dentro è vuota. Provai a scriverne la storia (nel 1959), ed è
quella del *Cavaliere inesistente*' (*RR*, 1: 1216).

5 'Direi che proprio *Il cavaliere*, dove i referimenti al presente sembrano più
lontani, dice qualcosa che tocca più da vicino le situazioni del nostro
tempo' (*RR*, 1: 1362).

6 For ease of reference, I quote here the passages in question: 'There was a
war on against the Turks. My uncle, the Viscount Medardo of Terralba,
was riding towards the Christian camp across the plain of Bohemia'
('C'era una guerra contro i turchi. Il visconte Medardo di Terralba, mio zio,
cavalcava per la pianura di boemia diretto all'accampamento dei cristiani'
[*RR*, 1: 367]). 'It was on the 15 of June 1767 that my brother, Cosimo Piovasco of Rondò, sat for the last time among us. I remember it as if it were
today. We were in the dining room' ('Fu il 15 di giugno del 1767 che
Cosimo Piovasco di Rondò, mio fratello, sedetter per l'ultima volta in
mezzo a noi. Ricordo come fosse oggi. Eravamo nella sala da pranzo' [*RR*,
1: 549]). 'Beneath the red ramparts of Paris lay marshalled the army of
France. Charlemagne was due to review his paladins. They had been waiting for more than three hours already; it was a hot, early summer afternoon, misty, a bit cloudy; the men inside the armour felt as if they were
boiling in pots over a slow fire' ('Sotto le rosse mura di Parigi era schierato
l'esercito di Francia. Carlomagno doveva passare in rivista i paladini. Già
da più di tre ore erano lì; faceva caldo; era un pomeriggio di prima estate,
un po' coperto, nuvoloso; nelle armature si bolliva come in pentole tenute
a fuoco lento' [*RR*, 1: 955]).

7 Calvino's always positive comments about Brecht are consolidated in Bertoni (1993, 200–1). Note in particular these comments from a 1984 interview: 'estrangement: that was an important theory for me, while I never
found Lukács's theories very interesting; ... between Brecht and Lukács, I
chose Brecht' ('l'estraniamento: questa teoria è stata importante per me,
mentre non ho mai trovato le teorie di Lukács molto interessanti; ... fra
Brecht e Lukács scelsi Brecht'; qtd. in Bertoni, 1993, 201).

8 I quoted this passage at the end of the previous chapter. (See the citation at
the top of p. 128 that begins 'I have no idea ...')

9 'Ma è anche un libro scritto in un'epoca di prospettive storiche più incerte

che non nel '51 o nel '57; con un maggiore sforzo d'interrogazione filosofica, che però nello stesso tempo si risolve in un abbandono lirico maggiore'
(RR, 1: 1216).

10 'Questi due personaggi [Agilulfo and Gurdulù] ... non potevano sviluppare
una storia; erano semplicemente l'enunciazione del tema che doveva essere
svolto da altri personaggi in cui l'esserci e il non esserci lottassero all'interno della stessa persona. Chi non sa ancora se c'è o non c'è, è il giovane;
quindi un giovane doveva essere il vero protagonista di questa storia ...
Rambaldo sarà la morale della pratica, dell'esperienza, della storia. Mi
serviva un altro giovane, Torrismondo, e ne feci la morale dell'assoluto, per
cui la verifica dell'esserci deve arrivare da qualcos'altro che se stesso ...

Per il giovane, la donna è quel che sicuramente c'è; e feci due donne: una,
Bradamante, l'amore come contrasto, come guerra, cioè la donna del cuore
di Rambaldo; l'altra – appena accennata –, Sofronia, l'amore come pace ... la
donna del cuore di Torrismondo' (RR, 1: 1216–17).

11 The most interesting discussion of Sartre's influence on Calvino I have come
across is in Bertoni 1993. I'm referring to Sartre's famous novel La nausée.

12 This could constitute an interesting point of departure for a discussion of
the *virtual* body proffered by modern technology and the ambiguous promise of unparalleled freedom to which it owes much of its appeal.

13 'L'unico modo per capirlo è porsi un compito ben preciso' (RR, 1: 996).
Colquhoun interprets this statement as a comment about Gurdulù and
translates it as 'The only way to cope with him is to give him a clear-cut job
to do.' But Rambaldo's question ('Why don't you make him realize that all
isn't soup ...?'), to which Agilulfo is replying, makes it clear that 'capir*lo*'
does not mean 'to understand *him*,' that is, Gurdulù, but rather 'to understand *it*,' that is, to understand that the world is not soup.

14 Colquhoun translates 'fino alla fine dei secoli' as 'for centuries,' which
seems inaccurate. In retrospect, the similarity in tone between this passage
and 'Becalmed in the Antilles' (published in English in the volume *Numbers
in the Dark*), the 1957 short story in which Calvino relied on a rather transparent allegory to criticize what he considered Togliatti's immobilism, is
compelling.

15 Calvino remarked that the idea to have Suor Teodora and Bradamante coin-
cide came to him very late in the composition (RR, 1:1219). This final twist
has been criticized for the alleged narrative inconsistencies that it gener-
ates. I agree that for much of the novel Suor Teodora and Bradamante function as separate characters. However, my argument is that there is a
constellation of meaning that finds a particularly appropriate, though by no
means necessary, expression in the final resolution. The surprise brings to

the surface what one may call a *narrative reason* that transcends the original authorial intention. And it is in this sense that the coup de théâtre can be called a stroke of genius.

16 I am using the '=' notation between the two names to remind the reader that the narrative has now acknowledged that Suon Teodora and Bradamante are one single character.

17 'Si comincia ad attraversare [in Pasolini's novels] ... una marmellata umana spalmata sugli squallidi bordi della città: ma a un certo punto c'è l'attrito d'un pensiero, d'un sentimento, d'un affiorare di coscienza ...

'Dalla letteratura dell'oggettività alla letteratura della coscienza ... Oggi, il senso della complessità del tutto, il senso del brulicante o del folto o dello screziato o del labirintico o dello stratificato, è diventato necessariamente complementare alla visione del mondo che si vale di una forzatura semplificatrice, schematizzatrice del reale. Ma il momento che vorremmo scaturisse dall'uno come dell'altro modo di intendere la realtà, è pur sempre quello della non accettazione della situazione data, dello scatto attivo e cosciente, della volontà di contrasto, della ostinazione senza illusioni' (*Una pietra*, 45).

18 'La resa all'oggettività ... nasce in un periodo in cui all'uomo viene meno la fiducia nell'indirizzare il corso delle cose ... perché vede che *le cose vanno avanti da sole*' (*Una pietra*, 41; emphasis added).

19 'Questa è infatti la tensione ideale che s'è logorata ... : è la crisi dello spirito rivoluzionario. Rivoluzionario è chi non accetta il dato naturale e storico e vuole cambiarlo' (*Una pietra*, 41).

20 '[S]e la ragione dell'universo trionfa su quella dell'uomo, è la fine del fare, della storia. Il barbaglio della ragione dell'universo è luce quando giunge a illuminare la vicenda limitata e ostinata del fare umano; ma se si sostiuisce ad essa è ritorno all'indistinto crogiuolo originario' (*Una pietra*, 44). I must confess I found this passage especially difficult to translate.

21 'Gli anni '50–60 formano uno spesso muro. Sono stati anni esteriormente non ingenerosi e il nostro benessere è aumentato. Ma in realtà sono stati anni duri, con alterne fasi di denti stretti, ventate di speranze, calate di pessimismo e di cinismo, gusci che ci siamo costruiti. Tutti abbiamo perduto qualcosa di noi stessi, poco o tanto. Conta quel che siamo riusciti a salvare, per noi e per gli altri. Da parte mia, è attraverso queste tre storie che credo d'aver salvato qualcosa di quel che c'era *di là* ...

'[I] tre romanzi qui raccolti sono nati da un bisogno che ogni volta mi veniva di esprimere una carica attiva, a suo modo ottimistica *senza mentire*' (*RR*, 1: 1222–3).

22 At a conference entitled *Masculinities and Cinema*, held in Newcastle-upon-

Tyne, UK, on 2–4 July 2001, Kaja Silverman delivered a stimulating paper on the cinema of Jean-Luc Godard. The theme of her intervention was that the dream of the nineteenth century (a dream from which we are still struggling to awake) is not commodification, as Walter Benjamin suggested, but mastery. I find an interesting and rich echo of this theoretical position in Calvino's concerns in *The Knight*.

Chapter 5 *The Watcher*

1 'La prima idea di questo racconto mi venne proprio il 7 giugno 1953. Fui al Cottolengo durante le elezioni per una decina di minuti. No, non ero scrutatore, ero candidato del Partito comunista ... E fu lì che mi venne l'idea del racconto, anzi il suo disegno ideale era già allora quasi compiuto come l'ho scritto adesso ... L'occasione di farmi nominare scrutatore al "Cottolengo" mi si presentò per le amministrative del '61. Passai al Cottolengo quasi due giorni e fui anche tra gli scrutatori che vanno a raccogliere il voto nelle corsie ... Insomma: prima ero a corto di immagini, ora avevo immagini troppo forti. Ho dovuto aspettare che si allontanassero ... e ho dovuto far maturare sempre più le riflessioni, i significati che da esse si irradiano' (qtd. in *RR*, 2: 1313–14).

2 'Dopo i quattro anni di silenzio narrativo, o quasi ("Io forse non scrivo più e vivo bene lo stesso," si legge in una lettera a Natalia Ginzburg del 12 maggio 1961 ...), che seguono il periodo d'intensa attività compreso tra le *Fiabe italiane* e *Il cavaliere inesistente*, Calvino si ripresenta in libreria con "il suo racconto più pensoso." Così recita il risvolto della prima edizione della *Giornata d'uno scrutatore* ... Si tratta infatti di "un libro di punti interrogativi," che in certo modo non viene a interrompere davvero quel silenzio ("In questo libro dò solo delle notizie sul mio silenzio")' (Falcetto in *RR*, 2: 1311).

3 '[*The Watcher* is] nello stesso tempo una specie di *reportage* ... e di *pamphlet* ... e anche di meditazione filosofica ... ma soprattutto, è una meditazione su se stesso del protagonista (un intellettuale comunista), una specie di *Pilgrim's Progress* d'uno storicista che vuole salvare le ragioni dell'operare storico insieme ad altre ragioni, appena intuite in quella sua giornata, del fondo segreto della persona umana' (Calvino qtd. in *RR*, 2: 1312).

4 'Erano gli anni della neoavanguardia, dei suoi maggiori trionfi e dei suoi attacchi contro il romanzo tradizionale, quello, per intenderci, che ancora seguitava imperterrito a proporre storie naturalistiche, o intimistiche, con personaggi dalle psicologie ben delineate ... In fin dei conti erano le tecniche del naturalismo ad essere esposte alle sventagliate critiche della

neoavanguardia. *La giornata d'uno scrutatore* sembra una provocazione' (Bonura 1972, 75–6).

5 I note that Bonura uses the term 'naturalism' to describe *The Watcher*. This raises an important issue (i.e., the distinction between naturalism and realism), which, however, is not crucial to my discussion of *The Watcher*.

6 'Si ha infatti l'impressione di essere di fronte alla denuncia drammatica di una crisi profonda che tocca le strutture stesse del raccontare e alla testimonianza di uno sforzo estremo per arrivare a superarla. Non solo, ma che il narratore sia giunto alle soglie di un limite oltre il quale non sembra esserci altro che l'impossibilità di raccontare: in altre parole, il silenzio' (Pautasso 1977, 1492).

7 'Passai al Cottolengo quasi due giorni ... Il risultato fu che restai completamente impedito dallo scrivere per molti mesi: le immagini che avevo negli occhi, di infelici senza capacità di intendere né di parlare né di muoversi, per i quali si allestiva la commedia di un voto delegato attraverso al prete o alla monaca, erano così infernali che avrebbero potuto ispirarmi solo un pamphlet violentissimo, un manifesto antidemocristiano, un seguito di anatemi contro un partito il cui potere si sostiene su voti ... ottenuti in questo modo. Insomma ... ora avevo immagini troppo forti. Ho dovuto aspettare che si allontanassero, che sbiadissero un poco nella memoria; e ho dovuto far maturare sempre più le riflessioni, i significati che da esse si irradiano' (qtd. in *RR*, 2: 1314).

8 'Nel volume del '63 c'è ... una riflessione esplicita sui fallimenti della razionalità utopica. Già nel secondo capitolo si sottolinea l'involuzione del movimento comunista internazionale, si lamenta il riprodursi dell'antica separazione tra governanti e governati; da un lato viene esaltato lo slancio delle democrazie nascenti, dall'altro viene denunciata la necrosi burocratica di cui soffrono partiti e Stati che pure di quello slancio si erano fatti interpreti. Riaffiorano così, in pagine che risultano a tratti soprendentemente solenni, questioni trattate su tutt'altro registro in opere quali "La gran bonaccia delle Antille," *Il barone rampante* o *Il cavaliere inesistente*' (*RR*, 2: xviii).

9 I should make clear that Togliatti's attitudes are being caricatured for polemical purposes. This is not the place for a detailed analysis of the merits and demerits of Togliatti's leadership. Rather, we are reflecting on the dangers that Calvino perceived in certain aspects of the PCI's cultural policy.

10 In 1958, the Italian publisher Feltrinelli secured its place in literary history by smuggling a copy of Pasternak's manuscript out of the USSR and publishing *Doctor Zhivago*. The critical debate that ensued exposed the ideolog-

ical basis of the PCI's sponsored battle for realism; and Pasternak's political views ensured that his work would be condemned by party critics. Like a number of other left-leaning intellectuals, Calvino, who had officially left the party by then, disagreed with the communist critics. Not surprisingly, his appraisal of Pasternak's work was much more balanced and insightful.

11 I remind the reader that, given the very close textual reading this chapter proposes and the crucial importance of the nuances of tone, the original passages in Italian are cited in the main body of the text, while the corresponding passages from William Weaver's excellent translation are in the notes, as here: 'Generic terms like "left-wing" party and "religious institution" are not used here to avoid calling things by their real name but because even declaring, d'emblée, that Amerigo Ormea's party was the Communist party and the polls were located inside Turin's famous "Cottolengo Hospital for Incurables" would represent a more apparent than real progress toward precision' (*The Watcher*, 5).

12 'Per spiegare cosa vuol dire *comunista* ho avuto bisogno di un periodo lunghissimo in cui tutti i significati fossero articolati in una struttura sintattica in cui la logica e la complessità fossero salvate insieme' (qtd. in *RR*, 2: 1313).

13 'In this journey he was making for the party, in the dawn as damp as a sponge' (*The Watcher*, 7).

14 'A final, anonymous heir of eighteenth century rationalism ... in the city where Pietro Giannone was kept in irons' (*The Watcher*, 8).

15 '[T]hen it was through the "inner contradictions of the bourgeoisie" or the "self-awareness of the declining class" that the class struggle had managed to bestir even the ex-bourgeois Amerigo' (*The Watcher*, 8)

16 '[T]his game many of whose rules seemed established and inscrutable and obscure, though you often felt you were helping establish them' (*The Watcher*, 8).

17 '[H]aving finally understood what wasn't really so hard to to understand: that this is only one corner of the immense world and that decisions are made – we won't say elsewhere, because "elsewhere" is everywhere – but on a vaster scale (and even here there were reasons for pessimism and reasons for optimism, but the former came more spontaneously to mind)' (*The Watcher*, 9).

18 'Following this train of thought, Amerigo was already content, as if it were all going for the best (apart from the dark prospects of the elections, apart from the fact that the ballot boxes were in an asylum, where they had been unable to hold political meetings, or stick up posters, or sell newspapers)' (*The Watcher*, 12).

19 'And with extremism, he could excuse his sloth, his indifference, he could immediately salve his conscience: if he could remain silent and motionless in the face of an imposture like this, if he was almost paralyzed, it was because in such situations it was all or nothing, either you accepted them or else: *tabula rasa*' (*The Watcher*, 25).

20 It might be useful to remember that Walter Benjamin (1977, 140–57; 1983, 95–6; 1968, 256) identified acedia as the affect haunting the modernist bourgeois intellectual.

21 'And Amerigo shut himself up like a hedgehog, in an opposition that was closer to aristocratic hauteur than to the warm, elementary partisanship of the people ... His thought raced in such an agile objectivity that he could see with the adversary's own eyes the very things he had felt contempt for a moment earlier, only to swing back, then, and feel with greater coldness how right his criticism was, and, finally, to attempt a serene judgment. Here again he was inspired not so much by a spirit of tolerance and of solidarity with his neighbor as a need to feel superior, capable of thinking all that was thinkable ... according to the prerogative of the true, liberal spirit.

   'In those years the Italian Communist party, among its many other tasks, had also assumed the position of an ideal liberal party, which had never really existed. And so the bosom of each individual Communist could house two personalities at once: an intransigent revolutionary and an Olympian liberal' (*The Watcher*, 25–6). For the problems related to the term 'liberal' see note 23 below. Weaver cannot but use it in this passage, but the result is that the paradox, and thus the satirical edge, is much weaker in English than in Italian.

22 After World War II, Croce's attitude toward communism was considerably less lofty, as he showed little hesitation in playing a significant role in the anti-communist crusade led by the DC. It is debatable whether this constituted an admission that the historico-philosophical significance of political struggle needed to be re-examined in view of Nazi and Fascist crimes, or whether he recognized in communism the class antagonist which Fascism was not.

23 In Italy a 'liberal' is a proponent of classical liberalism (from Locke to Adam Smith, etc.). Before and during Fascism, the liberal tradition included some progressive elements (the key figure here was Gobetti), and it is this tradition that the PCI will claim to have inherited. After World War II, however, the term 'liberal' took on an increasingly conservative meaning. The PLI was a right-wing, dogmatically laissez-faire party, though it did have some more progressive members. Therefore, it makes perfect sense to talk about a liberal-conservative attitude, an expression

that in North America sounds rather ridiculous. The U.S. notion of 'liberal' is, in this context, misleading.

24 Weaver translates 'Amerigo's historical attitude,' an interesting solution that conveys the general meaning but misses the allusion to the debates surrounding 'historicism' and what it meant to be a 'historicist' within the Italian cultural tradition, which we discussed in chapter 1 of this book.

25 It is perhaps hard for a contemporary North American audience to imagine how the PCI could credibly claim to be the heir of the 'liberal' tradition. Yet in the 1950s even an intellectual with as few sympathies for socialism as Norberto Bobbio (1955) took the claim quite seriously.

26 '[T]he more the militant individual lost inner richness, to conform to the compact, cast-iron bock, the more the liberal, housed in the same individual, gained new iridescent facets' (*The Watcher*, 26).

27 'They brought in one nun on a stretcher. She was young. Strangely, she was a beautiful woman. Dressed as if she were dead, her face flushed, she seemed composed, as if in the religious pictures hung in churches ... He [Amerigo] looked at it [a photograph of the nun] and was frightened. Even in its features, this was the face of a drowned woman, at the bottom of a well, shouting with her eyes, as she was pulled down into the darkness. He realized that everything in her was refusal; writhing: even her lying there motionless and ill' (*The Watcher*, 31).

28 'He didn't know what he would have liked; he understood only how far he was, he and everyone else, from living as it should be lived the life he was trying to live' (*The Watcher*, 31).

29 'And, after all, what could have changed in her? Not much: something still non-existent, which could therefore be thrust back into nothingness (at what point does a being become a being?), a mere biological potentiality, blind (at what point does a human become human?), a something that only a deliberate desire to make human could add to the ranks of human presences' (*The Watcher*, 54).

30 'The shrill cry came from a tiny red face, all eyes, the mouth opened in motionless laughter: a boy, sitting in bed in a white shirt, or rather not sitting, but emerging, trunk and head, from the bed's opening as a plant peeps up in a pot, like a plant's stalk that ended (there was no sign of arms) in that fishlike head, and this boy-plant-fish' (*The Watcher*, 55–6).

31 'The son had long limbs and a long face, which was also hairy and numb, perhaps half blocked by paralysis. The father was a peasant, also in his best suit, and in some ways, especially in the length of his face and his hands, he resembled his son. Not in the eyes: the son had the helpless eyes of an animal, while the father's eyes were half shut, wary, the eyes of an old farmer.

They were sitting obliquely on their chairs, at either side of the bed so they could stare at each other' (*The Watcher*, 57–8).

32 '"There," Amerigo thought, "those two, as they are, are necessary to each other." And then he thought: "There, this way of being is love." And then: "Humanity reaches as far as love reaches; it has no frontiers except those we give it"' (*The Watcher*, 64).

33 'From the moment he began *to feel less alien to those poor creatures*, the rigor of his political task had also become less alien to him. It was as if, in that first ward, the net of objective contradictions that held him in a kin of resignation to the worst had been broken, and now he felt lucid, as if everything were clear to him, as if he understood what should be demanded of society and what, on the other hand, couldn't be asked of society; but you had to achieve this awareness in person, otherwise it was useless.

'Everyone knows those moments when you seem to understand everything; perhaps the next moment you try to define what you've understood and it all vanishes' (*The Watcher*, 65; emphasis added).

34 Calvino's and Fortini's essays both appeared in *Il Menabò* 5 (1962), and I have discussed them already at some length in chapter 1.

35 'Oggi qualsiasi espressione letteraria che rappresenti una servitù in modo da rendere immediatamente possibile l'illusione di una libertà, serve una libertà illusoria ... Credo tocchi al marxista, al socialista coerente schernire oggi le nobili angosce di che il riformismo capitalistico cerca nascondere il suo sostanzioso ottimismo, la persuasione di avercela fatta ad assicurare al nostro paese progresso e democrazia' (Fortini 1962, 44).

36 'A chi si chiede ogni momento: "Ma non farò il gioco del capitalismo?" preferisco chi affronta tutti i problemi di trasformazione del mondo con la fiducia che ciò che è meglio serve per il meglio. Del resto, in questo stesso numero lo scritto di Fortini è un documento di come una tensione rivoluzionaria, se alimentata solo dalla passione per la teoria e non per l'operare pratico umano (e per le cose che di questo operare sono strumento e prodotto), si risolve nella scelta del nulla' (Calvino, *Una pietra*, 88).

37 Whether Calvino is correct in his assessment of Fortini's position is not the key issue. The most interesting aspect of the exchange is that it prefigures the polemic about 'structural reforms,' which would be hotly debated in the Italian left in the decades that follow.

38 'Doesn't the moment come, for any organization, when normal administrative routine takes over? (For Communism, too – Amerigo couldn't help wondering – would it happen with Communism, too? or was it already happening?)' (*The Watcher*, 14).

39 The voices of the New Left in Italy begin to be heard clearly in the debates

promoted by journals such as Raniero Panzieri's *Quaderni rossi*, founded in 1961, and Marco Bellocchio's *Quaderni piacentini*, founded in 1962.

40 '[T]he revolution meant discipline, preparation for responsibility, bargaining among powers even where the party wasn't in power (then Amerigo was attracted by this game many of whose rules seemed established and inscrutable and obscure, though you often felt you were helping establish them)' (*The Watcher*, 8).

41 From this root comes the English word 'inscrutable': 'That cannot be searched into or found out by searching; impenetrable or unfathomable by investigation; quite unintelligible, entirely mysterious' (*Compact Oxford English Dictionary*, 1: 1446).

Bibliography

Part 1 Calvino

A detailed bibliography of writings by Calvino has been compiled by Luca Baranelly and published in *Romanzi e racconti* (1994, 3: 1353–516). Once supplemented with Bertone (1994, 279–331), this should yield a virtually complete list of all traceable texts penned by the author. For a useful bibliography of non-fictional writings by Calvino see Ferretti (1989, 161–218), who also includes a list of the interviews Calvino published over the years.

The most extensive bibliographies of secondary literature on Calvino are listed in *Romanzi e racconti* (1994, 3: 1519). To these should now be added the one complied by Mario Barenghi, Bruno Falcetto, and Claudio Milanini and published in *Romanzi e racconti* (1994, 3: 1521–44), as well as Gabriele (1994, 166–70). A supplementary bibliography of secondary sources on Calvino's essays has appeared in *Saggi* (1995, 2: 3035–42).

My list below includes only works of specific relevance to my analysis.

Works by Italo Calvino Pertinent to This Study

Fiabe italiane: Raccolte dalla tradizione popolare durante gli ultimi cento anni e trascritte in lingua dai vari dialetti da Italo Calvino. 2 vols. Turin: Einaudi, 1971.
The Watcher and Other Stories. Trans. William Weaver. New York: Harcourt Brace Jovanovich, 1971.
The Path to the Nest of Spiders. Trans. A. Colquhoun. Hopewell, NJ: Ecco, 1976.
Una pietra sopra: Discorsi di letteratura e società. Turin: Einaudi, 1980.
Difficult Loves, Smog, A Plunge in Real Estate. London: Secker & Warburg, 1983.
The Uses of Literature. Trans. Patrick Creagh. New York: Harcourt Brace Jovanovich, 1986.

Lezioni americane: Sei proposte per il prossimo millennio. Milano: Garzanti, 1988.

I libri degli altri: Lettere 1947–1981. Turin: Einaudi, 1991.

Perché leggere i classici. Milan: Mondadori, 1991.

Romanzi e racconti. 3 vols. Ed. Claudio Milanini. Milan: Mondadori, 1991–4.

Our Ancestors. Trans. A. Colquhoun. London: Minerva, 1992.

Six Memos for the Next Millennium. Trans. Patrick Creagh. London: Cape, 1992.

Prima che tu dica «Pronto». Milan: Mondadori, 1993.

Eremita a Parigi. Milan: Mondadori, 1994.

Saggi. 2 vols. Ed. Mario Barenghi. Milan: Mondadori, 1995.

Numbers in the Dark. Trans. Tim Parks. Toronto: Vintage, 1996.

Book-length Studies on Italo Calvino

Adler, Sara Maria. *Calvino: The Writer as Fablemaker.* Madrid: Ediciones Jose Porrula Turanzas, 1979.

Baroni, Giorgio. *Italo Calvino: Introduzione e guida allo studio dell'opera calviniana, storia e antologia della critica.* Florence: Le Monnier, 1988.

Belpoliti, Marco. *Storie del visibile: Lettura di Italo Calvino.* Rimini: Luisè, 1990.

– *L'occhio di Calvino.* Turin: Einaudi, 1996.

– ed. *Italo Calvino, Enciclopedia: Arte, scienza e letteratura.* Milan: Marcos y Marcos, 1995.

Benussi, Cristina. *Introduzione a Calvino.* Bari: Laterza, 1989.

Bernardini Napoletano, Francesca. *I segni nuovi di Italo Calvino.* Rome: Bulzoni, 1977.

Bersellino, Italo. *Il viaggio interrotto di Italo Calvino.* Modena: Mucchi, 1991.

Bertone, Giorgio. *Il castello della scrittura.* Turin: Einaudi, 1994.

– ed. *Italo Calvino: La letteratura, la scienza, la critica.* Atti del Convegno nazionale. San Remo, 28–9 November 1986. Genoa: Marietti, 1988.

– ed. *Italo Calvino: A Writer for the Next Millennium.* Turin: Edizioni dell'Orso, 1998.

Bertoni, Roberto. *Int'abrigu int'ubagu: Discorso su alcuni aspetti dell'opera di Italo Calvino.* Turin: Tirrenia Stampatori, 1993.

Bloom, Harold, ed. *Italo Calvino.* Philadelphia: Chelsea House Publishers, 2001.

Bonura, Giuseppe. *Invito alla lettura di Italo Calvino.* Milan: Mursia, 1972.

Bresciani Califano, Mimma. *Uno spazio senza miti, scienza e letteratura, quattro saggi su Italo Calvino.* Florence: Le Lettere, 1993.

Calligaris, Contardo. *Italo Calvino.* Milan: Mursia, 1973.

– *Italo Calvino.* Ed. G.P. Bernasconi. New edition. Milan: Mursia, 1985.

Cannon, Jo Ann. *Italo Calvino: Writer and Critic.* Ravenna: Longo, 1981.

Carter, Albert Howard, III. 'Fantasy in the Work of Italo Calvino.' Diss. University of Iowa, 1971.
– Italo Calvino: Metamorphoses of Fantasy. Ann Arbor: UMI Research Press, 1987.
Castelnuovo Frigessi, Delia, ed. Inchiesta sulle fate: Italo Calvino e la fiaba. Pref. Cesare Segre. Bergamo: Lubrina, 1988.
Centofanti, Fabrizio. Italo Calvino: Una trascendenza mancata. Milan: Istituto Propaganda Libraria, 1993.
Chessa Wright, Simonetta. La poetica neobarocca di Italo Calvino. Ravenna: Longo, 1998.
Chubb, Stephen. I, Writer, I, Reader: The Concept of Self in the Fiction of Italo Calvino. Hull, UK: Troubadour, 1997.
Clerici, Luca, ed. Calvino e l'editoria. Milan: Marcos y Marcos, 1993.
Clerici, Luca, and Bruno Falcetto, eds. Calvino e il comico. Milan: Marcos y Marcos, 1994.
Corti, Maria. Il viaggio testuale. Turin: Einaudi, 1978.
De Caprio, Caterina. La sfida di Aracne: Sudi su Italo Calvino. Naples: Libreria Dante & Descartes, 1996.
Deidier, Roberto. Le forme del tempo: Saggio su Italo Calvino. Milan: Angelo Guerini, 1995.
Di Carlo, Franco. Come leggere I nostri antenati di Italo Calvino. Milan: Mursia, 1978.
Falaschi, Giovanni. Da Giusti a Calvino. Rome: Bulzoni, 1993.
– ed. Italo Calvino: Atti del Convegno Internazionale. Firenze, Palazzo Medici-Riccardi, 26–8 Feb. 1987. Milan: Garzanti, 1988.
Ferretti, Gian Carlo. Le capre di bikini: Calvino giornalista e saggista 1945–1985. Rome: Editori Riuniti, 1989.
– Le avventure del lettore: Calvino, Ludmilla e gli altri. Lecce: Piero Manni, 1997.
Finocchiaro Chimirri, Giovanna. Letteratura come storiografia. Catania: Giannotta, 1968.
– Italo Calvino tra realtà e favola. Catania: CUECM, 1987.
Flieger, Hanna. Il rapporto varianti/costanti nella poetica di Italo Calvino, modalità attanziali e implicazioni culturali. Turin: Poznan, 1994.
Folena, Gianfranco, ed. Tre narratori: Calvino, Primo Levi, Parise. Padua: Liviana, 1989.
Frasson-Marin, Aurore. Italo Calvino et l'imaginaire. Paris: Éditions Slatkine, 1986.
– ed. Italo Calvino: Imaginaire et rationalité. Acts of the Congress on Italo Calvino. Geneva: Slatkine, 1991.
Gabriele, Tommasina. Italo Calvino: Eros and Language. Cranbury, NJ: Fairleigh Dickinson University Press, 1994.

Hume, Kathryn. *Calvino's Fiction: Cogito and Cosmos*. Oxford: Clarendon; New York: Oxford University Press, 1992.

Jeannet, Angela M. *Under the Radiant Sun and the Crescent Moon: Italo Calvino's Storytelling*. Toronto: University of Toronto Press, 2000.

Lucente, Gregory L. *Beautiful Fables: Self-Consciousness in Italian Narrative from Manzoni to Calvino*. Baltimore: Johns Hopkins University Press, 1986.

Mengaldo, Pier Vincenzo. *La tradizione del Novecento: Da D'Annunzio a Montale*. Milan: Feltrinelli, 1975.

Milanini, Claudio. *L'utopia discontinua: Saggio su Italo Calvino*. Milan: Garzanti, 1990.

Mondello, Elisabetta. *Italo Calvino*. Pordenone: Edizioni Studio Tesi, 1990.

Montella, Luigi. *Italo Calvino: Il percorso dei linguaggi*. Salerno: Edisud, 1996.

Olken, I.T. *With Pleated Eye and Garnet Wing: Symmetries in Italo Calvino*. Ann Arbor: University of Michigan Press, 1984.

Pepe, Massimo, ed. *Conversazioni su Italo Calvino*. Atti del convegno dell'Università degli studi di Roma 'Tor Vergata.' Rome: Nuova cultura, 1992.

Pescio Bottino, Germana. *Calvino*. Florence: La Nuova Italia, 1967.

Pierangeli, Fabio. *Italo Calvino: Le metamorfosi e l'idea del nulla*. Soveria Mannelli: Rubettino, 1997.

Re, Lucia. *Calvino and the Age of Neorealism: Fables of Estrangement*. Stanford, CA: Stanford University Press, 1990.

Ricci, Franco, ed. *Calvino Revisited*. Ottawa: Dovehouse, 1989.

Scarpa, Domenico. *Italo Calvino*. Milan: Bruno Mondadori, 1999.

Weiss, Beno. *Understanding Italo Calvino*. Columbia: University of South Carolina Press, 1993.

Woodhouse, J.R. *Italo Calvino: A Reappraisal and an Appreciation of the Trilogy*. Hull, UK: University of Hull Press, 1968.

- *Il barone rampante*. Manchester: The University Press, 1970.

Articles Pertinent to the Five Novels Discussed in This Book

Amoroso, Vito. 'L'armonia di Calvino.' *Nuova corrente* 14 (1959): 68–71.

- 'Il cavaliere confuso.' *Nuova corrente* 18 (1960): 119–24.

Annoni, Carlo. 'Italo Calvino: La resistenza tra realtà e favola.' *Vita e pensiero* 51 (1968): 968–75.

Apollonio, Carla. '*Il dottor Jekyll e Mr. Hyde* di R.L. Stevenson e *Il visconte dimezzato* di Calvino: Divergenze e convergenze.' *Otto/Novecento* 3–4 (1984): 207–12.

Asor Rosa, Alberto. 'Calvino dal sogno alla realtà.' *Mondo Operaio* 3–4 (1958): 3–77.

- 'Il carciofo della retorica.' *Intellettuali e classe operaia.* Firenze: Nuova Italia, 1973. 139–47.
- 'Il cuore duro di Italo Calvino.' *La Repubblica* 1–2 December 1985: 17–18.
- 'Il punto di vista di Italo Calvino.' In Falaschi, *Italo Calvino.* 1988. 261–76.
Baldini, Pier Raimondo. 'Calvino: "Il più povero degli uomini"?' *Forum Italicum* 10 (1976): 189–202.
Barilli, Renato. 'Il mare dell'oggettività.' *Il Verri* 2 (1960): 158–61.
Barret, Tracy. 'The Narrator of Italo Calvino's *Il cavaliere inesistente.*' *Quaderni d'Italianistica* 13.1 (1992): 57–70.
Baudrillard, Jean. 'Les Romans d'Italo Calvino.' *Les temps modernes* 192 (1962): 1728–34.
Block, Alan A. 'The Utopian Reality of Italo Calvino's *Baron in the Trees.*' *Italian Quarterly* 30 (1989): 5–15.
Boselli, Mario. 'Italo Calvino: L'immaginazione logica.' *Nuova Corrente* 78 (1979): 137–50.
Bouissy, A., and Paul Renucci. 'Fantasie, fantastique, "fantascienza" dans les récits de Zavattini, Buzzati, Calvino et quelques autres (petit lexique).' *Letteratura e società.* Palermo: Palumbo, 1980. 649–66.
Bronzini, G.B. 'Dai Grimm a Calvino e la fiaba del Duemila.' *Cultura e scuola* 115 (1990): 53–61.
Bruscagli, Riccardo. 'Autobiografia (perplessa) di Italo Calvino.' *Paragone* 31 (1980): 82–7.
Bryce, Judith. 'Rousseau and Calvino: An Unexplored Ideological Perspective of *Il barone rampante.*' In *Moving in Measure: Essays in Honour of Brian Moloney.* Ed. Judith Bryce and Dough Thompson. Hull, UK: Hull University Press, 1989.
Byrne, Jack. 'Calvino's Fantastic "Ancestors": The Viscount, the Baron and the Knight.' *Review of Contemporary Fiction* 6.2 (1986): 42–53.
Caimmi Lamoureux, Augusta. 'Calvino e Vittorini: Modo di rifare la nuova realtà.' *Canadian Journal of Italian Studies* 3 (1979): 8–13.
Caretti, Lanfranco. 'Narrative di Calvino.' *Svizzera Italiana* 19 (1959): 41–4
Carlton, Jill Margo. 'The Genesis of *Il barone rampante.*' *Italica* 61 (1984): 195–206.
Cases, Cesare. 'Calvino e il "pathos della distanza."' In *I metodi attuali della critica.* Ed. Maria Corti and Cesare Segre. Turin: Edizione RAI, 1970. 53–8.
Cecchi, Emilio. 'Il visconte dimezzato.' Rev. of *Il visconte dimezzato,* by Italo Calvino. *Di giorno in giorno.* Milan: Garzanti, 1954. 310–13.
Ceserani, Remo. 'Quando Calvino leggeva "centopagine."' *Belfagor* 46 (1991): 706–9.

Citati, Piero. 'Fine dello storicismo (in risposta a Italo Calvino).' *Paragone* 6 (1955): 32–41.

De Lauretis, Teresa. 'Narrative Discourse in Calvino: Praxis or Poiesis?' *PMLA* 90 (1975): 414–25.

De Martini, Francesco. 'Strumenti scientifici nella dimensione fiabesca: Livelli di realtà in Italo Calvino.' *Narrare: Perscorsi possibili*. Ravenna: Longo, 1989.

De Tommaso, Piero. Rev. of *Il barone rampante*, by Italo Calvino. *Belfagor* 13 (1958): 492–5.

– 'Un'ambigua sfida al labirinto.' *Belfagor* 19 (1964): 88–91.

– 'Favola e realtà in Calvino.' *Narratori italiani contemporanei*. Rome: Edizioni dell'Ateneo, 1965. 203–16.

De Vivo, Albert. 'Calvino: politica e segni letterari.' *Forum Italicum* 25.1 (1991): 40–56.

Dulac, Paulette. 'Le cheminement de la dialectique dans *La journée d'un scrutateur*.' In Frasson-Marin, *Italo Calvino: Imaginaire et rationalité*. 1991. 67–75.

Edwards, Brian. 'Deconstructing the Artist and the Art: Barth and Calvino at Play in the Funhouse of Language.' *Canadian Review of Comparative Literature* 12.2 (1985): 264–86.

Falaschi, Giovanni. 'Calvino fra realismo e razionalismo.' *Belfagor* 26 (1971): 373–91.

– 'Italo Calvino.' *Belfagor* 27 (1972): 530–55.

Ferrata, Giansiro. 'Le due metà della *Giornata di uno scrutatore*.' *Rinascita* 20 (1963): 26.

Finocchiaro Chimirri, Giovanna. 'Realtà e favola in Italo Calvino.' *Teoresi* 21 (1966): 296–313.

Gabriele, Tommasina. 'Literature as Education and the Near-Perfect Protagonist: Narrative Structure in *Il barone rampante*.' *Stanford Italian Review* 11.1–2 (1992): 91–102.

Garboli, Cesare. 'Identità di Calvino.' *La stanza separata*. Milan: Mondadori, 1967. 209–14.

Gatt-Rutter, John. 'Calvino Ludens: Literary Play and Its Political Implications.' *Journal of European Studies* 5 (1975): 319–40.

Ghidetti, Enrico. 'Il fantastico ben temperato di Italo Calvino.' *Il Ponte* 43.2 (1987): 109–23.

Guardiani, Francesco. 'Optimism without Illusions.' *Review of Contemporary Fiction* 6.2 (1986): 54–61.

Heiney, Donald. 'Calvino and Borges: Some Implications of Fantasy.' *Mundus Artium* 3 (1968): 66–76.

Jonard, Norbert. 'Calvino et le siècle des Lumières.' *Forum Italicum* 18.2 (1984): 93–116.

Joseph, John Earl. 'Man, History, Subject, Object: Calvino in Crisis.' *Review of Contemporary Fiction* 6.2 (1986): 24–30.

Leroy, Hélène. 'Politique et littérature chez Italo Calvino.' In Frasson-Marin, *Italo Calvino: Imaginaire et rationalité*. 1991. 9–19.

Luperini, Romano. 'Calvino, Sciascia e lo scacco dell'ideologia nella narrativa degli anni cinquanta.' In *Il novecento*. Turin: Loescher, 1981. 760–71.

Manacorda, Giuliano. 'Nota su Italo Calvino.' *Belfagor* 12 (1957): 197–200.

Marabini, Claudio. 'La ricerca di Calvino.' *Nuova antologia* 554 (1985): 179–86.

Mazza, Antonia. 'Italo Calvino: Uno scrittore dimezzato?' *Letture* 26 (1971): 3–14.

– 'La parabola di uno "scrutatore."' *Letture: Libro e Spettacolo* 41 (1986): 291–308.

– 'Italo Calvino.' *Scrittori Italiani*. Milan: «Letture», 1989. 33–54.

Mengaldo, Pier Vincenzo. 'Aspetti della lingua di Calvino.' In Folena, *Tre narratori*. 1989. 9–55.

Migiel, Marilyn. 'The Phantasm of Omnipotence in Calvino's Trilogy.' *Modern Language Studies* 16.3 (1986): 57–68.

Milanini, Claudio. 'Introduzione.' *Romanzi e racconti*. By Italo Calvino. Vol. 2. 1992. xi–xxxvi.

Muckley, Peter A. 'A Senseless Cluster: A Note on Literary Allusion and Literacy in *The Baron in the Trees*.' *Italian Quarterly* 30 (1989): 17–22.

Nardella, Rosa. '*Il barone rampante*: Un Don Quijote della filosofia dei lumi.' *Italian Quarterly* 30 (1989): 23–30.

Olken, I.T. 'Spira Mirabilis: Italo Calvino's Progressionary Paradigms.' *Modern Language Quarterly* 49.2 (1988): 142–72.

Orioli, Giovanni. 'Calvino tra la favola e l'impegno.' *Elsinore* 1 (1964): 69–76.

Ossola, Carlo. 'L'invisibile e il suo "dove": "Geografia interiore" di Italo Calvino.' *Lettere italiane* 39.2 (1987): 220–51.

Palmieri, Pierre. 'Il sistema spaziale del *Barone rampante*.' *Lingua e stile* 23.2 (1988): 251–70.

Patuzzi, Claudia. 'Italo Calvino: Un intellettuale tra poesia e impegno.' *Nuova antologia* 527 (1976): 140–7.

Pautasso, Sergio. 'Favola, allegoria, utopia nell'opera di Italo Calvino.' *Nuovi Argomenti* 33–4 (1973): 67–94.

– 'Italo Calvino.' *I Contemporanei*. Milan: Marzorati, 1977. 1471–507.

Pescio Bottino, Germana. 'Italo Calvino tra fantasia e simbolo.' *Diogene* 2 (1960): 5.

Petroni, Franco. 'Italo Calvino: Dall'impegno all'arcadia neocapitalista.' *Studi novecenteschi* 5 (1976): 57–101.

– 'La discesa agli inferi: Archetipi e ideologia in Sartre, Calvino, e Fenoglio.' *Allegoria* 8 (1991): 35–55.

Ragusa, Olga. 'Italo Calvino: The Repeated Conquest of Contemporaneity.' *World Literature Today* 57.2 (1983): 195–201.

Sabbatino, Pasquale. 'Il secondo Novecento nelle lettere di Calvino.' *Otto/Novecento* 15.3–4 (1992): 107–32.

Sanguineti Katz, Giuliana. 'Le "adolescenze difficili" di Italo Calvino.' *Quaderni d'italianistica* 5 (1984): 247–61.

Sapegno, Natalino. 'Introduzione a Italo Calvino.' In Bertone, *Italo Calvino*. 1988. 17–19.

Sciascia, Leonardo. Rev. of *Il barone rampante*, by Italo Calvino. *Il ponte* 13 (1957): 1882–5.

Sobrero, Ornella. 'Calvino scrittore "rampante."' *Il caffè* 12 (1964): 28–42.

Spinazzola, Vittorio. 'L'io diviso di Italo Calvino.' *Belfagor* 42.5 (1987): 507–31.

Usher, Jon. 'The Grotesque as Metaphor in Calvino's *Giornata di uno scrutatore*.' *Bulletin of the Society for Italian Studies* 21 (1988): 2–14.

Varese, Claudio. 'Italo Calvino: Da *I racconti* a *Il cavaliere inesistente*.' *Nuova antologia* 95 (1960): 552–8.

– Rev. of *La giornata di uno scrutatore*, by Italo Calvino. *Nuova Antologia* 98 (1963): 120–3.

– 'Italo Calvino: Una complessa continuità.' *Rassegna della letteratura italiana* 84 (1984): 252–6.

Wahl, François. 'La logica dell'immagine in Calvino.' *Il caffè* 12 (1964): 36–7.

Weiss, Beno. 'Cottolengo: Calvino's Living Hell: The Speculating Intellectual at the Crossroads.' *Italian Culture* 10 (1992): 1045–58.

Woodhouse, J.R. 'Italo Calvino and the Re-Discovery of a Genre.' *Italian Quarterly* 12 (1968): 45–66.

Zago, Ester. 'The Romantic Baron of Italo Calvino.' *Proceedings of the Pacific Northwest Conference on Foreign Languages* 28.1 (1977): 78–80.

Part 2 Selected Background Readings

The Italian Context

Ajello, Nello. *Intellettuali e Pci: 1944–1958*. Rome: Laterza, 1979.

Alatri, Paolo. *Le occasioni della storia*. Rome: Bulzoni, 1990.

Alberoni, Francesco. *Italia in trasformazione*. Bologna: Il Mulino, 1976.

Albertoni, Ettore A., Ezio Antonini, and Renato Plamieri, eds. *La generazione degli anni difficili*. Bari: Laterza, 1962.

Alicata, Mario. 'La corrente *Politecnico*.' *Rinascita* 5–6 (1946): 116.

Asor Rosa, Alberto. *Scrittori e popolo*. Rome: Savelli, 1972.

– *Intellettuali e classe operaia: Saggi sulle forme di uno storico conflitto e di una possibile alleanza*. Florence: Nuova Italia, 1973.

– 'La cultura.' *Storia d'Italia: Dall'Unità a oggi*. Vol. 4, pt. 2. Turin: Einaudi, 1975.

– ed. *Letteratura italiana*. 6 vols. Turin: Einaudi, 1982.

– ed. *Letteratura italiana: Storia e geografia*. 3 vols. Turin: Einaudi, 1987.

Balestrini, Nanni. *Gruppo '63*. Milan: Feltrinelli, 1964.

Barberi Squarotti, Giorgio. *Poesia e narrativa del secondo Novecento*. Milan: Mursia, 1961.

– *La narrativa italiana del dopoguerra*. Bologna: Cappelli, 1965.

Barucci, Piero. *L'Italia del dopoguerra: La ricostruzione economica 1943–47*. Florence: le Monnier, 1978.

Bisacchia, Andrea. 'Dalla letteratura dell'oggettività alla letteratura della coscienza.' *Aspetti del secondo novecento: Pavese, Vittorini, Salvino*. Syracuse: Editrice Meridionale, 1973. 85–94.

Bo, Carlo. 'Il neorealismo, trent'anni dopo.' *Lettere italiane* 27.4 (1975): 396–409.

Bobbio, Norberto. *Politica e cultura*. Turin: Einaudi, 1955.

– *Profilo ideologico del Novecento italiano*. Turin: Einaudi, 1986.

Bonifazi, Neuro. *L'alibi del realismo*. Florence: La Nuova Italia, 1972.

Burgundio, Enrico. 'Sulle costruzioni fantastiche di sistemi non reali.' *Belfagor* 25.6 (1970): 642–8.

Candeloro, Giorgio. *Storia dell'Italia moderna*. 11 vols. Milan: Feltrinelli, 1986.

Cases, Cesare. *Marxismo e neopositivismo*. Turin: Einaudi, 1958.

Catalano, Gabriele, ed. *Da Verga a Eco: Strutture e tecniche del romanzo italiano*. N.p.: Tullio Pironti, 1989.

Colarizi, Simona. *La seconda guerra mondiale e la Repubblica*. Vol. 23 of *Storia d'Italia*. Ed. Giuseppe Galasso. Turin: UTET, 1984.

Cravieri, Pietro. *La Repubblica dal 1958 al 1992*. Vol. 24 of *Storia d'Italia*. Ed. Giuseppe Galasso. Turin: UTET, 1995.

De Felice, Renzo, ed. *Storia dell'Italia contemporanea*. 7 vols. Naples: Edizioni Scientifiche Italiane, 1983.

Di Pietro, John. 'La resistenza nel romanzo italiano del dopoguerra.' Diss. McGill University, 1979.

Eco, Umberto. 'Del modo di formare come impegno sulla realtà.' *Il Menabò* 5 (1962): 198–237.

Falaschi, Giovanni. *La resistenza armata nella letteratura italiana.* Turin: Einaudi, 1976.

Ferretti, Gian Carlo. *La letteratura del rifiuto.* Milan: Mursia, 1968.

– *Officina: Cultura, letteratura e politica negli anni Cinquanta.* Turin: Einaudi, 1975.

Fiaccarini Marchi, Donatella, ed. *Il menabò (1959–1967).* Rome: Ateneo, 1973.

Fini, Marco ed. *1945–1975 Italia: Fascismo, antifascismo, Resistenza, rinnovamento.* Milan: Feltrinelli, 1975.

Forti, Marco, and Sergio Pautasso, eds. *Il Politecnico.* Milan: Rizzoli, 1975.

Fortini, Franco. 'Astuti come colombe.' *Il Menabò* 5 (1962): 29–44.

– *Dieci inverni: 1947–1957: Contributi ad un discorso socialista.* Bari: De Donato, 1972.

– *Saggi italiani.* Bari: De Donato, 1974.

– *Verifica dei poteri.* Milan: Il Saggiatore, 1974.

Galli, Giorgio. *La sinistra italiana nel dopoguerra.* Milan: Il Saggiatore, 1978.

Gambetti, Fidia. *La grande illusione: 1945–1953.* Milan: Mursia, 1976.

Gambino, Antonio. *Storia del dopoguerra: Dalla liberazione al potere DC.* Rome: Laterza, 1975.

Garin, Eugenio. *Intellettuali italiani del XX secolo.* Rome: Riuniti, 1974.

Ginsborg, Paul. *A History of Contemporary Italy: Society and Politics, 1943–1988.* London: Penguin, 1990.

Golino, Ezio. *Cultura e mutamento sociale.* Milan: Edizioni di comunità, 1969.

– 'Il partito e l'intellettuale.' *Nuovi Argomenti* 1, 3rd s. (1982): 16–17.

Gramsci, Antonio. *Letteratura e vita nazionale.* Turin: Einaudi, 1950.

– *Gli intellettuali e l'organizzazione della cultura.* Turin: Einaudi, 1966.

– *La letteratura popolare.* Rome: Editori Riuniti, 1993.

Guarnieri, Silvio. *L'intellettuale nel partito.* Venice: Marsilio, 1976.

Guglielmi, Angelo. *Avanguardia e sperimentalismo.* Milan: Feltrinelli, 1964.

La Porta, Filippo. *La nuova narrativa italiana.* Turin: Bollati Boringhieri, 1995.

Luperini, Romano. *Il Novecento: Apparati ideologici, ceto intellettuale, sistemi formali nella letteratura italiana contemporanea.* 2 vols. Turin: Loescher, 1981.

Mammarella, Giuseppe. *L'Italia dopo il fascismo, 1943–1973.* Bologna: Il Mulino, 1974.

Marchi, Donatella, ed. *Il Menabò: 1959–1967.* Rome: dell'Ateneo, 1973.

Mazzarella, Arturo. 'Il Menabò: La ragione della storia.' *Lavoro critico* 11–12 (1977): 5–43.

Menabò di letteratura (Il). Ed. Elio Vittorini and Italo Calvino. Turin: Einaudi, 1959–67.

Migliori, Katia, ed. *Officina (1955–1959)*. Rome: Ateneo & Bizzarri, 1979.

Milanini, Claudio, ed. *Neorealismo: poetiche e polemiche*. Milan: Il Saggiatore, 1980.

Pintor, Giame. 'Lettera al fratello Luigi.' In Milanini, *Neorealismo*. 1980. 35–7.

Politecnico (Il). Ed. Elio Vittorini. Turin: Einaudi, 1945–47.

Romanò, A. 'Osservazioni sulla letteratura del Novecento.' *Officina* 11 (1957): 417–44.

Romano, Massimo. *Gli stregoni della fantacultura: La funzione dell'intellettuale nella letteratura italiana del dopoguerra (1945–1975)*. Turin: Paravia, 1977.

Roversi, Roberto. 'Digressione per "I gettoni,"' *Officina* 4 (1955): 158–64.

Salinari, Carlo. *Preludio e fine del realismo in Italia*. Naples: Morano, 1967.

– *Tra politica e cultura*. Milano: Teti, 1980.

Scalia, Gianni. 'La letteratura di partito.' *Officina* ns 2 (1959): 51–6.

Secchi, Mario. '*Officina* e il tempo dell'ideologia.' *Lavoro critico* 7/8 (1976): 5–56.

Tarizzo, Domenico. 'L'esperienza del *Politecnico* tra mitologie di massa ed élites del sapere.' *Nuova corrente* 18 (1960): 55–72.

Togliatti, Palmiro. *I corsivi di Roderigo: Interventi politico-culturali dal 1944 al 1964*. Ed. Ottavio Cecchi, Giovanni Leone, and Giuseppe Vacca. Bari: De Donato, 1976.

Valente, Mario. *Ideologia e potere: Da 'Il politecnico' a 'Contropiano' 1945/1972*. Turin: ERI, 1978.

Vittoria, Albertina. *Togliatti e gli intellettuali: Storia dell'Istituto Gramsci negli anni Cinquanta e Sessanta*. Rome: Editori Riuniti, 1992.

Zancan, M. *Il progetto 'Politecnico.'* Venice: Marsilio, 1984.

Zangrandi, Ruggero, and Marcello Venturoli. *Dizionario della paura*. Pisa: Nistri-Lischi, 1951.

Zolla, Elemire. *Eclissi dell'intellettuale*. Milan: Bompiani, 1959.

Theoretical and Methodological Works

Angenot, Marc. 'The Absent Paradigm.' *Science-Fiction Studies* 6 (1979): 9–19.

Bakhtin, Mikhail M. *The Dialogic Imagination: Four Essays*. Ed. Michael Holquist. Trans. Caryl Emerson and Michael Holquist. Austin: University of Texas Press, 1981.

– *Problems of Dostoevsky's Poetics*. Ed. and trans. Caryl Emerson. Manchester: Manchester University Press, 1984.

– *Rabelais and His World*. Trans. Helene Iswolsky. Bloomington: Indiana University Press, 1984.

Barthes, Roland. *S/Z*. Paris: Seuil, 1970.

Benjamin, Walter. *Illuminations*. Trans. Harry Zohn. New York: Harcourt, Brace & World, 1968.

– *The Origin of German Tragic Drama*. Trans. John Osborne. London: NLB, 1977.

– *Charles Baudelaire: A Lyric Poet in the Era of High Capitalism*. Trans. Harry Zohn. London; New York: Verso, 1983.

– *Reflections: Essays, Aphorisms, Autobiographical Writings*. Ed. Peter Demetz. Trans. Edmund Jephcott. New York: Schocken, 1986.

Bernstein, Richard J., ed. *Habermas and Modernity*. Cambridge, MA: MIT Press, 1985.

Binni, Walter. *Poetica, critica e storia letteraria*. Bari: Laterza, 1963.

Bolongaro, Eugenio. 'From Litereariness to Genre: Establishing the Foundations for a Theory of Literary Genres.' *Genre* 25 (1992): 277–313.

Braudel, Fernand. 'La longue durée.' *Annales ESE* 13 (1958): 725–53.

Deleuze, Gilles. *Foucault*. Paris: Minuit, 1986.

Deleuze, Gilles, and Félix Guattari. *L'Anti-Œdipe*. Paris: Minuit, 1972.

– *Mille plateaux*. Paris: Minuit, 1980.

Eco, Umberto. *The Role of the Reader*. Bloomington: Indiana University Press, 1979.

– *Semiotics and the Philosophy of Language*. Bloomington: Indiana University Press, 1984.

– *Opera aperta*. Milan: Bompiani, 1988.

Foster, Hal, ed. *The Anti-Aesthetic: Essays on Postmodern Culture*. Seattle: Bay, 1983.

Foucault, Michel. *L'ordre du discours*. Paris: Gallimard, 1971.

– *Surveiller et punir*. Paris: Gallimard, 1975.

– *Language, Countermemory, Practice: Selected Essays and Interviews by Michel Foucault*. Ed. Donald F. Bouchard. Trans. Donald F. Bouchard and Sherry Simon. Ithaca, NY: Cornell University Press, 1977.

– *Power/Knowledge: Selected Inteviews and Other Writings 1972–1977*. Ed. Colin Gordon. Trans. Colin Gordon, Leo Marshall, John Mepham, Kate Soper. New York: Pantheon, 1980.

– *The History of Sexuality*. 3 vols. Trans. Robert Hurley. New York: Vintage, 1980–6.

Gramsci, Antonio. *Quaderni del carcere*. 4 vols. Ed. Valentino Gerratana. Turin: Einaudi, 1975.

Guillén, Claudio. *Literature as System*. Princeton, NJ: Princeton University Press, 1971.

Habermas, Jürgen. *Knowledge and Human Interests*. Trans. Jeremy J. Shapiro. Boston: Beacon, 1971.

– 'Modernity – An Incomplete Project.' In Foster, *The Anti-Aesthetic*. 1983. 5–15.

– *The Philosophical Discourse of Modernity: Twelve Lectures*. Trans. Frederick G. Lawrence. Cambridge, MA: MIT Press, 1987.

Ingarden, Roman. *The Cognition of the Literary Work of Art*. Trans. Ruth Ann Crowley and Kenneth R. Olson. Evanston, IL: Northwestern University Press, 1973.

Iser, Wolfgang. *The Act of Reading: A Theory of Aesthetic Response*. Baltimore: Johns Hopkins University Press, 1978.

Jewell, Keala. *The Poiesis of History: Experimenting with Genre in Postwar Italy*. Ithaca, NY: Cornell University Press, 1992.

Kant, Immanuel. *Critique of Pure Reason*. Trans. Norman Kemp Smith. London: Macmillan, 1933.

Lukács, Georg. *The Historical Novel*. Trans. Hannah and Stanley Mitchell. Boston: Beacon, 1963.

– *History and Class Consciousness*. Trans. Rodney Livingstone. Cambridge, MA: MIT Press, 1971.

Mannheim, Karl. *Ideology and Utopia*. 1936. Trans. Luis Wirth and Edward Shils. New York: Harcourt, Brace & World, [1970].

Marcuse, Herbert. *One-Dimensional Man*. Boston: Beacon, 1964.

– *Negations: Essays in Critical Theory*. Trans. Jeremy J. Shapiro. Boston: Beacon, 1968.

McCarthy, Thomas. *The Critical Theory of Jürgen Habermas*. Cambridge, MA: MIT Press, 1981.

Ricoeur, Paul. *Le conflit des interprétations*. Paris: Seuil, 1969.

– *Hermeneutics and the Human Sciences*. Ed. and trans. John B. Thompson. Cambridge, UK: Cambridge University Press, 1981.

Sartre, Jean-Paul. *Qu'est-ce que la littérature?* Paris: Gallimard, 1948.

– *Between Existentialism and Marxism*. Trans. John Mathews. New York: Morrow Guill, 1979.

Suvin, Darko. *Metamorphoses of Science Fiction: On the Poetics and History of a Literary Genre*. New Haven, CT: Yale University Press, 1979.

– *Victorian Science Fiction in the UK: The Discourses of Knowledge and Power*. Boston: G.K. Hall, 1983.

– *Positions and Presuppositions in Science Fiction*. Kent, OH: Kent State University Press, 1988.

Taylor, Charles. *Sources of the Self*. Cambridge, MA: Harvard University Press, 1989.

White, Hayden. *Tropics of Discourse: Essays in Cultural Criticism*. Baltimore: Johns Hopkins University Press, 1978.

Williams, Raymond. *Keywords: A Vocabulary of Culture and Society*. London: Fontana, 1988.

Index